ELECTROSTATIC LOUDSPEAKER

DESIGN AND CONSTRUCTION

RONALD WAGNER

 TAB BOOKS Inc.
Blue Ridge Summit, PA 17214

This book is dedicated to my children Karen and Linda, and especially to the memory of Michael, a young man who truly made the world a better place to live.

FIRST EDITION
FIRST PRINTING

Copyright © 1987 by TAB BOOKS Inc.
Printed in the United States of America

Reproduction or publication of the content in any manner, without express permission of the publisher, is prohibited. No liability is assumed with respect to the use of the information herein.

Library of Congress Cataloging in Publication Data

Wagner, Ronald.
Electrostatic loudspeaker design and construction.

Includes index.
1. Electrostatic loudspeakers—Design and construction—Amateurs' manuals. I. Title.
TK9968.W34   1987   621.38′028′2   87-1924
ISBN 0-8306-0832-X
ISBN 0-8306-2832-0 (pbk.)

Questions regarding the content of this book should be addressed to:

Reader Inquiry Branch
Editorial Department
TAB BOOKS Inc.
P.O. Box 40
Blue Ridge Summit, PA 17214

Contents

Preface

The most obvious reason for writing a book on electrostatic speakers is that it hasn't been done before. Beyond that, there are a number of other factors that are more important. First, there is the fact that existing books on speakers and acoustics only present some of the theory of how an electrostatic speaker operates. Very few, if any, ever indicate how to build one. Second, in addition to the construction details, this book can be used as a reference source for the theory and history of electrostatic speakers and transducers. For the reader who is interested in pursuing the subject in more detail, the text contains patent numbers.

Acknowledgments

I would like to express my appreciation to the many inventors and technologists who have written or patented ideas on electrostatic speakers. Their material has provided the background for this book. In addition to them, a special "thank you" goes to Gordon Svendson of Ampex Corp., and Richard Smith of Hewlett Packard. Both of these gentlemen contributed many hours of their time and were a major force in the project to design and build the first full range electrostatic loudspeaker. A special thanks is also extended to Mr. Peter J. Walker of the Acoustical Manufacturing Co. Ltd. for permission to reprint his article "A Wide Range Electrostatic Loudspeaker," and to Mr. Charles Malme of BBN Laboratories for loaning me the original photos from his article "A Wide Range Electrostatic Loudspeaker," and for his permission to reprint this informative article.

Also used in this book are the following registered trademarks and trade names.

Masonite is a registered trade name of the Masonite Corp.
Mylar is a registered trade name of E.I Dupont Corp. Wilmington Delaware.
Quad is a registered trademark of the Acoustical Manufacturing Co. Ltd. of Huntingdon England.

Introduction

This is both a "how-to" book and an informative text on electrostatic speakers. It will provide the reader with a step-by-step sequence for building full range electrostatic speakers, and it will acquaint the reader with the speakers' basic operating principles. The book also describes the important parameters of an electrostatic speaker and indicates how each affects the performance.

The book is intended for the audio amateur, musician, craftsman, or anyone else who is not only interested in this type of speaker, but would also like to obtain the very best in sound reproduction. The book also serves one other purpose. If you become familiar with building an electrostatic loudspeaker, then the material should also provide to you the knowledge of how to repair one. This will be useful to those readers that have older models of commercial electrostatic speakers.

There are a number of prerequisites for successfully completing the speaker project described in the following pages. First, you should have some skill as a woodworker, preferably in the area of cabinet construction. This book does not require any exotic construction skills, but only a familiarity with power tools and their limitations, and the ability to work to close tolerances. It is also desirable for the reader to have some knowledge of both electricity and electronics. This knowledge is needed to build the high voltage power supplies and to wire the speaker panels. In addition to these two requirements, the material requires the ability to follow directions and to translate the written instructions and pictorial diagrams into physical action.

Chapter 1 begins with a history of the electrostatic transducer. It not only covers the early attempts at making an electrostatic transducer, but it indicates the appropriate patent numbers. The chapter also describes some of the more recent electrostatic speaker inventions.

In many ways, a speaker can be considered as a two way street. The part that produces the sound influences the medium that propogates the sound. At the same time, the medium affects the speaker's ability to produce a sound. To explain this interaction, Chapter 2 begins with a discussion of the basics of sound. It relates how a conventional speaker produces a sound, and then describes how it is influenced by the medium.

To determine a speaker's quality, a number of tests can be performed. Chapter 3 describes the more common ones and indicates how the reader, with some basic audio equipment, can make similar performance tests.

Chapter 4 introduces the reader to the mechancal and electrical properties of an electrostatic loudspeaker. It begins with an introduction to the principles of electric charge. It illustrates how an electric charge can produce a force, and how this force can be used to create a movement. The chapter builds on this material and shows how these concepts are used to make both a single-ended and a push-pull speaker.

Although many articles have been written about electrostatic loudspeakers, very few have addressed the problem of diaphragm stability. The principal reason for this is that most articles only describe *how* the speaker is supposed to operate. To overcome this problem, the book introduces a new concept for the stability problem called the diaphragm spring rate. This factor is created by the force, and if the diaphragm is to be stable it must be offset by a counterforce. The text indicates how to calculate the diaphragm spring rate and how to establish the required counterforce for making the diaphragm stable.

The construction of an electrostatic speaker begins in Chapter 5. This chapter describes the materials that are needed to build a support structure, and then delineates the plate material that can be used to make a speaker. Following this, a description is given on how to prepare plastic plates for use as an electrostatic speaker. These are the materials used for the speakers covered in this book.

Chapter 6 describes the construction details for the frame and the rib assemblies. These are the main structural components for the plate assembly described in Chapter 5.

Chapter 7 winds up this first section by describing the steps that are necessary to assemble the speaker's subassemblies.

After the parts are assembled, a preliminary test of the speaker's insulating coating is performed. This procedure is described in Chapter 8.

One of the most important tools for making an electrostatic speaker is a stretching frame. This tool is used to establish the counter force for the diaphragm spring rate. Its use will ensure that all of the speakers have the same diaphragm tension. Chapter 9 describes how to build a stretching frame.

After the speaker assembly has been tested, the panels can be placed in the stretching frame, and Chapter 10 describes the final assembly steps. Of special interest in this area is the conductive coating that is applied to the diaphragm. While most construction articles have used graphite, there is an alternate material that is easily obtained that overcomes the problems of using graphite.

When all of the speaker panels are assembled, a supporting cabinet is required. The requirements for an electrostatic speaker are different from those of a conventional speaker. In Chapter 11, two types of supporting structures are described. The first is a utility frame, and it can be used for testing and general purpose use. The other type is more decorative, and it is intended for use in a living room.

After all of the speaker panels have been built, it is time to connect them to the appropriate electronics. Chapter 12 describes how to build a high voltage power supply. It also indicates some of the important characteristics of the audio transformer and how they can be measured.

Chapter 13 is intended to describe some of the basic measurements that can be made on speakers, and to describe what the reader can do to evaluate the speakers that he has built.

For purpose of comparison, Chapter 14 describes the characteristics of commercial electrostatic speakers. Besides familiarizing the reader with alternate designs, it should create an interest in trying different concepts.

Chapter 15 contains reprints of three articles

that have appeared on the subject of electrostatic speakers. The three articles are frequently used as a reference for other articles. While the material is very old, the concepts that are presented are important, and it is hoped that their inclusion will help the reader.

The Appendix contains four sections. The first is a speaker material list. The second section defines the electronic parts that are needed for the speaker. The third section contains a list of suggested tools, and the last section is a list of materials that are needed for the stretching frame.

Chapter 1

How It Began

It is difficult to define a specific event as the beginning of sound reproduction. We might, for instance, consider the starting point to be February 19, 1878. On that date, Edison patented his "Tin Foil Phonograph" (No. 200521). However, as we look at Fig. 1-1, we may wonder about the events that lead up to this example of man's ingenuity. As we continue to search back in time we might pause at March 7, 1876. On this date, a patent was issued (174,465) to Alexander Graham Bell for his invention of the telephone.

This event could also be considered the starting point. It was here that the words "Mr. Watson, come here I want you." became the first example of faithful sound reproduction. The instrument that achieved this historic event is shown in Fig. 1-2. From this point on, the science of faithful sound duplication was expanded to include music as well as voice reproduction.

However, even before Bell's marvelous invention, a patent of considerable importance was is-

sued to Ernest W. Siemens, founder of the Siemens Co. of Germany. This patent (149,797) was issued on April 14th, 1874 and it indicated how an electric current, flowing through a coil of wire, could create a mechanical motion. The Siemen's patent was a significant contribution to sound reproduction. It not only became the basis for several electromechanical devices, but it is also the principle mechanism used in electromagnetic loudspeakers. If this patent is that important, perhaps it is the starting point.

Siemens, however, was not the first to work on the concept of electric current and magnetism. Before Siemens, the American physicist Joseph Henry described the principle of electromagnetic induction. In his honor the basic unit of inductance is named the henry.

Another important scientist of that period was the French physicist and mathematician Andre Marie Ampere. In the 1820's, Ampere determined that there was a relationship between electric cur-

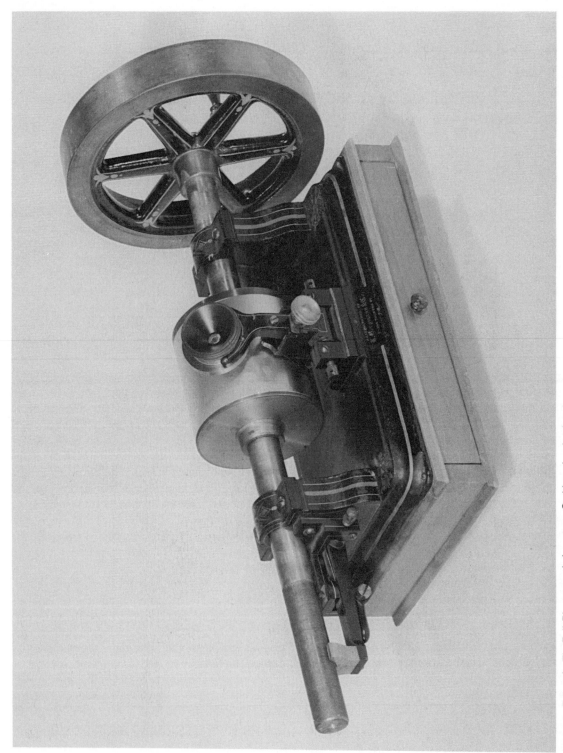

Fig. 1-1. Edison's Tin-Foil Phonograph (courtesy Smithsonian Institute).

Fig. 1-2. Bell's liquid transmitter (courtesy Smithsonian Institute).

rent and magnetism. In addition, he also made many other contributions. For instance, he defined some of our modern electrical terms. Such factors as galvanometer, electrodynamic, electromagnetic, and electrostatic were but a few of his definitions.

It wasn't Ampere, however, who discovered the principle of electromagnetism. This honor goes to the Danish physicist Hans Christian Oersted. He discovered, in 1819, that a compass needle would deflect at right angles to a wire carrying an electric current. His experiment established the link between magnetism and electricity.

Although each of the above names has an associated invention, they were not the only people working on the ideas. This situation sometimes created another difficulty. When more than one person is engaged in the same activity, the question often arises "Who is the inventor?" Even after a patent is granted it does not always define the real inventor. For instance, the work of Henry stimulated the thinking of Michael Faraday. Although Faraday published his papers on electromagnetic induction before Henry, historians believe that Henry's work preceded that of Faraday. The telephone is another example of "Who is the inventor?" In the 1870's there were many inventors besides Bell, who were trying to develop this instrument. Thomas Edison worked on it, but his main contribution occurred after the Bell patent.

Another contender for the telephone patent was Professor Amos Dolbear. At the Paris Electrical Exhibition of 1881, Dolbear successfully demonstrated his electrostatic transducer for the telephone. See Fig. 1-3. He also obtained a pair of patents (April 5, 1881 (239,742) and April 26, 1881 (240,578)) for his device. The purpose behind Dolbear's patent was to circumvent the Bell invention. The patentee, in this case, had to be established by a court of law. This was achieved in 1887, when the court case on patent infringement identified Bell as the inventor of the telephone. Because of this decision, the scientific community directed its efforts towards improving some of the other telephone components. In this area, one of the elements that became an important part of the telephone was Edison's carbon microphone.

WHO INVENTED THE PHONOGRAPH

Another controversial invention was the phonograph. In addition to Edison, there were a number of others with the same idea. In 1877, for instance, Charles Cros described a method of recording on a flat disc. Before that, in 1857, Leon Scott invented the phonautograph. This later device (see Fig. 1-4) used many of the principles contained in the modern phonograph, but it was basically a device for viewing sound patterns. Thus, it was similar to a modern chart recorder. To record the sound vibrations, Scott used a horn in reverse. The air vibrations were transformed into a mechanical movement by a bristle and a stretched diaphragm that was located at the apex of the horn. As the sound patterns caused the diaphragm to move, their waveforms were traced on a paper that had been coated with lamp black and mounted on a revolving cylinder. This device was closer to the modern phonograph than was Edison's "Tin Foil Phonograph."

One of the differences between the phonautograph and Edison's phonograph was the movement of the bristle. The former design used a lateral movement while Edison used one that was vertical. Unfortunately, Scott did not take any additional steps to produce an instrument like the phonograph.

Besides Scott, another contender for the "phonograph hall of fame" was F.B. Fenby. His patent, issued in England on January 13th, 1863, was called "An Electromagnetic Phonograph." One of the interesting facts about this patent was the word "phonograph" that appeared in the title. While it was the first one to use the word, Fenby's patent does not follow its present definition, and in fact became the basic mechanism for the player piano.

One interesting fact about the "Tin Foil Phonograph" is also related to its title. Edison did not claim to be the inventor of the phonograph. His patent title was "An Improvement in Phonograph or Speaking Machines." He essentially considered the invention to be an improvement over Scott's phonautograph. After receiving the patent, Edison did not pursue its development until after 1887. While Edison's attention was focused on the elec-

4

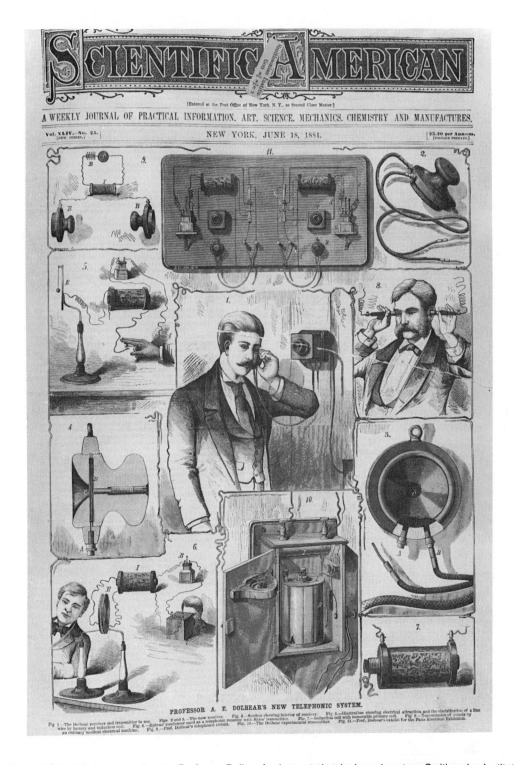

Fig. 1-3. Cover of *Scientific American* showing Professor Dolbear's electrostatic telephone (courtesy Smithsonian Institute).

Fig. 1-4. Leon Scott's Phonautograph (courtesy Smithsonian Institute).

tric light, Bell and his associates at the Volta laboratories, were busy with their own ideas about the usefulness of the phonograph. This interest caused Edison to return to his invention and to work on it until it became a commercial product.

Following Edison's patent, a more classical approach appeared in an 1895 patent (534,543) by Emile Berliner. The practical aspects of this patent indicated how the grooves could guide the needle across the record. It also described how a flywheel could maintain a constant velocity.

All of the above events occurred during the 1800s and it seems appropriate to call this time "The age of the great inventors." As for the technology of sound reproduction, each one of the above inventions became an important link in making the modern stereo system a reality.

ELECTROSTATIC TRANSDUCERS

Following the age of the great inventors, a British scientist, L.F. Richardson, came up with an idea for improving the safety of oceangoing ships. Although his timing was a little off, his purpose was to provide a means for detecting large underwater objects. His patent was applied for in 1912, and it occurred a short time after the sinking of the Titanic. As is often the case, one idea will lead to another. In this instance, Richardson's work inspired a Russian electrical engineer, Constantin Chilowski. His idea was to apply Richardson's principles to submarine detection. Chilowski wanted to do echo ranging with high frequency signals. He was able to bring his idea to the attention of the French physicist Paul Langevin. After considering several possibilities, Langevin turned to electrostatics. On the 29th of May 1920, the French issued a patent (502,913) in both their names. As it turned out, there were many problems with the electrostatic transducer and it was later replaced, in 1916, by a piezoelectic device.

In 1918, Edward C. Wente described how electrostatics could be used to build a condenser microphone. The outside diameter of his microphone was 3.0 inches, and the diaphragm diameter was 1.5 inches. Electrically it had a capacity of 300 picofarads. Because this is a small value, it forced the associated electronics to be located in the same case. In this application, the electrostatic microphone became a precision piece of laboratory equipment.

LOUDSPEAKERS

Throughout the history of sound reproduction, there is evidence that the electrostatic transducer was considered as a viable alternative to the electromagnetic speaker. The electrostatic speaker, however, did not appear until 1929. In fact, before 1924, sound reproduction beyond what was necessary for the telephone was virtually impossible. The reason behind this was the lack of a suitable amplifier. In the early 1920s, two researchers, Rice and Kellog, set out to create a hornless loudspeaker. They immediately recognized the need for a suitable quality laboratory amplifier, and their first project was to design and build one. A paper published by them in 1925, on the design of a hornless loudspeaker, marked the beginning of high quality sound reproduction. The implementation of this design eliminated most of the other speakers from the commercial market.

Although the Rice and Kellog speaker was very successful, there were problems which needed further attention. One of the first was the relationship between speaker width and sound wavelength. Good low frequency reproduction is obtained when the speaker has a cone with a very large diameter. In addition to its size, the cone mounting structure must also be rigid. The application of these principles will force the speaker's output to become directional with increasing frequency. Above a specific value (see the "ka" factor in Chapter 2), the speaker's acoustic output will decrease with increasing frequency.

In contrast, if the speaker is made small so that it can reproduce the high frequencies, the cone movement will also be small. The speaker will not have enough cone movement, at the lower frequencies, to achieve a sufficient acoustical volume. The early researchers soon recognized this problem and used two different approaches to solve the contradictory requirements. One group chose to divide the cone, by mechanical means, into smaller sec-

7

tions. At low frequencies, the entire cone is rigid and moves like a piston. When the frequency is increased, the cone radiates from a smaller section. At very high frequencies, the speaker radiates from an area next to the center of the cone. The other group separated the audio band into several frequency spectrums and then used a separate speaker for each band of frequencies. One advantage of this method is that the speaker bandwidth is now determined by how many speakers are used in the entire system. The designer is free to choose any number that he likes.

In addition to the work on radiators, other inventors were involved with speaker baffles. They were trying to use the sound that was radiated from the rear of the speaker. Their investigations have produced such speaker systems as the bass reflex, acoustical labyrinth, and the folded horn. After World War II, this development work continued and there was a proliferation of speaker systems. An interesting viewpoint is the claim, by each one, that their sound was the most faithful reproduction.

One of the major events that began in the early 1950s was the regional high fidelity show. A visit to any of them usually provided the audio enthusiast with an abundance of information. Because Madison Avenue had not discovered the audio business, there was often a free exchange of technical information. A technical discussion at any component booth might involve the system designer, the chief engineer, or the president of the company. Often the same person was all three. Not only was this situation true in the speaker area but it also applied to the other audio components as well. The regional audio shows provided a stimulus that created the present stereo industry.

Almost all of the shows were related to the component market. They were, however, often attended by many of the "high tech" recording companies. These companies were usually demonstrating the newest thing in high fidelity or stereo recording. This would often consist of either a disc with a few outstanding selections or a major symphony. Recordings that used multiple "mix downs" were unheard of, and these live recordings appeared at most of the demonstration booths. This gave the customer the opportunity to compare the same program material on many different systems, and to obtain answers to technical questions from people who were qualified to answer them.

By the early sixties, the attendance at the audio shows had significantly deteriorated. The declining attendance was produced by the change from a technical exposition to a glorified audio store. To eliminate the technical aspects, Madison Avenue decided to keep the engineers in the lab. This meant that only sales people went to the shows. In addition, they chose to reduce the attendance even further by charging an attendance fee.

It was during this time that two scientists, Thiele and Small, began treating a loudspeaker system like an electrical filter. This was a significant advantage because an electrical filter can be described by a set of mathematical equations. As with many great ideas, this concept was not immediately recognized. Speaker manufacturers did not indicate or specify the Thiele/Small parameters until the end of the seventies and into the early eighties. Today, most well known loudspeaker manufacturers list the associated Thiele/Small values for their speakers. In this way, the audio enthusiast or experimenter is able to design and build a speaker system that will fit his particular needs.

ELECTROSTATIC SPEAKERS

Returning to the subject of electrostatics, and in particular to electrostatic speakers, the required craftmanship can be divided into two subcategories. The first group performed their research and development work before World War II. During the ten years 1925 to 1935, there were a number of patents as well as technical articles on electrostatic speakers. Despite this activity, the speaker never seemed to progress beyond the development stage. One of the reasons was the lack of suitable materials. Electrostatic speakers use a high voltage to create the electrostatic field. Designers of that day were forced to rely on either the diaphragm or the air gap for protection from electrical breakdown. This imposed some very severe limits on both the applied voltages and the amount of audio power that the speaker could produce.

Early Electrostatic Speakers

As mentioned, the early scientists lacked suitable materials. The patent for mylar, the principle component in a modern electrostatic speaker, was not issued until March 22, 1949 (2,465,319). Mylar is a registered trade name of E.I. DuPont Corp. Still, the researchers were very ingenious. A patent by Colin Kyle (1,644,387) was one of the first to describe an electrostatic speaker. The patent shows a speaker with a perforated metal back plate that also has a corrugated surface. A flexible diaphragm is stretched over the rear plate, and it bridges across the depressions in the plate. Cemented to the diaphragm was a thin flexible conductive coating. The conductive coating was located away from the plate by placing it on the opposite side of the diaphragm. A cross sectional view of this concept is shown in Fig. 1-5. The material used to make the conductive coating was beaten leaf. It had a thickness of less then 0.0001 inches. The diaphragm was made of a very thin metal foil, and it was centered between two parallel perforated plates. Two insulating rings were used for separation.

The diagram of Fig. 1-6 shows another concept for building an electrostatic speaker. An article describing this speaker was written by P. E. Edelman in 1931. The speaker consists of two flexible electrode diaphragms separated by an air gap of variable dimensions. One diaphragm is a cloth with flexible metal strips. The other diaphragm is also

flexible and it has a metal foil fastened to it. The spacers consist of a series of spacer threads. This is shown in the enlarged diagram of Fig. 1-7. On the reverse side of the front diaphragm, a dust of mica or talcum was applied. This prevented adhesion to the rear electrode. The conductive coating was made from an aluminum foil and it was held in place with either cerowax or gold size japan varnish. This method provided a flexible, light weight, laminated diaphragm with an approximate dielectric constant of three. The supporting frame for the front diaphragm was held under tension by springs that were placed at the expandable corners. This prevented the diaphragm from having any wrinkles. The rear diaphragm was supported by either the same frame or another auxiliary frame. One interesting fact is that Edelman had six patents (1,759,809/1,776,112/1,759,810/1,759,811/1,767,656/1,767,657) on electrostatic speakers.

Another patent for an electrostatic speaker was granted on December 4, 1934 to Edward W. Kellog (1,983,377). While Kellog's patent does not describe the construction, it does cover the subject of segmentation. Segmentation is a technique used to separate the various sections of an electrostatic speaker. It provides a function that is similar to the method of mechanically separating the cone segments of an electromagnetic speaker. The patent describes a method to segment both a single-ended as well as a push-pull electrostatic speaker. The concept of segmentation was also used by inven-

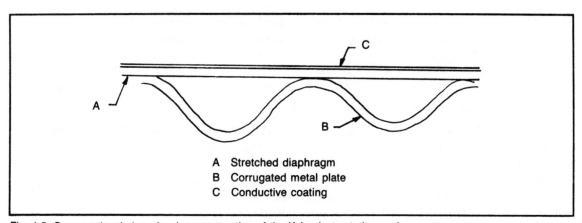

A   Stretched diaphragm
B   Corrugated metal plate
C   Conductive coating

Fig. 1-5. Crosssectional view showing construction of the Kyle electrostatic speaker.

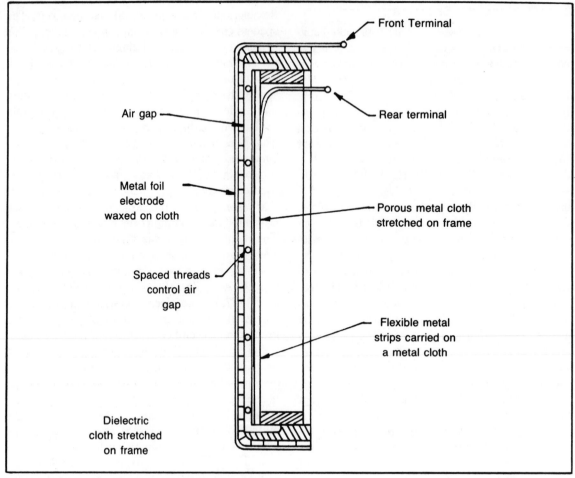

Fig. 1-6. Construction details for Edelman's electrostatic speaker.

tors after World War II. In a segmented speaker, each section is electrically connected to its neighbor by either a resistor or an inductor. This configuration makes each section equal to a low pass filter. When the opposition of each speaker section is equal to the value of its associated resistor or inductor, the audio output will fall by 3 dB. Any further increase in frequency will decrease the output from this section even further. During this time, the principle audio output will be produced by one of the adjacent segments.

Another early description of an electrostatic speaker appeared in the magazine Wireless World on May 29, 1929. The article contained a descrip-

tion by a Berlin correspondent, about the "Voght Electrostatic Loudspeaker." This speaker had a diameter of 15 inches and a depth of 2 inches. The electrical capacity was 1000 picofarads and it used a push-pull configuration (see Chapter 4).

Electrostatic Speakers After World War II

The second group of inventors developed electrostatic speakers after World War II. This group can be subdivided into two additional parts. The first part is made up of the years from the end of World War II until about 1965. The second subdivision covers the remaining years to 1986.

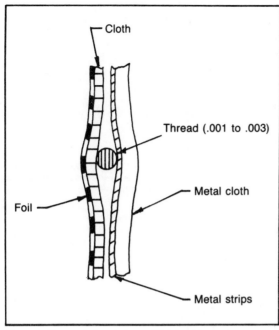

Fig. 1-7. Crosssectional view of Edelman's speaker showing how spacers are made from threads.

During the 1950's, the research on electrostatic speakers was carried on in both the United States and the United Kingdom. The U.S. effort was directed by Arthur Janzen. Peter Walker of the Acoustical Manufacturing Co. carried on the effort in the United Kingdom. Janzen received his first patent (2,631,196) on March 10, 1953. This patent as well as his next describe an electrostatic tweeter. The second patent (2,896,025) (see Fig. 1-8) was issued on July 21, 1959. One interesting aspect of this later patent is the technique for obtaining the fixed conductive plates. Instead of using a perforated metal plate, Janzen used wires. His patent also describes a technique for winding the wires around a plastic form. See Fig. 1-9.

The fad of that day was to combine the Janzen tweeters with an electromagnetic speaker system called the AR-1. This was the first bookshelf type speaker system produced by the Acoustic Research Corp. Following the successful implementation of a tweeter, Janzen turned his attention to a full range speaker. To obtain more volume, the spacing be-

Fig. 1-8. Front and end views of the Janzen electrostatic tweeter.

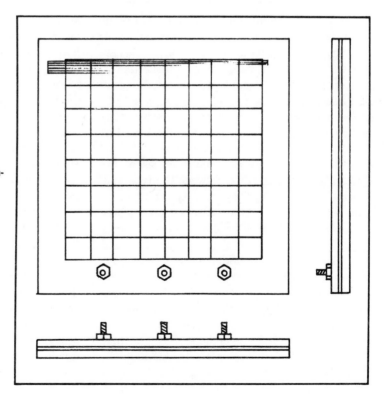

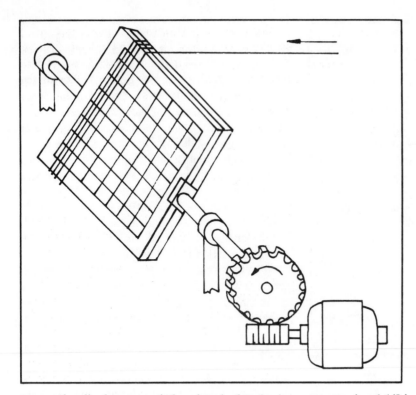

Fig. 1-9. Diagram shows the method used to wind the wire for the plates of the Janzen electrostatic tweeter.

tween the diaphragm and the plate had to be increased. The spacing for the bass speaker panels was changed from 0.012 inches to 0.100 inches. The completed loudspeaker system consisted of 10 woofers and one 4 1/2 inch tweeter located on each of the two panels. The woofer dimensions were 11 inches by 11 inches. The final result of this effort was the model KLH-9 speaker system. In 1962, Mr. Janzen custom built a full range speaker for Mr. Ewing Nunn, a well known audio enthusiast of that time. The main difference between the two units was the physical size. The custom speaker had 1/3 more diaphragm area. This speaker contained three six foot panels while the standard speaker had only two.

While Janzen was working on his speakers, Peter Walker was building the first Quad electrostatic speaker system. Mr. Walker used a different approach in his design than the one followed by Janzen. The Quad was a short speaker, as compared to the KLH-9, which was six feet high. The quad design is shown in Chapter 14. In this unit, the tweeter is a 1 1/2 inch wide strip located in the center of the speaker. This panel has a lower cutoff frequency of 7 kilohertz. In the outer sections, the spacing was increased so that they could be used for mid-range and bass. The polarizing voltages for the tweeter was 1.5 kilovolts, while 6.0 kilovolts was used for the bass panels. Following many years of successful production, Mr. Walker set out to improve his original speakers. The culmination of this effort was a patent (3,773,984) which later became the model ESL 63. The unusual segmenting features of this speaker are described in Chapter 14.

Another major contributor to the field of electrostatic speakers, although he never built one, was Professor F.V. Hunt. In 1954, Professor Hunt wrote a book on electroacoustics. His book described, in mathematical terms, the advantages of using the push-pull arrangement for an electrostatic speaker. Although some researchers were already using this arrangement, Professor Hunt's book provided the justification, in mathematical terms, for the superiority of this speaker.

In 1963, Charles Malme wrote an article for the Journal of the Audio Engineering Society. This work described his research on electrostatic speakers and became part of his thesis at M.I.T. The concepts were also patented (3,014,098). Malme's speaker had several unique features. First, it did not use perforated plates. Instead, he used metal rods. This technique made segmentation an easy task. The rods could be connected in parallel until the required width was achieved. They then were connected by a resistor to the next segment. Another unusual characteristic of this design was the large spacing between the plates and the diaphragm. Of all the electrostatic speakers, Malme's design had the greatest separation (1/4 inch). Although this gave the speaker the ability to have a large diaphragm movement, it also created another problem. To move the diaphragm over the entire spacing, a special high voltage amplifier had to be built. This amplifier was directly connected to the load (no transformer) and the output voltage was approximately 5 kilovolts rms. The circuit diagram for this amplifier is also shown in the article. See the reprint in Chapter 15.

Dayton Wright Speaker

A different, and interesting, approach is described in a patent issued on Dec. 11, 1973 to Dayton Wright of Ontario, Canada. This electrostatic speaker, which has been commercially marketed, had several unique features. First, the physical dimensions of the enclosure were much larger than most other speakers of this type. The cabinet was 40 by 48 by 8 inches. The speaker was capable of accepting 250 watts of input power without experiencing any damage.

The one characteristic that makes this speaker exceptional was the use of a gas (sulphurhexafluoride or perfluoropropane). The gas was sealed in an enclosure that completely surrounded the speaker elements (see Fig. 1-10). The properties of this gas benefit the speaker performance in a number of ways. The sound wave traveling through the gas will have a velocity that is 1/3 of its velocity in air. At the boundary between the two mediums, there will be a deflection of the sound waves. In effect, the boundary will act as a lens. The orientation of the electrostatic speaker panels inside the gas chamber (see Fig. 1-11 and Fig. 1-12) can change the wavefront from the speaker. This orientation can either focus the sound into a particular area or it can separate and spread the sound over a larger area.

Beveridge Speaker

On November 20, 1973, a patent (3,773,976) was granted to Harold Beveridge. This speaker was also unusual because it used a specially designed cabinet that contained an acoustic lens in front of the electrostatic speaker panel. The purpose of the lens was to spread the sound. It accomplished this by arranging each of the channels shown in Fig. 1-13 so that their effective sound paths were equal. This caused the emitted sound to have a circular wavefront in the horizontal plane. Vertically, the speaker was like a cylinder. The patent also indicated an important relationship between the width of the channel for the acoustic lens, and the frequency that it must reproduce. For best performance, the width should be 2/3 of the highest radiated frequency.

In addition to the features just mentioned, there are two internal volumes that have a critical relationship. Volume 1 which is open to the rear of the radiator should be about 10 times that of volume 2. The purpose of volume 1 is to absorb the rear radiation. In addition to this, the cabinet contains some sound absorbing material for frequencies above 300 Hz.

Other factors that are important in the design are the width of the throat at position "A" in Fig. 1-13. This should be about 3 inches. The lens opening at the front of the cabinet is 7 inches, while the active diaphragm is about 1 foot in width and 23 inches in length. The entire speaker system is housed in a cabinet that is 36 inches wide, 18 inches deep, and 72 inches high. This is a very large cabinet for an electrostatic speaker. Another factor in the speaker design was its location in the listening room. The speaker was designed to be placed in

13

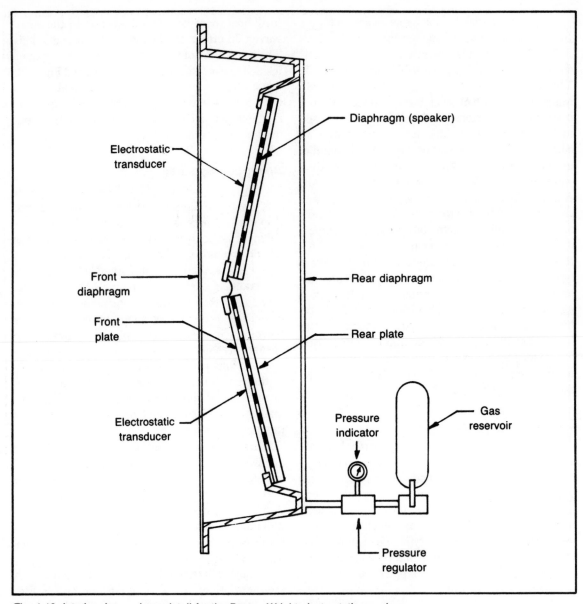

Electrostatic transducer

Diaphragm (speaker)

Front diaphragm

Rear diaphragm

Front plate

Rear plate

Electrostatic transducer

Pressure indicator

Gas reservoir

Pressure regulator

Fig. 1-10. Interior view and gas detail for the Dayton Wright electrostatic speakers.

the center of the room against the longest wall. This allowed the lenses to spread the sound over the maximum radiated angle.

The electronics for this speaker was also fairly extensive. By using a bridge circuit, the plates of the speaker were directly connected to the amplifier output. Because of this, the output devices were

vacuum tubes. A block diagram of the electronics is shown in Fig. 1-14.

Acoustat

Two recent patents (4,323,950 and 4,324,950) on electrostatic speakers were issued in April of 1982. Mr. James Strickland, of Ft. Lauderdale,

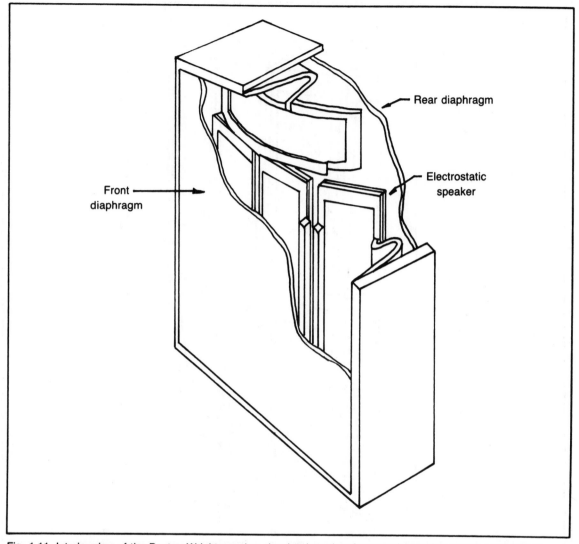

Rear diaphragm

Electrostatic speaker

Front diaphragm

Fig. 1-11. Interior view of the Dayton Wright speaker showing how the electrostatic speaker panels are oriented.

Florida, was the inventor. The first patent is for an audio step-up device (transformer) for driving an electrostatic speaker. This is shown in Fig. 1-15. In this application, the audio spectrum is separated into two frequency ranges. A transformer is used for each range. One transformer is optimized for driving the bass panels. It covers a frequency range of 30 Hz to 5 kilohertz. The step-up ratio is 200 to 1. The second transformer is designed to cover the frequency range from a few hundred hertz to 20 kilohertz. Its step up ration is 60 to one. Besides

the transformers, the patent also shows a number of resistors and capacitors. They are used as filters so that the correct frequencies are fed to the correct transformer.

The second patent covers the design of an amplifier that is directly connected to the speaker. The output stage of this amplifier uses vacuum tubes for the high audio voltages. Power for these tubes is obtained from a 5 kilovolt power supply. The audio output signal is approximately 4.0 kilovolts RMS. The schematic diagram is shown in Fig. 1-16.

Fig. 1-12. Another view of the interior of the Dayton Wright electrostatic speaker showing a different speaker panel orientation.

Civitello

A recent patent on electrostatic loudspeakers (4,289,936) was granted to John Civitillo on Sept. 15, 1981. Mr. Civitello's design configures the speaker system as a geodesically curved surface. The patent claims that this configuration will broaden both the horizontal and the vertical radiation patterns.

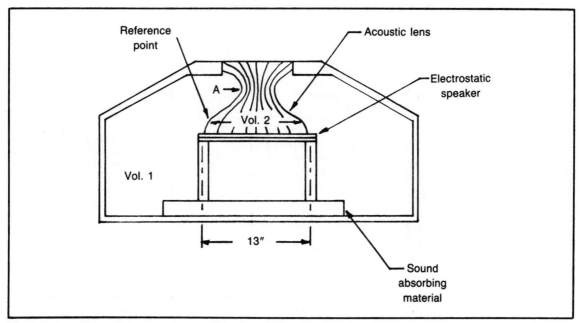

Fig. 1-13. Location and component parts of the Beveridge electrostatic speaker.

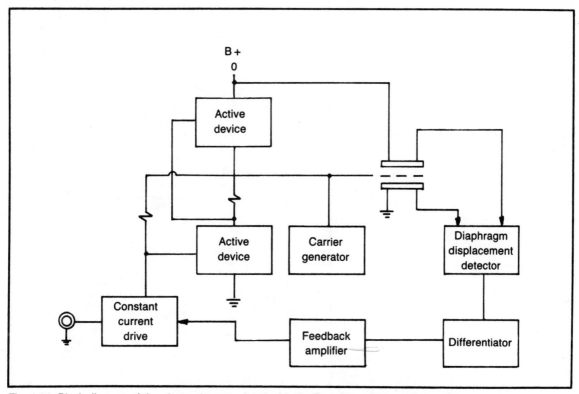

Fig. 1-14. Block diagram of the electronics associated with the Beveridge electrostatic speaker.

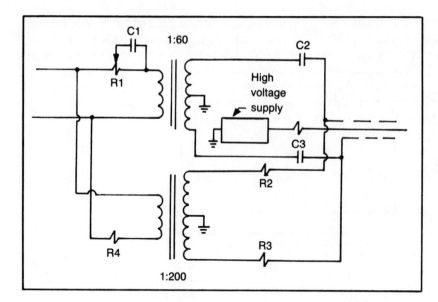

Fig. 1-15. Circuit diagram of the Acoustat frequency selective transformer circuit.

Fig. 1-16. Transformerless output circuit for the Acoustat electrostatic speakers.

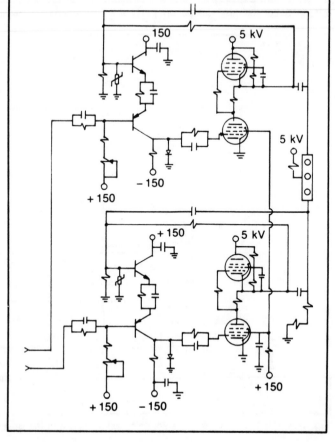

This chapter has shown that electrostatics have been used for sound reproduction as early as 1881. These early devices were designed for use in telephone applications. The first electrostatic speakers came into existence in the early 1920's. Unfortunately, they had several problems that limited their commercial use. After World War II there was a rebirth of interest in this type of speaker. This renewed interest was created by the outstanding sound quality and the availability of newer materials. While the sales of electrostatic speakers do not compare with those of electromagnetics, there is a constant and growing interest in them. Later chapters of this book will explain the construction techniques needed to build an electrostatic speaker.

Chapter 2

Electromagnetic Speakers

Before starting a discussion on speakers, it is appropriate to learn something about the medium of sound transmission.

ACOUSTICAL PROPERTIES OF AIR

Sounds can be created by many different devices. The source of the sound can be separated into two categories. The first one consists of sounds that are produced naturally, such as, birds singing, the wind in the trees, or the sound of water splashing against the shore. The second category consists of sounds that are manmade. Unfortunately, not all of these manmade sounds are pleasant. Some of the more unpleasant ones include sounds produced by airplanes, motorcycles, and car horns. In addition to this last group, there are sounds that provide a pleasant sensation. This feeling can be created by a musical instrument such as a piano or a clarinet. The vibrating string of a well played violin is another possibility. The sound produced by a high quality radio or stereo system can also produce a pleasing sensation. All of these later manmade

sounds have one thing in common. The sound is usually created by a transducer.

By definition, a transducer is a device that converts power from one form to a related value in another form. In the strictest sense a stretched string of a guitar is a transducer. When the string is plucked, the mechanical power required to move the string causes it to vibrate. This mechanical vibration produces a change in the atmospheric pressure adjacent to the string. In this instance, the mechanical force has been transferred to an acoustic force.

Pressure Variations

As stated, the oscillation of a guitar string causes vibration of the air molecules adjacent to the string. This movement of the molecules is transmitted through the air as particle vibrations. If the vibrations are received by the ears of a human, the brain will interpret the resulting air pressure variations as a sound. In the diagram of Fig. 2-1, a string has been stretched between two supports.

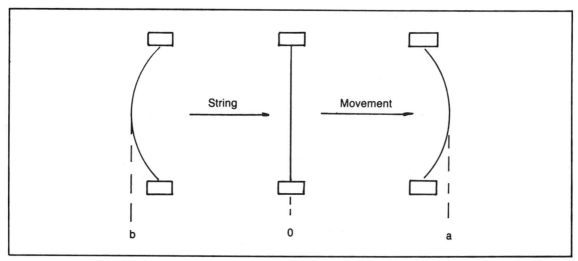

Fig. 2-1. A stretched string.

When the string is at the point marked zero, it is in the normal or non-vibrating position. The two positions "a" and "b" indicate displacements from the normal position.

Let us suppose that the string is moved from the zero position to the point marked "b." This movement of the string will require an amount of energy to be expended. If the string is held at position "b," the energy that caused the string to move is stored in the string as potential energy. When the string is released it will move away from position "b" and travel toward the position marked "a." The potential energy that was stored in the string is now converted to kinetic energy. As the string moves toward "a," it pushes the air molecules in front of it. Because of the air mass, this movement compresses the air molecules in front of the string. The compression of the molecules will produce an increase in the normal atmospheric pressure.

The movement of the string from "b" to "a" is shown in Fig. 2-1. The graph of Fig. 2-2A indicates the changing air pressure in front of the moving string. When the string was moved from its zero position to point "b" there was a reduction in the air pressure in front of the string. Therefore, when the string is released, the air pressure graph will begin at a negative value. If, during the initial move-

ment, the string is held in position "b" for a length of time the air pressure will return to its normal position. Because this will equalize the air pressure, the graph will begin at zero. This is shown by the dotted line in Fig. 2-2A. The arrival of the string at position "a" produces two results. First, it produces the greatest increase in the air pressure. Second, the string will stop its forward motion and, for a moment, it will be stationary. The kinetic energy of the moving string is now transformed back into potential energy. If the string is not held in this position it will immediately begin moving back towards position "b" and the potential energy will again become kinetic. The arrows of Fig. 2-1 will now be in the opposite direction. The result of this movement is shown in Fig. 2-2B.

If the pressure graphs of Fig. 2-2A and Fig. 2-2B are connected together, the result would be the instantaneous change in atmospheric pressure over one cycle of the string movement. This is shown in Fig. 2-3. The increase in atmospheric pressure at any instant in time can be calculated by:

$$P = Pp \times (\sin\theta).$$

Where P =   the instantaneous pressure.

Pp =   the maximum or peak value of the pressure.

$\sin\theta$ =   the vertical component angle in degrees.

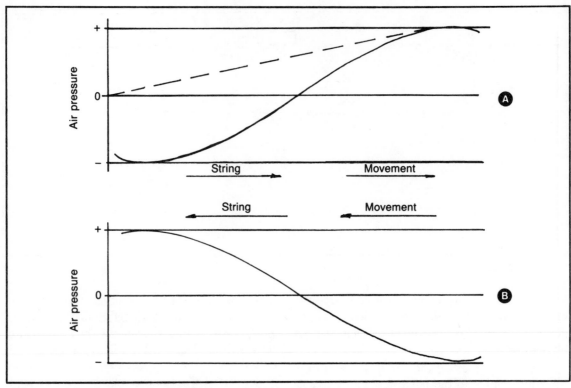

Fig. 2-2. Diagram showing how a string moves and how this movement changes the air pressure.

At position "a" in Fig. 2-1, the sin of theta is equal to one and P = Pp. Conversely at "b" the sin of theta is equal to negative one and P = −Pp. While this calculation will provide the instantaneous value, most computations use the root mean square or rms value. The rms value is related to the peak value by:

$$P_{[rms]} = (0.707) \times Pp$$

Where $P_{[rms]}$ = the root mean square value of the pressure.

Pp = the peak value of the pressure.

Period and Frequency

Another important characteristic of the moving string, is the time required for it to travel from position "b" to "a" and back to "b." A complete movement between these two points is a cycle, and the time that it takes to complete the movement is the period. The frequency of this movement is the number of cycles that are completed in one second and its unit of measurement is the Hertz. The period and the frequency are the reciprocal of each other, and are related by the following formula.

$$T = 1/F$$

Where T = the period between any two equal points in seconds.

F = the number of cycles in Hertz.

As an example, suppose the string is made to vibrate and it completes one cycle of oscillation (from "b" to "a" and back to "b") in 0.001 seconds. The frequency of this oscillation is:

$$F = 1/T$$
$$F = 1/(0.001)$$
$$F = 1000 \text{ Hertz}$$

Therefore the string will make 1000 round trips between the two positions in one second.

22

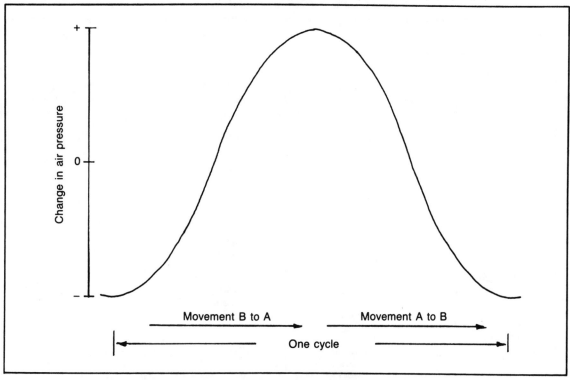

Fig. 2-3. Total air pressure change over one cycle of the strings movement.

Velocity

In Fig. 2-1, the string stops its forward motion at position "a." The molecules, however, continue and begin to spread out in large concentric circles. If the air pressure is measured at some distance from the string, there will be a time difference between the two equal pressure points. The speed or velocity of propagation can be obtained by dividing the distance between the moving string and the observation point by the time that it takes for the pressure points to change to an equal value. The velocity of sound, in air, is shown in Table 2-1.

In scientific work, most measurements are based on the metric system. The length is measured in meters, mass and weight in kilograms and time in seconds. This system of measurement is abbreviated as MKS, and it will be used as much as possible throughout this book. However, occasionally the CGS system will be required. In this system the length is measured in centimeters, mass and weight in grams and time in seconds.

Wavelength

In Fig. 2-3, the wavelength is equal to the distance between two corresponding equal points of the curve. The wavelength can be calculated by dividing the velocity by the frequency. That is:

$$\lambda = c/f$$

Where λ = the wavelength of the sound in meters, centimeter or inches.

c = the velocity in meters, centimeters or inches.

f = the frequency in Hertz.

For a 1000 cycle tone, using the MKS units, the wavelength is:

$$\lambda = 343/1000$$
$$= 0.343 \text{ meters}$$

This calculation can be converted to the English units of inches/ second by multiplying the answer by 39.37. The wavelength for a 1000 cycle tone is approximately 13.5 inches.

23

Table 2-1. MKS and CGS Units of Measurement.

	MKS	CGS	English	
Velocity	343 Meters/ sec.	34300 Centimeters/ sec.	1130 Feet sec.	13440 Inches sec.
Work	Joules (Newton/ meters)	ERGS (Centimeters/ dyne)	Foot pounds	
Volume Velocity	Cubic meters/ sec.	Cubic centimeters/ sec.		
Air Density	1.18 kg Cubic Meter	$1.18*10^{-3}$ Grams Cubic Centimeter		
Pressure	10^5 Newtons square meters	10^6 Dynes square centimeter		
Microbars	0.1 Newtons square meter	1 Dyne square centimeter		
Acoustic Impedance	405 Rayls	40.5 Rayls		

Air Resistance

When something moves, there is usually a corresponding opposition to that movement. In an electrical circuit, this opposition is called a resistance. It is equal to the voltage divided by the current. That is:

$$R = V/I$$

Where
R = the resistance in ohms.
V = the voltage across the resistance.
I = the current flowing through the resistance.

In an acoustic system, the resistance is related to the characteristics of the medium. For a plane sound wave, the value is equal to the pressure divided by the particle velocity. This resistance can be calculated by:

$$R = P/u$$

Where
R = the acoustic resistance of the medium.
P = the rms pressure in dynes/cm^2.
u = the particle velocity in cm/sec.

One other way to determine R is to multiply the density of air (Kg/m^3 or grams/cm^3) by the velocity (m/s or cm/sec). Most acoustic text books indicate the acoustic resistance as a factor called pc. In this instance p is the density and c is the velocity. For a plane sound wave, the pressure and the particle velocity are in phase. Table 2-1 provides a value for R in both the MKS and the CGS system of measurement.

This preceding material has shown that air has at least three properties that relate it to the transmission of sound. If a loudspeaker is to create a sound, the moving speaker cone must also change the atmospheric pressure. The variation in the pressure will travel through the medium at a rate that is equal to the velocity of propagation. The air resistance will oppose the moving cone and it will affect the speaker's ability to produce a sound. Before discussing the relationship between the moving cone and the resistance, an explanation will be given about the principles that force the cone to move.

ELECTROMAGNETIC SPEAKERS

The operational performance of an electromagnetic speaker is a function of many different factors. Most of them can be classified into one of three categories. The two most common to the audio enthusiast are the electrical and the acoustical parameters. The third factor takes into account the mechanical properties of the cone, the mounting system and the force needed to move the cone. This section will attempt to explain some of these factors and how they influence the speakers performance. The following chapter "Measuring Speaker Parameters" will indicate how some of these speaker parameters can be measured. In this chapter, some of the details on how a speaker works have been simplified. The reason for this approach is to acquaint the reader with how the speaker operates and not how to design one.

Magnetic Principles

As children, almost everyone has at one time or another experimented with two magnets. One of the first things that was discovered is that each magnet has two distinct magnetic sides. One side was the North pole while the other side was the South pole.

If the two magnets had like poles (North or South) facing each other, a force tried to push the magnets apart. On the other hand, if the poles nearest each other were of opposite designation, the force between them was one of attraction. These conditions are illustrated in Fig. 2-4.

To better understand the properties of a magnetic field, it is helpful to visualize it as being made

up of magnetic lines. The lines radiate outwards from the North pole and return to the magnet at the South pole. This is shown in Fig. 2-5. The strength of the magnetic field is related to the number of lines per unit area. At the ends of the magnet, the lines are very concentrated and this creates a strong magnetic field. A strong magnetic field produces a strong force. Along the sides of the magnet, the lines are far apart and this creates both a weak magnetic field and a small force.

One of the other properties of a magnetic line is that it cannot cross another line. When the magnets shown in Fig. 2-6A are near each other, the lines of force from one magnet will collide with the lines from the other magnet. The result of this collision is that each magnet will push the lines from the opposite magnet to one side. In this way the lines can return to their own magnetic pole. Because the lines cannot cross each other, there is a repelling force between the two magnets.

In Fig. 2-6B, the magnets have opposite poles facing each other. In this configuration some of the lines leaving the North pole of magnetic one will enter the South pole of magnet two. The lines that enter magnet two will pass through this magnet and come out its North pole. After leaving the North pole of magnet two, the lines will return to the South pole of magnet one.

In addition to the lines linking both magnets there will also be some lines which are associated with each individual magnet. As shown, they will leave the North pole of their magnet, Fig. 2-6B, and return to their respective South pole. As the two magnets are moved closer more and more of the lines from magnet one will enter magnet two. If the two magnets actually touch, then all of the lines from magnet one will enter magnet two. In effect, the two magnets no longer exist. They have been replaced by one large magnet. The principles of attraction and repulsion, between poles of a magnet, are why an electromagnetic speaker functions.

Before the forces created by a magnet can be used in a speaker, they will need some modification. In the above discussion, both magnets were permanent. In a speaker, one is permanent and one

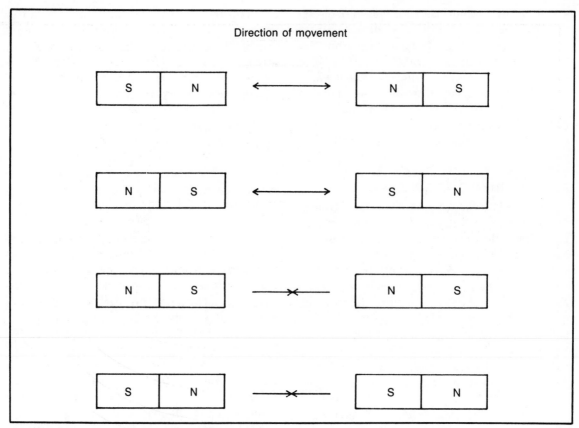

Fig. 2-4. Directions of magnetic force around two permanent magnets.

is an electromagnet. An electromagnet is made by taking a wire and winding it into a coil. A pictorial diagram as well as a schematic of an electromagnet is shown in Fig. 2-7.

To make the coil function as a magnet, an electric current must flow through the wires of the coil. If a voltage source is connected to the coil, there will be a current flowing in the wire. This current will create a magnetic field around the coil. In the diagram of Fig. 2-8A, the magnetic lines leave the top end of the coil and return to the bottom. This makes the top the North pole and the bottom the South pole. The unique properties of an electromagnet are that it can be turned on and off and that the direction of its magnetic field can be reversed. If the polarity of the battery terminals are reversed, the electric current will flow in the opposite direction. This is shown in Fig. 2-8B. The lines will now

leave the bottom of the coil (North pole) and return at the top (South pole).

In the diagram of Fig. 2-7, if a battery is connected to the coil so that the terminal marked "A" is the North pole then it will be repelled by the North pole of the permanent magnet. Reversing the battery polarity will create a force of attraction between the two magnetic poles.

An electromagnet used in a speaker must have one other feature before the speaker will work. In addition to being able to control the direction of the field, it must also be variable. To achieve this, consider the circuit diagram shown in Fig. 2-9. If the arm of the variable resistor is adjusted to point "A" the top of the coil will be connected to ground. In this condition, no current will flow through the coil and the magnetic field will be zero. As the arm is moved toward position "B," the current in the

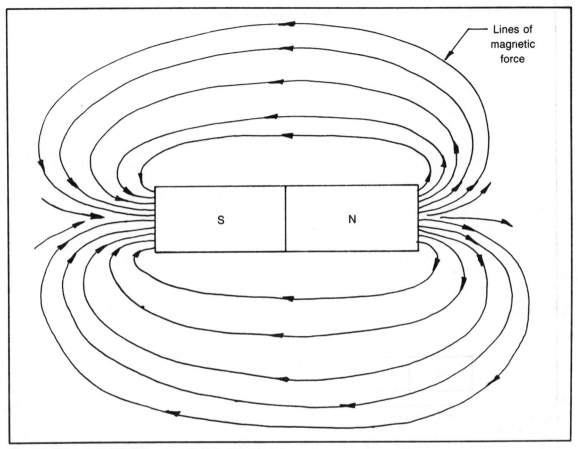

Fig. 2-5. Electromagnetic lines around a bar magnet.

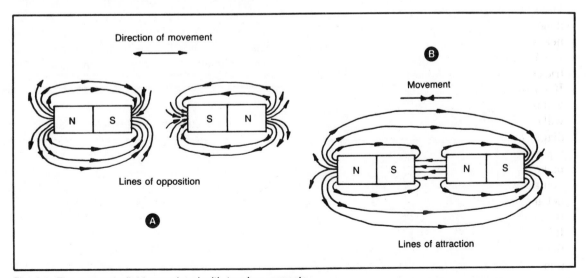

Fig. 2-6. The magnetic field associated with two bar magnets.

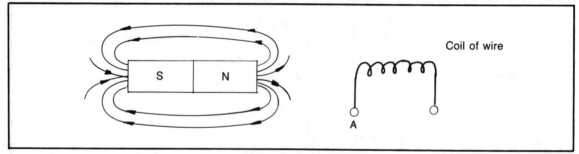

Fig. 2-7. The magnetic field around a magnet and the electrical symbol used for a coil of wire that becomes an electromagnet.

wires of the coil and the strength of the magnetic field increases proportionately. At position "B," the current and the field strength will be at their maximum value. Reversing the polarity of the voltage, as in Fig. 2-8B, will cause the magnetic field to vary in the opposite direction.

Electromagnetic Force

In the preceding diagrams, the permanent magnet and the coil have been two separate components. In the diagram of Fig. 2-10A, a wire is placed inside a magnetic field. As indicated, if the wire does not carry any current it will not disturb the magnetic field between the two magnets. A wire, however, that is carrying an electric current will be surrounded by a magnetic field of its own. This is shown in Fig. 2-10B. The polarity sign at the end of the wire indicates that the current is flowing into the wire. The arrows around the wire indicate the direction of the magnetic field. When this wire is inserted into the magnetic field, of Fig. 2-10A the

magnetic lines between the two poles will bend around the wire. This is shown in Fig. 2-10C. The force between the two magnetic fields will deflect the wire downwards. The force can be calculated by:

$$F = BLI\sin(\theta)$$

Where F = the force in newtons.
B = the flux density in webers/m^2.
L = the length of the wire (inside the magnetic field in meters).
I = the current flowing in the wire.
sin(θ) = the angle between the magnetic field of the wire and that of the magnet.

In the diagram, the magnetic field of the wire is at right angles to the magnetic field of the magnet. This makes the value of sin(θ) equal to one and the force is at its maximum. Because the conductor has mobility, it will move from a region that has a strong magnetic field, toward one that is weaker.

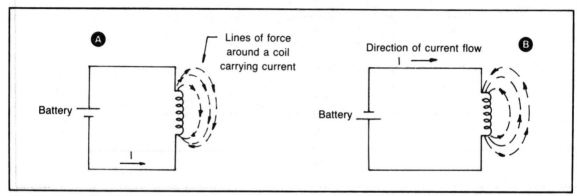

Fig. 2-8. The magnetic lines around an electromagnet.

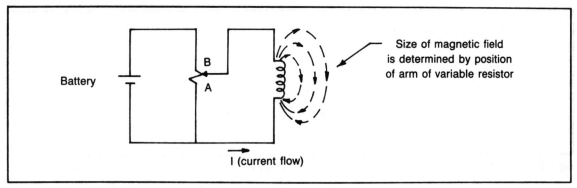

Fig. 2-9. Diagram shows a simple method for making an electromagnet variable.

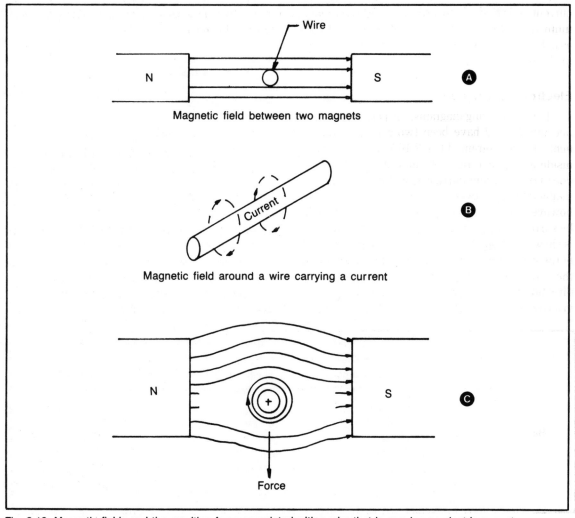

Fig. 2-10. Magnetic fields and the resulting force associated with a wire that is carrying an electric current.

Reversing the polarity of the current, flowing in the wire, will deflected the wire upwards.

In the above formula, the force is dependent upon four factors. The first, "B," represents the flux density or the amount of magnetic lines that exist between the poles of the magnet. To change this value would require a new magnet. Another factor is the angle, $(\mathrm{Sin}(\theta))$, between the two magnetic fields. In this application, the angle is 90 degrees and therefore the $\mathrm{Sin}(\theta)$ is equal to one. This is the maximum value that can be obtained. The last two items, the length of wire and the current, are the easiest ones to change. Both of these factors have some limitations. The wire, for instance, has a resistance. When an electric current flows through a resistance, it produces heat. The more current that flows, the hotter it gets. If the wire gets too hot, the insulation around the wire will melt. This will short out the coil, and make the speaker inoperative. To prevent this, most speakers have a power rating. As long as this value is not exceeded, the speaker will not be damaged by excessive current.

This leaves the length of wire as the only other factor that could be changed. Suppose, as shown in Fig. 2-11A, that the number or wires in the magnetic field is doubled. This will make the value of "L" in the force equation equal to 2L. The force will also double. The easiest way to increase the number of wires is to wind them into a coil. This is shown in Fig. 2-11B. Using this method, the number of wires can be increased until the space between the two poles of the magnets is full. This is the limitation on how much wire (length) can be placed inside of the magnetic field. Therefore, if the force must be increased, the easiest method is to increase either the number of turns of wire, or the current flowing in the wire.

At this point, you should have a some conceptual idea of how a magnetic field will produce a force of attraction or repulsion. Also, you should have an appreciation for some of the factors needed to create that force. In the following section, a brief description will be given about the construction of an electromagnetic speaker.

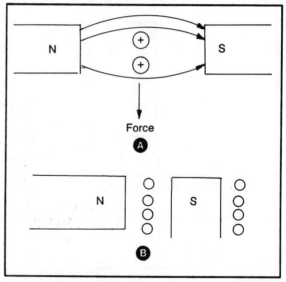

Fig. 2-11. Diagram shows (A) one method for increasing the force produced by a magnetic field, and (B) how more turns of wire can be added inside a magnetic field.

Speaker Construction

The material just covered has shown that the forces of attraction and repulsion can be used to produce a movement. Before describing how this principle is used to make a speaker function, a description will be given on how a speaker is made. Figure 2-12 is a cross sectional view of a typical speaker. In the center of the frame is a permanent magnet. A coil of wire is wound on a form, called a bobbin, and it is attached to the cone of the speaker. The suspension system holds the cone in place. Two wires, which are the electrical connections to the coil, are brought out to two terminals. Connecting a battery to these terminals, such as was done in Fig. 2-7, will make the coil move either toward or away from the permanent magnet. The exact direction is determined by which way the coil is polarized in respect to the fixed magnet. If the direction is such that the poles are of opposite polarity then the coil will move inward toward the magnet. If the coil polarity is the same as the fixed magnet, then the coil will move outwards.

Because the speaker cone is attached to the coil, it will follow the motion of the coil and a click

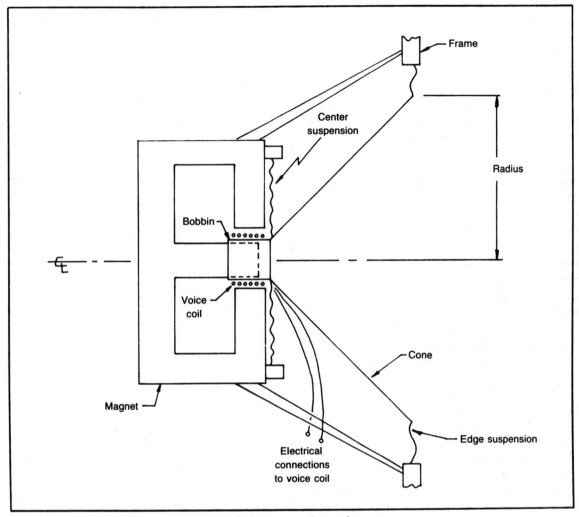

Fig. 2-12. Crosssectional view of a conventional electromagnetic speaker.

will be heard from the speaker. The magnitude of this movement is a function of battery voltage. The greater the voltage applied, the greater the current flowing, the greater the force generated, and the farther the cone will move. There are, of course, limits to both the movement and to how much voltage can be placed across the voice coil.

The suspension system limits the amount of cone travel. The speaker power rating determines the maximum voltage and the current. Exceeding either of these values can permanently damage the speaker.

How a Speaker Produces Sound

The preceding sections have described how a speaker is built, and also the principles of magnetics that are used to make the speaker cone move. This section will now indicate how a speaker produces a sound. First, when a speaker is part of an audio system, it is not connected to a battery. Instead, it receives an audio signal from an amplifier. The output voltage from the audio amplifier forces an electrical current through the voice coil of the speaker. The electrical connections are shown in the diagram of Fig. 2-13A. The waveform of Fig.

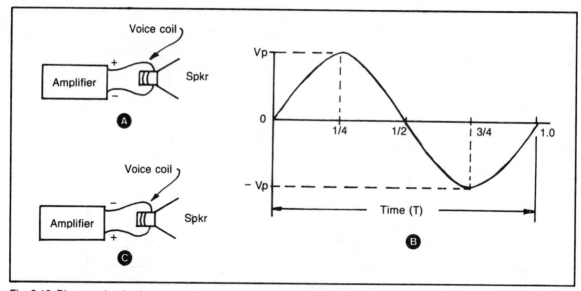

Fig. 2-13. Diagram showing how a speaker is connected to an amplifier and the time relationship of the voice coil current.

2-13B represents one cycle of the current that is flowing through the voice coil. As indicated in the diagram, the amplitude is zero when "T" equals zero, one-half and one. On the other hand, when "T" is equal to one quarter of the cycle the output signal is at its maximum positive value. This is Vp. When "T" is equal to three-quarters of a cycle the output has reached its maximum negative value. This is – Vp.

In Fig. 2-13B, the current flow is increasing in value from when "T" equals to zero until it reaches its maximum at "T" equal to 1/4 of a cycle. At 1/4 of the cycle, the current will reach its greatest amplitude and this will produce the strongest magnetic field. As a result, the voice coil and the attached speaker cone will move to their maximum displacement.

Note—the exact direction is dependent upon the polarity of the permanent magnet and the magnetic field which surrounds the voice coil.

The mechanical parts of the speaker cone suspension system is similar to a string. At Vp, the spring, which makes up the suspension system, will be stretched by the forces created in the magnetic field. From the time when "T" is equal to 1/4 to

the time when it equals 1/2 cycle, the amplitude of the current is decreasing. This will decrease the strength of the magnetic field. As the magnetic field decreases, the force produced by the stretched spring will make the cone return to its normal position. When the current and the magnetic force equal zero, the cone will have returned to its normal position.

In Fig. 2-13C, the output current from the amplifier has reversed its polarity. This will cause the current to flow in the opposite direction. As the electrical current increases in the voice coil, the magnetic field also increases. However, the polarity of the current is now opposite to the preceding one. This will make the coil and the cone move in the opposite direction. When the cone reaches the position at – Vp, the suspension spring will now be compressed. As the current decreases, the compression forces of the spring will push the cone back to its normal position at "T" equal to one.

If the frequency of the signal, in Fig. 2-13B, is 1000 Hz, then the coil and the cone will move back and forth 1000 times in one second. This motion of the cone will, in turn, cause the air molecules to vibrate, and this will create a corresponding change in the atmospheric pressure. Variations of the pressure will be propagated through the medium just like it did when the source was a string. Our ears and brain will again detect and interpret these variations as sound coming from the speaker.

PERFORMANCE FACTORS

The above discussion briefly describes how a speaker can produce a sound and how the surrounding medium reacts to the sound disturbance. This section will describe some of the other factors that affect a speaker's ability to produce sound.

Sound Power

In the process of making the string of Fig. 2-1 vibrate, some work had to be done. This work was initially performed by moving the string from its sured in Joules (newton/meters), ergs (dynes/centimeter) or in foot pounds. This is shown in Table 2-1. The factors used in calculating work are the force and the distance, and work is equal to the force multiplied by the distance (Work ^{5} Force × Distance). As an example, suppose the magnetic field applies a force of 3.937×10^{-3} newtons (approximately 0.000976 pounds) to the cone of a speaker. If this force causes the cone to move 2.54×10^{-4} meters (about 0.01 inches) the amount of work that was done is:

$$Work = Force \times Distance$$
$$= (3.937 \times 10^{-3}) \times (2.54 \times 10^{-4})$$
$$= 10^{-6} \text{ newton/meters or Joules}$$

Power and work are related factors. Power is the time needed to perform the required amount of work. If the speaker, in the above example, performs the indicated amount of work in one millisecond (0.001 seconds) then the power is equal to:

$$Power = Work/Time$$
$$= 10^{-6} \text{ Joules}/10^{-3} \text{ seconds}$$
$$= 10^{-3} \text{ watts}$$
$$= 1 \text{ milliwatt}$$

Although the calculations were for a speaker, the result is not a function of the speaker. The solution only indicates how much power was required to perform the indicated amount of work. The power that is radiated by a speaker is also a function of the cone diameter, the baffle (if any), the frequency, and the radiation impedance.

Radiation Impedance

As the cone moves, the air molecules next to the cone will resist this movement. This opposition consists of two components. The first one, the radiation resistance, is directly related to the resistance of the air. The second component is due to the air mass, and the combined effect is the radiation impedance.

To learn more about the characteristics of the radiation impedance, an electrical circuit can be used as an analogy. By comparing the impedances in an electrical circuit with those of an acoustic circuit, a better understanding of the radiation impedance will be obtained. For instance, in Fig. 2-14A, the current flow (I) is proportional to the applied voltage and to the total impedance.

The total impedance in this circuit, is a function of the components marked "L" and "R." The opposition created by the inductance "L" is $j\omega L$. Omega (ω) is equal to 6.28 times the frequency of the source voltage. The value of "L" is the inductance in henries. The "j" term indicates that the opposition created by "L" uses a different reference point then the one used by the resistor. Because of this difference, the two values cannot be directly added together. A pictorial diagram of this relationship is shown Fig. 2-14B. To find the impedance (Z), the values of R and $j\omega L$ must be combined as the square root of the sum of the squares. That is: $Z = (R^2 + (\omega L)^2)^{1/2}$.

As an example, suppose that the frequency of the source, in Fig. 2-14A, is 1000 Hz and the inductance equals 0.1 Henries. The value of (ω) is equal to $6.28 \times f$ ($6.28 \times 1000 = 6280$) and the opposition produced by "L" is:

$$j\omega L = 6280 \times 0.1 = j628 \text{ ohms.}$$

If "R" is a 100 ohms resistor the equivalent impedance diagram is shown in Fig. 2-14C. The total

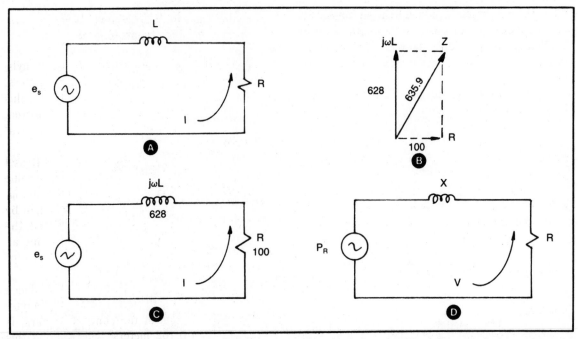

Fig 2-14. Diagram showing the similarity between the electrical impedance in a circuit and the acoustical impedance as seen by a speaker cone.

impedance in this circuit is equal to:

$$Z = (R^2 + (\omega L)^2)^{1/2}$$

Where Z = the total impedance in ohms.
R = the resistance of the resistor in ohms.
L = the inductance in Henries.
jωL = the impedance of the inductor in ohms.
ω = $2 \times pi \times f$

Using the values shown in Fig. 2-14C, the total impedance of this electrical circuit is equal to:

$$Z = ((100)^2 + j(638)^2)^{1/2}$$
$$= 635.9 \text{ ohms.}$$

The difference between the reference point for the inductor and that of the resistor is the phase angle. This value can be calculated by:

Phase Angle(θ) = $\tan^{-1}$ (jωL/R)
Where θ = the phase angle in degrees.

For the values used in this example, the phase angle is:

Phase Angleθ = $\tan^{-1}$ (628/100)
= 81 degrees

Because the phase angle is positive and very large, it indicates that the impedance is mostly dependent on "L." At a frequency of 10 Hertz this same analysis would show that the resistor is the controlling factor.

Any resistance in an electrical circuit, such as Fig. 2-14C, is often referred to as the real part of the impedance. The opposition associated with jwL is the imaginary part. In a resistor, power is being dissipated as heat. This is real and can be measured. The inductor, on the other hand, dissipates no power but stores the energy in its magnetic field. At some later time, this energy will be returned to the circuit.

The circuit shown in Fig. 2-14D is an electrical representation of an acoustic circuit. The resis-

34

tance in this circuit is radiation resistance of the air while the inductance represents the air mass. In an electrical circuit, current flow is produced by the application of a voltage source. This creates a difference in voltage throughout the electrical circuit.

In an acoustic circuit, the air molecules move because there is a difference in the atmospheric pressure. This value is Pr in Fig. 2-14D. In the electrical circuit, the current flow is the result of the moving electrons. The measurement unit is the ampere. In an acoustic circuit, the particle velocity is due to the movement of the air molecules. This movement is in units of cubic meters/second or in cubic centimeters/second. Because the circuit of Fig. 2-14D resembles that of Fig. 2-14A, the acoustic circuit will have properties that are similar to those of the electrical circuit.

The ka factor

The ka factor is very important and appears in many of the calculations for a loudspeaker. In one area, for instance, it relates the size of the speaker to the dimensions of its acoustical output. The value of k is the wave number and it is equal to Omega divided by the velocity. That is: $k = \omega/c = (2 \times pi \times f)/c = 6.28 \times f/\lambda$. For c in meters, this factor is equal to $1.831 \times 10-2 \times f$. The value of k is also equal to $1.826 \times 10-4 \times f$ when c is in centimeters. The value of "a" equals the radius of the speaker cone. The units for this function must be the same as those used for c in the wavelength equation.

For the acoustical diagram of Fig. 2-14D, the acoustic resistance of the air must include the characteristics of the speaker. The value of the radiation resistance (Rr) is equal to:

	Rr	=	pcAR1(2ka)
Where	Rr	=	the radiation resistance.
	pc	=	the resistance of the media.
	A	=	the area of the cone in meter^2.
	R1	=	a Bessel function
	k	=	$6.28/\lambda$

λ = 343/f
f = the frequency in Hertz.
a = cone radius in meters.

In the MKS system, the value of pc is 405 rayls, and "A" is the area of the cone in square meters. Because most speakers have circular cones, this value is equal to pi multiplied by the radius squared. Symbolically this can be written as $A = pi \times a^2 = 3.1416 \times a^2$.

In the above equation, the term R1 is a Bessel function. Although this sounds formidable, its value can be obtained from either the graph shown in Fig. 2-15, from the values contained in Table 2-2, or by direct calculation. Whichever method is used, the actual process is no more difficult than some algebraic exercises. In this equation, the values for k and a have already been identified.

As an example, suppose that you have an 8 inch speaker and you wish to determine its radiation resistance. The radius of the cone, in meters, is $(4 \times 2.54 \times 10^{-2})$ 0.102 meters^2. Substituting this value together with the other known values makes the equation for the radiation resistance equal to:

$$Rr = 405(A)R1(3.72 \times 10^{-3} \times f)$$
$$= 1.51 \times A \times R1 \times f$$

The area of the cone is equal to:

$$A = 3.1416(4 \times 2.54 \times 10^{-2})^2$$
$$= 32.4 \times 10^{-3} \text{ meters}^2$$

Inserting this value into the equation provides the following result.

$$Rr = 1.51 \times (32.4 \times 10^{-3}) \times R1 \times f$$
$$= 4.9 \times 10^{-2} \times R1 \times f$$

As already indicated, there are a three possible methods for obtaining the value of R1. One approximation is to let $R1 = x^2/8$. In this equation, the value of x is equal to 2ka. Before doing this calculation, a frequency must be selected. For this example, suppose the frequency "f" is equal to 268.8

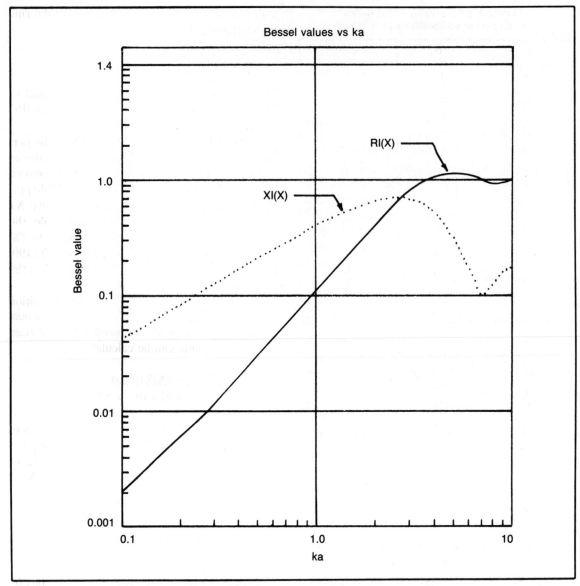

Fig. 2-15. A graph that relates the Bessel function to the acoustic factor ka.

Hertz. This makes the value of k equal to:

$$k = (6.28/343) \times f$$
$$= (18.31 \times 10^{-3}) \times 268.8$$
$$= 4.921$$

The ka factor is obtained by multiplying this last number by the radius of the speaker (ka =

$4.921 \times 0.102 = 0.502$). If this value is doubled then R1 is equal to $(1)^2/8$ and this is equal to 0.125. With this last calculation, all of the factors for the radiation resistance have now been defined. The calculated value of Rr is equal to:

$$Rr = 4.9 \times 10^{-2} \times R1 \times f$$
$$= 4.9 \times 10^{-2} \times (0.125) \times f$$

x	R1(x)	X1(x)
0.0	0.0000	0.0000
0.1	0.0020	0.0424
0.2	0.0050	0.0847
0.3	0.0113	0.1272
0.4	0.0198	0.1680
0.5	0.0308	0.2120
0.6	0.0443	0.2486
0.7	0.0600	0.2968
0.8	0.0779	0.3253
0.9	0.0991	0.3816
1.0	0.1199	0.3969
1.1	0.1438	0.4296
1.2	0.1695	0.4624
1.3	0.1969	0.4915
1.4	0.2257	0.5207
1.5	0.2561	0.5460
1.6	0.2876	0.5713
1.7	0.3201	0.5924
1.8	0.3539	0.6134
1.9	0.3883	0.6301
2.0	0.4233	0.6468
2.2	0.4946	0.6711
2.4	0.5665	0.6862
2.6	0.6378	0.6925
2.8	0.7073	0.6903
3.0	0.7740	0.6800
3.2	0.8367	0.6623
3.4	0.8946	0.6381
3.6	0.9470	0.6081
3.8	0.9932	0.5733
4.0	1.0330	0.5349
5.0	1.1310	0.3232
6.0	1.0922	0.1594
7.0	1.0013	0.0989
8.0	0.9413	0.1219
9.0	0.9455	0.1663
10.0	0.9913	0.1784

$$= 6.13 \times 10^{-3} \times (268.8)$$
$$= 1.65 \text{ ohms}$$

This is the resistance of R in Fig. 2-14D.

The method just used for determining R1 is usually adequate. As stated, however, there are several other ways to obtain its value. The approximation used in the example was the first term of a power series. The graph shown in Fig. 2-15 will provide another approximation. Although this value is not as accurate, it does have the advantage of being quick and convenient. If more accuracy is desired, the power series can be expanded. The following equation shows the second and third terms of the series.

$$R1(x) = (x^2/8 - x^4/192 + x^6/9216)$$

Using this formula, the value of R1 is equal to 0.1199. This will make the radiation resistance (Rr) equal to 1.58 ohms.

If a number of these calculations must be performed, the process can become quite tedious. While you could use a computer, the values shown in Table 2-2 will do the same thing. This table provides the value of R1 as well as a term called X1 for each value of "x." In the above example, the value of "x" was equal to 1.000. Referring to Table 2-2, the corresponding value for R1(x) is 0.1199. This is the same number that was obtained in the above calculation.

In the previous electrical circuit, the opposition created by "L" was indicated by $j\omega L$. In the acoustic diagram, the opposition caused by the air mass is X_r and its value can be calculated by:

$$X_r = pc(A)X1(2ka)$$
$$= 4.91 \times 10^{-3} \times X1 \times f$$

X1 is another Bessel function and the first term of its power series is equal to $4(x)/3 \times pi$. At the point where "x" is equal to one (268.8 Hz), the value of X1 is 0.424, and the radiation impedance X_r is equal to:

$$X_r = 4.91 \times 10^{-3} \times 0.424 \times f$$
$$= 2.08 \times 10^{-3} \times f$$
$$= 5.60 \text{ ohms}$$

For quick results, the value of X1 could be obtained from the graph of Fig. 2-15. There are two methods that can be used to increase the accuracy of this calculation. First, more terms of the series can be used. The equation shown below is an expansion of the power series for the factor X1.

$$X1 = (4/pi) \times (x/3 - x^3/45 + x^5/1575)$$

The second method is to use a corresponding value from Table 2-2.

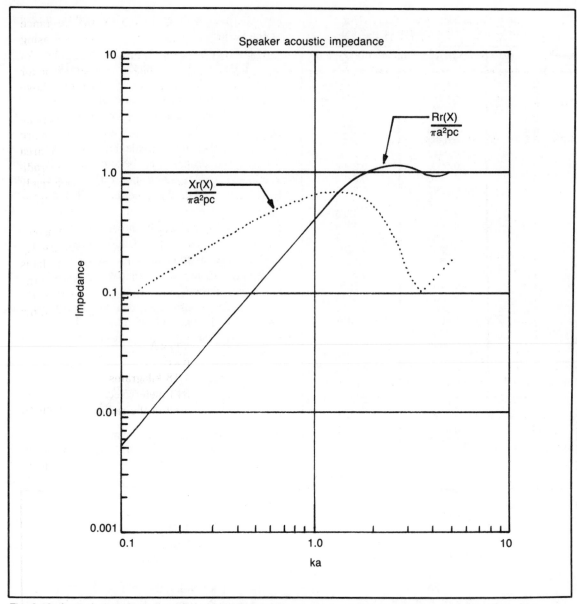

Fig. 2-16. A graph that shows the relationship between the speaker's radiation resistance and the value of ka.

In the electrical circuit, the total impedance is obtained by combining the real and imaginary impedances. This method could also be used to determine the total acoustic impedance for the above example. Combining the two values will produce the following result.

$$Z_r = ((R_r)^2 + (X_r)^2)^{1/2}$$
$$= ((1.65)^2 + (5.60)^2)^{1/2}$$
$$= 5.83 \text{ ohms.}$$

The associated phase angle is 73.5 degrees. This large positive number indicates that the reactance

38

of the air mass is greater than the resistance. As such, it will be the main factor that affects the speaker acoustic output. Most books do not combine these terms. A graph of the radiation resistance (R_r) and the radiation impedance (X_r) is shown in Fig. 2-16.

Radiated Power vs Frequency

In the graph of Fig. 2-17, the speaker frequency response has been divided into sections. Each section is controlled by some component of the speaker. At first glance, the most notable area is the peak which occurs in section "B." The peak is the resonant frequency of the speaker. The height of the peak is a function of both the electrical and the radiation resistance.

In section "A," below the resonant frequency, the response is controlled by the compliance of the suspension system. The output in this region falls rapidly and is equal to 12 db/octave.

In region "C," the speaker output is controlled by the air mass. The curves of Fig. 2-16 indicate how the speaker radiation impedance (X_r) and its radiation resistance (R_r) vary. This variation is a function of the wave number "k" and the radius of the piston "a." The curves are for a speaker mounted on an infinite baffle. Below the point where ka is equal to two, the air mass (X_r) is the predominate factor. In this region, the reactance of X_r rises in direct proportion to the increasing frequency. It reaches a maximum value when ka is between one and two. Below this value, the air mass keeps the speakers output constant. Above this point the value of X_r decreases.

In section "C," the value of R_r is also increasing. In this case, the value goes up by the square of the increase in frequency. Except for the area around the point where ka is equal to one, the radiation resistance is less the reactance. As already stated, the air mass controls the speaker performance in region "C."

In section "D" of Fig. 2-17, the fall in the acoustic output is due to the radiation resistance R_r. This region is located above the point where ka is equal to two. As already noted, the reactance of the air mass (X_r) falls to a value that is less then R_r. In this region, the value of R_r can be calculated by:

$$\begin{aligned} R_r &= 405 \times A \\ \text{Where} \quad 405 &= p \times c \\ p &= 1.18 \text{ kilograms.} \\ c &= 343 \text{ meters/sec.} \\ A &= \text{area of the radiator in meters.} \end{aligned}$$

As indicated, the point where ka equals two is important. Above this point, the speaker radiation an-

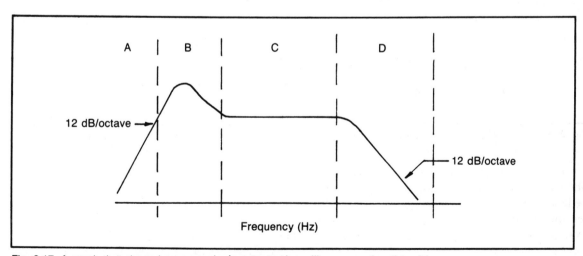

Fig. 2-17. A graph that shows how a speaker's output value will vary as a function of frequency.

gle decreases, for increasing frequency, and the speaker becomes directional.

Directivity

The ka factor also appears in the calculations for speaker directivity. The polar plot of Fig. 2-18 indicates how the radiation angle changes as a function of ka and how the acoustic output decreases with this change.

Although the polar plot of Fig. 2-18 only indicates the radiation pattern for specific values of ka, the loss for any value can be calculated by:

$$P/P_{ref} = (2 \times [J_1(x)]/(x))$$

Where P = the acoustic power at some angle that is referenced to the speakers axis.

P_{ref} = Acoustic power at the same distance but on axis with the speaker.

$J_1(x)$ = Bessel function.

(x) = $ka \times \sin\theta$

The diagram shown in Fig. 2-19 pictorially indicates how these quantities are related. As an example suppose that we want to know the acoustic output, at an angle of 45 degrees, for an 8 inch speaker. The first step in the process is to determine the value of "x." Previously the value of k was calculated as being equal to $1.831 \times 10^{-2} \times$ f. The radius (a) is 0.102 meters. The value of ka is 1.863×10^{-3} and for an angle of 45 degrees the value of "x" equal to:

$$x = 1.831 \times 10^{-3} \times f \times \sin\theta$$
$$= 1.831 \times 10^{-3} \times f \times 0.707$$
$$= 1.320 \times 10^{-3} \times f$$

If f equals 268.8 Hz, then "x" equals 0.355. The power at P_{45} is equal to:

$$P_{45}/P_{ref} = (2 \times [J_1(0.355)]/0.355)$$
$$= 5.63 \times [J_1(0.355)]$$

The value of J_1 can be obtained from Table 2-3 and the number corresponding to 0.355 is 0.1722. This makes P_{45} equal to:

$$P_{45} = 5.63 \times (0.1722) \times P_{ref}$$

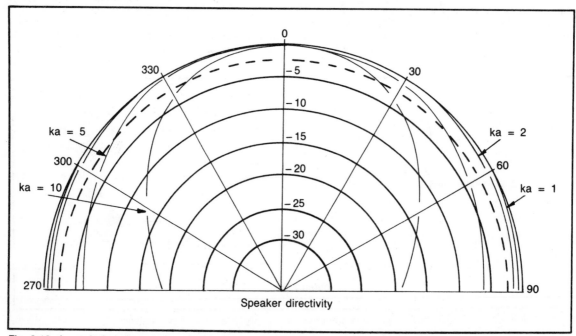

Fig. 2-18. A graph that shows how a speaker's acoustic directivity as a function of ka.

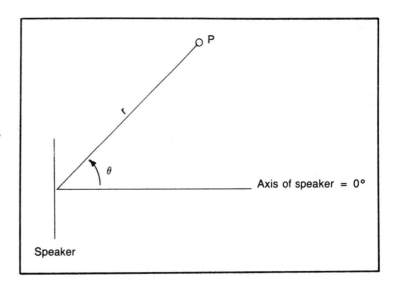

Fig. 2-19. A diagram that indicates how a speaker's directivity is determined.

In the diagram: P, r, θ, Axis of speaker = 0°, Speaker

If P_{ref} is assumed to be unity then P_{45} equals:

$$P_{45} = 5.63 \times (0.1722)$$
$$= 0.9695$$
$$= -0.27 \text{ db.}$$

This calculation indicates the value of the radiated power at an angle of 45 degrees. As shown, it is slightly less than the power produced on axis with the center of the speaker.

For the above calculations, there are two methods which can be used to determining the value of the Bessel function. The first method is to use the Bessel value from column two of Table 2-3 and some basic calculations. An alternate method is to use the last column in Table 2-3. The value shown here has already been calculated for the function $(2 \times [J_1(x)]/(x))$. If the value of P_{45} is determined from this table, the result is 0.9941 and that is equal to -0.052 db.

This same procedure can also be used for values of ka between 2 and 3. A calculation corresponding to these values of ka indicates that the power radiated by the speaker will be down -4.78 and -12.9 decibels respectively. This drop in acoustic power indicates why it is desirable to keep the radiation pattern hemispherical.

Because a hemispherical pattern only occurs when ka is less then one, the diameter of the speaker must be reduced as the frequency is increased. Commercial speaker manufacturers use one of two methods to maintain wide radiation angles. One technique is used in the so-called extended range speakers. In this type of speaker, the size of the cone is decreased by mechanical means, so that radiating area gets smaller. Suppose the 8 inch speaker is made so that above 268.8 Hz the radiating area is decreased to 2 inches. The frequency where ka will equal one is now increased from 268.8 to 2150 Hz.

Another approach to overcoming the directivity problem is to use a number of separate speakers. Each speaker is connected through a crossover network so that the system covers the audio range. This technique is more expensive then using a single cone speaker. However, it does have the advantage of extreme flexibility. The output of each speaker can be tailored to the specific requirements for the ka factor.

OTHER FACTORS THAT AFFECT CONE MOVEMENT

Once the cone can be made to move, there are several factors that can affect the speakers performance. Some of the factors are: the strength of the magnetic field, the length of the voice coil, the type of material that is used to make the cone, the stiffness or compliance of the cone mounting system,

Table 2-3. Bessel Valves That Relate to a Speaker's Directivity. (x = ka sin θ)

	$J_1(x)$	$\dfrac{2J_1(x)}{x}$
0.0	0.0000	1.0000
0.1	0.4990	0.9980
0.2	0.0995	0.9950
0.3	0.1483	0.9887
0.4	0.1960	0.9802
0.5	0.2423	0.9692
0.6	0.2867	0.9557
0.7	0.3290	0.9400
0.8	0.3688	0.9221
0.9	0.4059	0.9009
1.0	0.4401	0.8801
1.1	0.4709	0.8562
1.2	0.4983	0.8305
1.3	0.5220	0.8031
1.4	0.5419	0.7743
1.5	0.5579	0.7439
1.6	0.5699	0.7124
1.7	0.5778	0.6799
1.8	0.5815	0.6461
1.9	0.5811	0.6117
2.0	0.5767	0.5767
2.2	0.5560	0.5054
2.4	0.5202	0.4335
2.6	0.4708	0.3622
2.8	0.4097	0.2927
3.0	0.3391	0.2260
3.2	0.2613	0.1633
3.4	0.1792	0.1054
3.6	0.0955	0.0530
3.8	0.0128	0.0068
4.0	−0.0660	−0.0330
5.0	−0.3276	−0.1310
6.0	−0.2767	−0.0922
7.0	−0.0047	−0.0013
8.0	0.2346	0.0587
9.0	0.2453	0.0545
10.0	0.0435	0.0087

briefly discuss each of these components. Those readers who wish to explore the subject further are referred to the appendix for references to other appropriate material.

Mass of the Cone

The first factors to be considered is the mass of the cone. This component is identified in Fig. 2-20 as X_m. The mass of a speaker is determined by the material used to make the cone. If the cone is paper, it will have a different mass then if it is polypropolene. The force that is required to move the cone is related to the mass by the following equation.

$$F = m \times a$$

Where
F = the force in newtons.
m = Mass of the cone in kilograms.
a = the acceleration in seconds^2.

As an example of this calculation, suppose that a speaker cone has a mass of 0.05 kilograms. Also assume that the cone must move 0.01 inches in 250 microseconds (250 microseconds equals 0.000250 seconds). Before the acceleration can be determined, the velocity of the moving cone must be calculated. Velocity is equal to the distance traveled divided by the time. For this example the velocity can be calculated by:

$$v = \text{distance/time} = 0.01/0.00025$$
$$= 40 \text{ inches/second}$$

and how well the speaker is matched to the air load. While these are not all of the factors that determine a speaker's performance, they are some off the most important ones. Other factors, such as cabinets, are used to improve the results obtained from the speaker. This subject is adequately covered in other books on speaker systems.

Speaker Model

A simple electrical representation of a speaker is shown in Fig. 2-20. The following material will

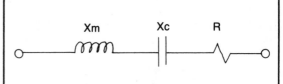

Xm = Mass of the speaker cone

Xc = Compliance of the speaker suspension system

R = Dc resistance of the voice coil

Fig. 2-20. The basic mechanical and electrical components of an electromagnetic speaker.

Acceleration is a term used to indicate a change in the speed or velocity. The acceleration is related to the velocity by:

$$a = (v1 - v0)/time$$

Where
v1 = final velocity
v0 = beginning velocity
a = acceleration in inches/sec.^{2}

In this example, it is assumed that the initial velocity is zero and the final velocity is equal to the calculated value. Inserting the values for the velocity and the time into the formula the speaker cone is accelerated to:

$$a = (40 - 0)/0.00025$$
$$= 1.6 \times 10^5 \text{ inches/sec}^2$$

Before this value can be used in the force equation it must be converted from inches/sec^2 to meters/sec^2. This is accomplished by multiplying the above answer by 2.54×10^{-2}.

$$a(\text{meters/sec}^2) = a(\text{inches/sec}^2) \times (2.54 \times 10^{-2})$$
$$= (1.6 \times 10^5) \times (2.54 \times 10^{-2})$$
$$= 4.064 \times 10^3 \text{ meters/sec}^2$$

For ease in the following calculation this answer will be rounded out to 4.1×10^3 meters/sec^2.

Now that a value for mass and acceleration is known, a corresponding value for the force can be calculated. This value will indicate the amount of force that will be necessary to move the cone the indicated distance in the specified time. The required force is:

$$F = m \times a$$
$$= (0.05) \times (4.1 \times 10^3)$$
$$= 205 \text{ newtons}$$

To most people, a force of 205 newtons will not mean much. However, this value can be converted to pounds by multiplying it by 0.248. When this is done, the result is:

$$F(\text{pounds}) = F(\text{newtons}) \times 0.248$$
$$= 205 \times 0.248$$
$$= 50.84 \text{ pounds}$$

This value indicates that if a cone with a mass of 0.05 kilograms must move 0.01 inches in 250 microseconds, then the required force must be 50.8 pounds. As already indicated, this force must come from the electromagnetic field.

Compliance

The next factor that will be considered is the speaker cone compliance. This is identified in Fig. 2-20 as Xc. Compliance, or stiffness, is a function of the cone mounting system. These two terms are frequently associated with the characteristics of a spring. If a spring is compliant, then it can be stretched or compressed easily. If it is very compliant, then the spring can easily be stretched or compressed but may not return to its original position after the force is removed. This situation cannot be tolerated in a speaker. If the force which moves the speaker cone is removed, then the cone must return to its zero position. On the other hand, if the spring has very little compliance, then an excessive amount of force will be needed to make the cone move. The value of the compliance "C" is equal to:

$$C = x/F$$

Where
C = the compliance in meters/newton.
x = the displacement in meters.
F = the force in newtons.

Examples of this type of calculation are indicated in the compliance section of Chapter 3.

Resistance

The last item shown in Fig. 2-20 is resistance. This is the resistance of the voice coil. Its value is determined by the diameter and length of the wire used to make the coil.

Linearity

Linearity is a relationship between the input

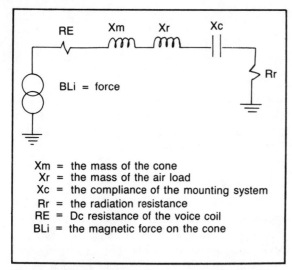

Xm = the mass of the cone
Xr = the mass of the air load
Xc = the compliance of the mounting system
Rr = the radiation resistance
RE = Dc resistance of the voice coil
BLi = the magnetic force on the cone

Fig. 2-21. All of the components that determine how an electromagnetic speaker operates.

and output characteristics of a speaker. The input is the electrical current and the output is the movement of the cone. If the speaker is perfectly linear, then the cone movement per unit of electrical current will always be the same. Within certain boundaries this will be true. However, as the cone is required to move further and further, it may reach a region that is non-linear. In this region, the current does not force the cone to move the same amount and therefore some distortion will be introduced.

The preceding discussion has shown that there are a number of factors that can and do affect the performance of a speaker. It would seem appropriate, at this point, to combine all of these parameters into one composite diagram that can be used to represent an electromagnetic speaker. This diagram is shown in Fig. 2-21.

Chapter 3

Speaker Measurements

After reading Chapter 2, you should have a basic understanding of how an electromagnetic speaker operates. In addition to this, you should also be familiar with some of the factors that affect the speakers' ability to produce a sound. This chapter will explore these factors a little further, and will provide a technique to measure the major components of a speaker.

Measurements on a speaker can be divided into two groups. Tests in the first group are related to the mechanical and electrical properties of the speaker, and the second group measures the speakers acoustic output.

MECHANICAL AND ELECTRICAL PARAMETERS

With the acceptance of the Thiele/Small relationship, it has become popular to measure a loudspeaker system performance and from this determine the best enclosure for a particular speaker. The one problem with this technique is that it does not reveal why two similar drivers may

have slightly different performance characteristics. Information of this type can only be obtained by determining which of the major components has different characteristics. The following material should provide some of these details.

Determining the Cone Mass

In the last chapter, under the section titled "Other Factors that Affect Cone Movement" the analysis began with the mass of the cone. This section will continue this dialog and show how to measure the mass of a speaker cone.

At all frequencies, the speaker performance is influenced by both the mass of the cone and by its compliance. At the resonant frequency however, the two reactances (X_m and X_c of Fig. 2-20) are equal but opposite in sign. When that happens, the two values cancel each other and this produces a significant increase in the speaker acoustic output. At this point, if either X_m or X_c is altered, there will be a corresponding change in the resonant frequency. A requirement for changing either one of the components is that it must not damage the speaker. With this constraint, the easiest part to change is the mass of the cone. When this is done there will be a new resonant frequency. The original mass of the cone can be determined from the two resonant frequencies and the value of the added mass.

The initial step in determining the mass of the cone is to measure the speaker free air resonant frequency. This can be done by first connecting the circuit shown in Fig. 3-1. Next, vary the frequency of the audio oscillator from 10 to 100 Hz. As the oscillator frequency approaches the speaker resonant frequency, the voltmeter reading will increase. The peak reading will correspond to the speakers resonant frequency.

During this test process, it is a good idea to keep the voltmeter reading near a value of one volt. Too small a value can introduce errors due to noise. Too large a signal may cause the cone to exceed the limits of its suspension system, and this will also introduce errors in the readings.

The equation for the resonant frequency of an electrical circuit is:

$$fr = (1.59 \times 10^{-1})/(L \times C)^{1/2}$$
Where L = the inductance in the circuit.
  C = the capacitance in the circuit.

A similar type of equation is used to determine the resonant frequency of the speaker mechanical system. The equation for the resonant frequency of a mechanical function is:

$$fr = (1.59 \times 10^{-1})/(m \times C)^{1/2}$$

Where m = the mass of the mechanical system.
  C = the compliance of the mechanical system.

To solve this equation, two of the three factors must be known. The above procedure, for the resonant frequency, provides one of the factors. To obtain a second factor, the mass must be changed and a new resonant frequency must be measured. When an additional mass is added to the cone, the equation for the resonant frequency is:

$$fr + frc = (1.59 \times 10^{-1})/[(m + ma) \times C]^{1/2}$$
Where frc = the change in the resonant frequency caused by the added mass.
  ma = the value of the added mass.

If fr_1 is the original free air cone resonance, then fr_2 is the new resonant frequency caused by the added mass. In the above equation, $fr^2 = (fr + frc)$. Substituting these changes into the equations for the resonant frequency produces the following result.

$$fr_1 = (1.59 \times 10^{-1})/(m \times C)^{1/2}$$

and

$$fr_2 = (1.59 \times 10 - 1)/[(m + ma) \times C]^{1/2}$$

Both equations have one common factor, and because of this they can be solved simultaneously for the compliance. After completing this step the result is:

$$m = [ma \times (fr_2)^2]/[(fr_1)^2 - (fr_2)^2]$$

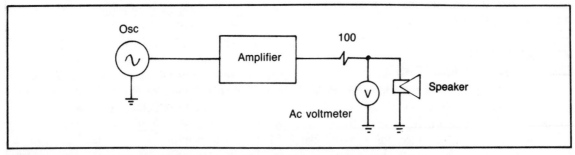

Fig. 3-1. A test system for determining the mass of an electromagnetic speaker.

With a little simplification this can be reduced to:

$$m = ma/[(fr_1)^2/(fr_2)^2 - 1]$$

As already noted, the easiest method for changing the mass of the speaker cone is to add a weight of known value, to the cone. This will be *ma* in the above equation. The effect of the added weight is to increase the mass of the cone and this will produce a lower resonant frequency. After adding the weight, sweep the oscillator frequency over the 10 to 100 Hz range. The voltmeter reading should again rise to a peak value, and this will correspond to the new resonant frequency. This is fr_2 in the above equation. At this point, all of the factors in the last equation are known and it can be solved for the mass.

When performing this test, make sure that the added weight doesn't rattle. Use several pieces of sticky tape to hold the weight to the center of the cone. Failure to have the weight securely held can produce errors in the calculated results.

To test the above procedure, a measurement was made on an eight inch speaker. This speaker was manufactured by Radio Shack and its part number is 40-1021. It was chosen for this initial test because the manufacturer specifies the mass of the cone. This information can be used to check both the measurement accuracy as well as the procedure.

As an initial step, two readings were taken of the speaker free air cone resonance. When making this measurement, do not use the frequency dial on the oscillator as an indication of the frequency. Most of them are inaccurate. The resonant frequency in this example, was measured with an oscilloscope. For very accurate results use an electronic counter. Table 3-1 indicates the measured results as well as the manufacturers specification.

Once the free air cone resonance is known, the next step is to add some additional weight to the cone. The value of this weight must be accurately known. One object that seems to fulfill this requirement is a 25 cent coin. To determine the possible weight variation, three coins were measured on a laboratory gram scale. The results indicated that the coin weight did not vary by more then 5% (0.21 grams). The measured value for each of the three coins was 5.58, 5.71, and 5.50 grams. The average weight for all three was 5.6 grams.

After taping one of the quarters to the center of the speaker cone, the resonant frequency was remeasured. For accuracy, two readings were also taken of this measurement. Table 3-1 indicates the result of this measurement. A calculation based on

Table 3-1. Measurement Values for Determining the Mass of a Speaker Cone.

	Test #1	Test #2	Ave.	Mfg. Data
Free air resonance With qtr #1 With qtr #2	34.48 30.3 30.3	35.71 30.3 30.3	35.09 30.3 30.3	30 (+/− 8)
Calculated values of the mass				
With qtr #1 With qtr #2	16.74 16.12	16.74 16.12	16.74 16.12	16.5

The value of the mass was calculated according to the following formula.

$$M = M1/((f1/f2)^2 - 1)$$

Where M = the mass of the speaker cone
M1 = the mass of the added weight
f1 = the free air cone resonance
f2 = the cone resonance with the added weight

the average values suggests that the mass of speaker cone was 16.4 grams. Radio Shack literature specifies the mass as 16.5 grams. This is a measurement error of less than 1%. As an added accuracy check, Table 3-1 also indicates the results of a second test. This test used a different coin and the results were only slightly different than the first reading.

Compliance Measurement

The second component in the diagram of Fig. 2-20 is X_c. Its value is a function of the compliance associated with the cone mounting system. As you might expect, compliance is another parameter that is important in the operation of the speaker, and one that is seldom if ever identified.

The compliance (C) can be determined from the measurements taken for the mass of the cone. The previous equations for the resonant frequencies, can be manipulated so that the solution will indicate the value of the compliance instead of the mass. When this is done the result is:

$$C = [(fr_1)^2/(fr_2)^2 - 1]/[m \times 39.48 \times (fr_1)^2]$$

Radio Shack does not define the compliance for its 8 inch speaker. However, the accuracy obtained in measuring the mass would indicate that a similar accuracy should be obtained for the compliance. Using the average numbers from Table 3-1, the compliance is 1.253×10^{-6} cm/dyne.

There are several methods that can be used to check the accuracy of this measurement. As a reference point, suppose that the mass of the cone specified by the manufacturer, is used to calculate the value of X_m. Numerically, this will be equal to the value of X_c. At the resonant frequency a mass of 16.5 grams will have an opposition (Xm) that is equal to 3572 ohms. Inserting this value into the equation for Xc and solving for the compliance provides a value of 1.293×10^{-6} cm/dyne. This is a measurement error of less 3.1% in the above value. Another way to determine the measurement accuracy is to substitute the values obtained for the mass and the compliance into their respective formulas and then solve for Xm and Xc. If the mea-

surement procedure is correct, these two values should be equal.

Determining the Magnetic Force

One other factor that is rarely ever specified is the magnetic force. This force, which moves the speaker cone, is very important in the operation of the speaker. It affects both the efficiency and the speaker power handling capability. As indicated in Chapter 2, the factors which contribute to the force are the strength of the magnetic field and the length of the voice coil inside that field. Of course, the amount of current that is flowing through the wire is also a factor. While text books on speaker design will treat each of these factors separately, it is difficult to make any test on a completed speaker that will indicate a value for either the field strength or the length of the wire. Because the magnetic field and the length of the voice coil are fixed by the speaker manufacturer, they will be treated as a single factor.

In Chapter 2, the force that moved the cone was identified as being equal to the Bl product multiplied by the current flowing in the voice coil. In equation form this is written as:

$$F = Bl \times I$$

Where F = the force in Newtons
B = Flux density in Webers/M^2
l = the length of the voice coil in meters
I = current flowing in the voice coil in amperes

The procedure for determining the Bl product is to apply an external force to the speaker cone. Next, measure how much current will be necessary to return the cone to its state of equilibrium. With these two factors, the value of the Bl product can be obtained by calculation. Figure 3-2 is a diagram of a fixture that can be used for this purpose. For this measurement, place the speaker face up on your work surface and connect the electrical components as shown in the diagram.

Before actually performing this test, a circular cardboard disc should be placed over the apex of the cone. A convenient source for the cardboard is the back of a writing tablet. Turn the tablet over and, with a compass, draw a circle that is larger than the center of the cone but smaller than its outside diameter. The one that was made for the Radio Shack speaker had a diameter of five inches. The purpose of the disc is twofold. First, it provides a flat surface for measuring the movement of the cone and, second, it acts as a safety precaution in case something is dropped on the cone.

As shown in Fig. 3-2, the fixture needed to measure the force is relatively simple. First, take a piece of stiff wire and bend it so that it can be fastened to a screw that will be inserted in one of the speaker mounting holes. The other end of this wire is bent until it just touches the cardboard disc. After assembling the fixture and positioning the wire so that it touches the cardboard disc, place a weight on top of the disc. The weight does not have to be held down because the cone will not be vibrating. When the weight is placed on the disc, it should deflect the cardboard disc about 1/32 of an inch. For this part of the experiment, a convenient weight is several quarters.

Now that the weight is in place on the cardboard disc, the next step is to connect the voice coil to the indicated circuit. Be sure to set the variable

resistor to its maximum resistance. Turn on the voltage source and gradually decrease the value of the resistance. Check to see which direction the cone is moving. If it is moving away from the wire, reverse the connections to the voice coil. When the cone moves toward the wire, continue decreasing the resistance until the wire just touches the cardboard disc. When this happens, the cone has moved back to its original position and the equation $F = Bl \times I$ is balanced. The force in this case is equal to the weight of the quarters. The current flowing in the voice coil, can be read from the milliammeter. This measurement has now provided two of the three factors in the force equation and it can be solved for the Bl product.

One small problem exists at this point and that is the system of units. The equation for the force is in MKS units, while the measured values are closer to the CGS system of units. If the results are needed in MKS units, then a correction factor will have to be added to the equation. When this is done the equation to determine the Bl product is:

$$Bl = k(M/I) \text{ gauss.}$$

Where
- M = the added weight in grams.
- I = the current in milliamperes.
- k = 9.8×10^6 which is a factor used to convert the equation to the proper units.

Another problem with this simple setup was being able to determine when the wire and the cardboard actually touch. If they don't quite make it (although it may look like it to the eye), the force calculation will be high. On the other hand, if the cardboard disc pushes the wire upwards then the force calculation will be low.

To overcome this, a strip of pressure sensitive copper conductive tape was placed on top of the cardboard disc. The copper strip used for this measurement was 1/4 inch wide and 4 inches long. The actual dimensions are not really important. It just needs to be large enough so that a connection can be made to the strip and so that it will touch the wire. Pressure sensitive conductive tape is used to make prototype pc boards and the material can be obtained from Bishop Graphics and electronic supply houses.

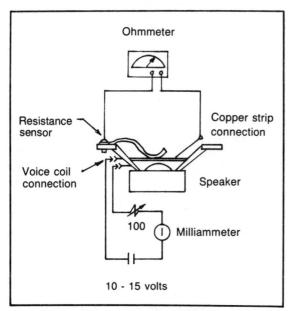

Fig. 3-2. A test fixture for determining the BL product in a conventional electromagnetic speaker.

Once the tape is in place, the disc can be installed on top of the speaker cone and the wire adjusted until it touches the copper strip. The next step is to connect an ohmmeter between the tape and the wire. The ohmmeter should indicate a value of zero between the two components. Now place the weights on top of the cardboard disc. Use as many quarters as necessary so that the meter indicates an open circuit. Connect the electrical circuit to the voice coil. Make sure that the polarity is correct, and adjust the variable resistor until the ohmmeter again indicates a short. This technique will give an exact value for the electrical current, and will improve the accuracy for calculating the Bl product. After completing the above procedure, the values can be inserted into the equation to determine the Bl product.

For the Radio Shack speaker, the added weight was equal to four quarters and the current required to return the cone back to its original position was 42 milliamps. Inserting these values into the equation for the Bl product provides the following answer.

$$Bl = (9.8 \times 10^6 \times (5.6 \times 4))/42$$
$$= 5.23 \times 10^6 \text{ gauss}$$

Another way to make this measurement is to clamp a bar across the center of the speaker frame. Next place a small ruler against the bar and let it rest on the cardboard disc. Make a note of where the rule touches the bar and then place some additional weight on the cardboard disc. Adjust the current until the ruler has returned to the same mark. The result of this measurement can then be inserted into the above equation and the value of the Bl product can be obtained.

Resistance

The last element shown in Fig. 2-20 is the resistance R. This is the dc resistance of the voice coil. Its value can be measured with an ohmmeter. If accurate results are required, a digital ohmmeter can be used for this measurement. For the Radio Shack speaker, the value was 6 ohms.

Impedance of the Voice Coil

One factor that is not shown in Fig. 2-20 is the impedance of the voice coil. The diagram of Fig. 3-3 indicates how the impedance of the voice coil varies as a function of the frequency. Like the acoustic impedance, the total impedance "Z" of the voice coil, is made up of a real and an imaginary value. The real part is the dc resistance of the coil. Its value is a function of both the length and the size of the wire used to make the coil. It is a constant value that is independent of the frequency. The imaginary or reactive part of the impedance is equal to:

$$X_L = 6.28 \times f \times L$$

Where X_L = the reactance of the coil in ohms.
  f = the frequency.
  L = the inductance of the coil in henries.

The easiest way to measure the value of X_L is to use the circuit shown in Fig. 3-4. After connecting the indicated components, adjust the output of the oscillator until the voltmeter has some convenient reading. After setting the oscillator frequency, measure the voltage across the voice coil. This value is designated as e_{vc}. Next, move the voltmeter connection to the position marked "A." Take another reading and record this value as e_a. Using the two voltage readings, the value of Z can be calculated by:

$$Z = (e_{vc} \times R)/(e_a - e_{vc})$$

This is the total impedance. It is related to the component parts by the following formula.

$$Z = (R^2 + X_L^2)^{1/2}$$

Where R = the resistance of the coil and the resistor in ohms.

X_L = the reactance of the coil in ohms.

To obtain X_L subtract the dc resistance of the coil from the value of Z. Remember the values must be

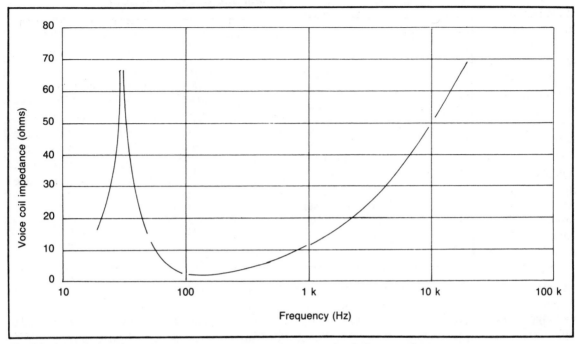

Fig. 3-3. A graph that shows the voice coil impedance of a conventional electromagnetic speaker.

subtracted as vectors. For the Radio Shack speaker, the values of Z and X_L are shown in Table 3-2 for a number of frequencies.

Linearity Measurement

If a speaker is to reproduce the input signal, the cone must move in exact proportion to the applied current. Because there are physical limitations in the cone mounting system, a doubling of the voice coil current will not necessarily produce twice the movement. The best way to check the linear-

ity is with the speaker cone in a vertical configuration. This is a difficult test to perform. An acceptable alternative, although it applies a small amount of bias, is to lay the speaker on a table so that the cone is horizontal. The bias is created by the force of gravity. It produces a slight offset from the true center position of the cone. In this test, the important factor is the total movement per unit of applied current. The electrical connections for this test are shown in Fig. 3-5.

The difference between the two circuits shown in the diagram are a change in the power supply

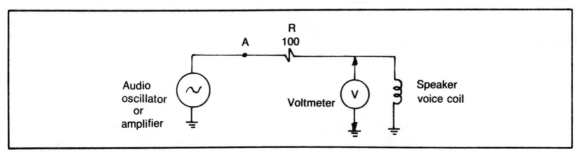

Fig. 3-4. The electrical circuit used to measure a loudspeaker's voice coil impedance.

Table 3-2. Measurements for the Voice Coil Impedance of a Speaker.

Freq. (Hz)	e_a (volts)	e_{vc} (volts)	Imped. Z (ohms)	Coil Imped. (ohms)
20	2.3	0.300	15.0	13.7
25	1.35	0.295	28.0	27.3
30	0.74	0.300	68.2	67.9
40	1.5	0.305	25.4	24.7
50	2.55	0.300	13.3	11.9
75	4.6	0.300	6.98	3.6
100	5.4	0.315	6.19	1.52
250	5.0	0.300	6.38	2.17
500	4.0	0.300	8.1	5.4
1000	2.95	0.300	11.3	9.6
2500	1.8	0.300	20.0	19.1
5000	1.3	0.300	30.0	29.4
10000	0.93	0.300	47.6	47.2
15000	0.80	0.300	60.0	59.7
20000	0.73	0.300	69.8	69.5

polarity and the type of transistor. The two transistors are the small TO-66 power devices. If the five ohm resistor does not allow enough current to flow, its value can be reduced. However, do not operate the circuit without any resistance in this position. The resistor is rated at four watts.

With the cone facing upwards, clamp a bar to the rim of the speaker. Next place a ruler against

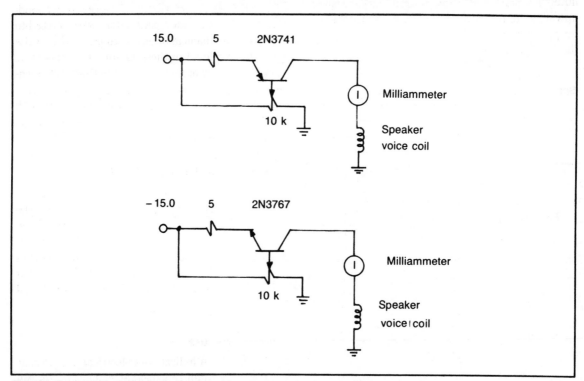

Fig. 3-5. Two electrical circuits that are used to measure a loudspeaker's cone linearity.

the bar so that it is resting on the center of the cardboard disc. Note the cone's position on the ruler. Now apply a dc voltage and adjust the current so that the ruler moves at least one or two graduations. Do not use graduations that are too large because you will not be able to determine the speakers linearity. Make a note of the distance that the cone moved and how much current was needed to achieve this movement. Now change the current by an equal amount. Again, note how far the cone moves. Record the movement as well as the current. Continue this process until the cone movement vs. the applied current no longer changes in equal increments. At this point, the speaker cone has achieved the maximum peak linear movement in one direction. To obtain the corresponding movement in the other direction, use the other circuit shown in Fig. 3-5. After connecting the circuit, repeat the above steps. When this is finished, you should be able to make a table similar to Table 3-3. Figure 3-6 is a graph of this data. As previously noted, the bias caused by having the cone facing upwards can be subtracted out by making the center position, on the linearity curve, equal to 1/2 of the total movement.

Table 3-3. Measured Values Relating the Speaker's Voice Coil Current to the Cone Movement.

	Voice Coil Current (Amps)	Cone Movement (Inches)
Reverse	0.0	0.0000
	0.04	0.0156
	0.088	0.0313
	0.125	0.0469
	0.180	0.0625
	0.250	0.0781
	0.340	0.0938
	0.462	0.1094
Forward	0.000	0.0000
	0.05	0.0156
	0.074	0.0313
	0.125	0.0469
	0.180	0.0625
	0.248	0.0781
	0.340	0.0938
	0.462	0.1094

Speaker Phasing

One factor that should be determined, if the speaker system uses more than one radiator, is the speaker phasing. In multiple speaker systems, it is important to have all the cones move in the same direction at the same time. This can be achieved by momentarily connecting a 1.5 volt battery across the speaker voice coil and observing the direction of the cone movement. At this point, take some red paint or finger nail polish and mark the speaker terminal that is connected to the positive lead of the battery. Repeat this step on all of the speakers for a stereo pair. On the cabinet, mark the terminal which corresponds to the red speaker terminal. All of the terminals should be connected, through their associated crossover networks, to the same terminal on the stereo amplifier. When there is a positive signal on the output of the amplifier, the cones will all move in the same direction.

This section has tried to explain how some simple measurements can be used to determine some of the intrinsic parameters of a direct radiating loudspeaker. The indicated parameters were related to either the mechanical or electrical properties of the speaker. While all of these factors are important, they are usually of more interest to the speaker engineer than to the audio amateur. There are, however, other properties which are of interest to both the engineer and the audio enthusiast alike. These are the acoustical properties of the speaker.

ACOUSTICAL PARAMETERS

The four most important acoustical parameters are the sound pressure, the sound power, the speaker efficiency, and the overall frequency response. Acoustical measurements indicate the sum total of all the factors that are part of the speakers performance. One of the first factors of interest is the amount of sound pressure that can be produced by the speaker.

Sound Pressure

Figure. 3-7A indicates an electrical current that is flowing through the speaker voice coil. As the current in the voice coil increases from zero, it

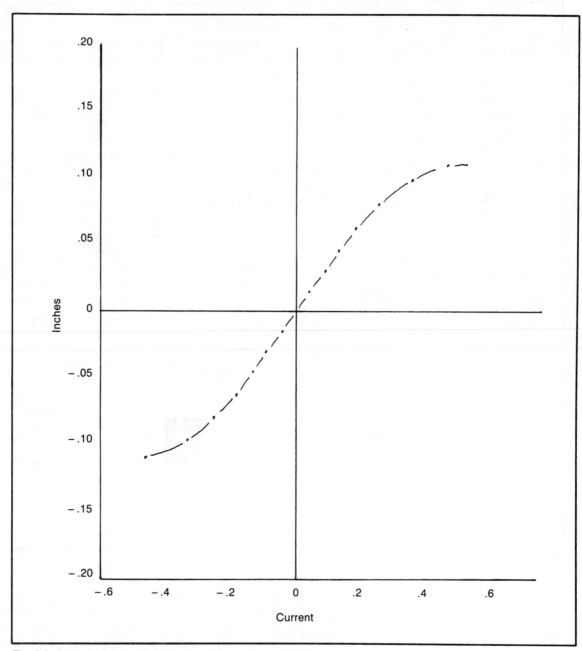

Fig. 3-6. A graph showing the linearity of an eight inch speaker cone.

forces the cone to move toward the position marked "FM" in Fig. 3-7B. This point is the maximum forward travel of the cone. It is obtained when the electrical current reaches its maximum value at I_p.

During the forward movement, the air particles directly in front of the cone are compressed. This produces an increase in the nominal atmospheric pressure. The maximum increase in pressure will

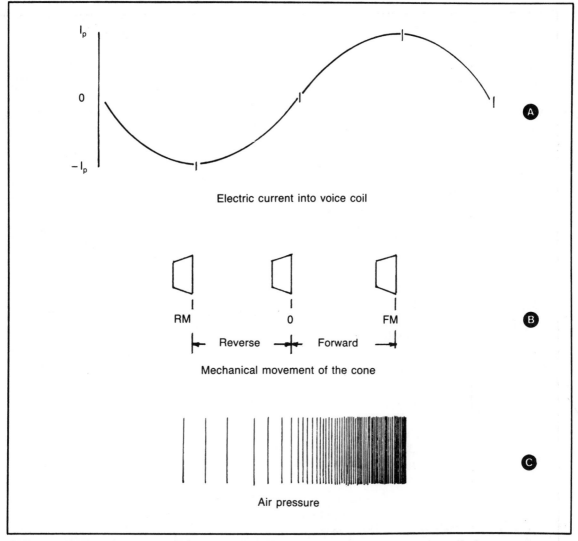

Fig. 3-7. A diagram that shows the relationship between the electrical current (in the voice coil), the cone movement, and the resulting change in the air pressure.

occur at the point marked "FM."

After the current reaches its maximum value at I_p, it will reverse itself and the cone begins to move in the opposite direction. This backward movement continues until the current reaches its maximum movement at $-Ip$. At that point, the cone will have moved to position RM in Fig. 3-7B. Since the motion is backwards, it produces a rarefaction of the air particles and this will decrease the nominal atmospheric pressure in front of the speaker. If the pressure in front of the speaker is plotted against time, it should be a replica of the mechanical cone movement. The instantaneous pressure change at any point in time is equal to the increase or decrease in pressure minus the nominal atmospheric pressure. This later value is equal to 1.013×10^5 Newtons/M^2.

Instruments which measure sound pressure do not respond to the instantaneous change in air pressure. Instead they indicate the root mean square value (rms) of the pressure variation over one cycle. This root mean square value is equal to 0.707 × the peak change in the atmospheric pressure.

Sound pressure is measured in microbars and one microbar equals 0.1 N/M². The instruments that are used by sound engineers indicate the sound pressure in a unit called decibels (dB). This instrument measures the change in sound pressure and indicates the result on a meter that is calibrated in dB. This type of meter is a sound level meter.

As an example of the above measurement, suppose that the cone movement of Fig. 3-7B produces an rms sound pressure level of one microbar. This value of sound pressure can be expressed in decibels (dB) by the following equation.

$$SPL = 20 \times \log(P/0.0002) \text{ dB.}$$

Where SPL = the sound pressure level in dB
  P = the root mean square sound pressure level in microbars.
  0.0002 = the reference sound pressure level in microbars.

For the above situation, where a speaker cone is producing a sound pressure level of one microbar, the associated level in decibels is:

$$SPL = 20 \times \log(1/0.0002)$$
$$= 20 \times \log(5000)$$
$$= 73.98 \text{ dB.}$$

This number indicates the sound pressure level produced by the back and forth movement of the cone. In Fig. 3-7B, this movement is between the points marked "FM" and "RM." If a sound level meter is placed directly in front of this speaker, it would have a meter reading of 74 dB.

Sound Power

A speaker's acoustic power can be determined from the sound pressure level. The following equation changes the sound pressure reading into a sound power value.

$$PWL = SPL + 20 \times \log(r) + 10.5 \text{ dB.}$$
Where PWL = the acoustic power level in dB.

SPL = the sound pressure level in dB.
r = the distance in feet between the source and the point of measurement.

For the example where a speaker is producing a SPL of 74 dB, the acoustic power level would be 94 dB if the measuring distance is one meter (3.3 feet). The calculation for this is:

$$PWL = 74 + 20 \times \log(3.3) + 10.5$$
$$= 74 + 9.54 + 10.5$$
$$= 94 \text{ db}$$

When the acoustic power is known, the efficiency of the transducer can be calculated. Efficiency is a ratio of two power levels. It determines how much of the electrical input power is converted into sound power. To determine the efficiency, the sound power level (PWL) must be expressed in watts. This can be done by rearranging the following equation.

$$PWL = 10 \times \log(W/10^{-13})$$
Where W = the acoustic power in watts
  10^{-13} = the reference power level

Solving this equation for the power in watts (W) produces the following results.

$$W = \text{Log}^{-1}\{(PWL/10)] \times 10^{-13}$$

Using the numbers from the above example the acoustic power in watts is:

$$W = \log^{-1}(94/10) \times 10^{-13}$$
$$= 0.000254 \text{ watts.}$$
$$= 250 \text{ microwatts.}$$

The efficiency of a speaker is the ratio of the power output to the power input. That is:

$$\text{Spkr efficiency} = (P_{out}/P_{in}) \times 100$$

If the amplifier for this example supplied an input power of 25 milliwatts (0.025 watts), and the acoustic output power was 250 microwatts, speaker efficiency is one percent.

At this point, you may wonder what happened to the other 99% of the power. In Chapter 2, the opposition to the movement of the speaker cone consisted of the air resistance plus the air mass. The diagram of Fig. 2-16 showed that the opposition caused by the air mass is larger than the value of the resistance. This is true for all values of ka less than one. Under these conditions, most of the power supplied to the speaker is stored in the reactance of the air mass. Only a small amount is dissipated as real power by the acoustic resistance.

Frequency Response

One of the last measurements to be described is the speaker frequency response. This measurement indicates how the acoustic power changes as a function of the frequency. Ideally, the acoustic output should be constant over the entire audio range.

In essence, a frequency response test is an extension of the one used for sound pressure readings. In this instance, the input voltage across the speaker terminals is held constant. The frequency of the source is now varied over the range of interest. The acoustic output of the speaker is measured with a sound level meter. A typical test set up is shown in Fig. 3-8.

Although the diagram implies that this is a very

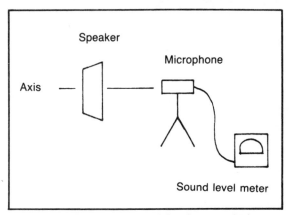

Fig. 3-8. A test set-up for determining the acoustical output from a loudspeaker.

simple test, there are many factors that can introduce a considerable amount of error. This is especially true if the measurements are taken inside of a room with reflective walls and ceilings. There are two possible choices for eliminating the measurement errors created by the room reflections. The easiest way, and one that can also be done by the audio amateur, is to perform the test outside. This must be done away from reflecting walls. It does, however, have some problems of its own. One, of course, is the weather. It is difficult to do any testing when it is raining or if the temperature is very low. Other possible problems are wind or man-made noises.

To overcome these problems, manufacturers often use an anechoic chamber. This room is designed so there are no reflecting surfaces. Rooms of this type are very expensive to build and not all speaker manufacturers have one. Those that do not must resort to either the outside tests or, as is sometimes done, conduct no test at all.

This later condition is usually justified by some type of comparison test. The performance of the speaker under test is compared against some other well known speaker system. In another type of test, people that are supposed to have "golden ears" are sometimes used to judge the speakers' overall performance. While the measurement by instruments may not reveal all the little nuances of the speakers performance, the judgement by the "golden ear crowd" is very subjective and is probably not repeatable.

For the listener, the biggest problem associated with any test is one of correlation. When a speaker is placed in a living environment, it may perform differently than it did in the test situation. To achieve the best performance, a speaker should be moved around the listening area. At each location, a frequency response as well as a listening test should be conducted. The final placement should be the position that provides the flattest response and sounds the best to the listener.

The last two chapters have presented information related to an electromagnetic speaker. This device is very complex and the ability to achieve the best performance is dependent on many factors.

Very few audio amateurs have ever tried to build an electromagnetic speaker. This doesn't mean that it cannot be done (See Audio, July 1962, "Thirty Pounds of Magnet and an 18 inch Cone" by J. Russell). It is just extremely difficult. There is, however, a speaker that the home experimenter can build. The prerequisite is some woodworking skills coupled together with a little care and patience in making the individual parts. The speakers that will be described in the next chapters of this book are this type of device. They are called electrostatic loudspeakers.

Chapter 4

Electrostatic Loudspeakers

In chapter two, sound was created by the movement of a speaker cone. The force that created this movement was produced by an electromagnetic field. Although this is the most common technique, it is not the only method available. This chapter will introduce some of the basic principles of electrostatic speakers. This type of speaker uses an electric field to create a force of attraction or repulsion. The thrust of this effort will cause a lightweight diaphragm to move and this produces a sound.

ELECTRIC FIELD

Previous exposure to the principle of an electric field, for many of us, has been by static electricity. For instance, when you walk across a nylon carpet with rubber-soled shoes, and then reach for a metal door knob, the resulting spark is created by the electric charge on your body. Electrons were transferred from the carpet to your body. In effect you acquired a negative charge.

Charge

Many high school and college students become familiar with the basics of an electric field in science courses and demonstrate the principles of an electric field by producing an electric charge. If materials such as amber, ebonite, or hard rubber are rubbed with wool or fur, they acquire a negative charge. On the other hand, if a glass rod is rubbed with silk it will acquire a positive charge. Although the two rods have opposite charges, they cannot, because of their weight, be used to demonstrate the principles of electrostatics. To overcome this limitation, the charge on each rod is transferred, by contact, to two light pith balls. If one ball is touched with the glass rod and the other with the rubber rod, both balls will acquire a charge. The polarity on each ball will be the same as the rod that touches it.

Field Strength

The diagram shown in Fig. 4-1 is used to illus-

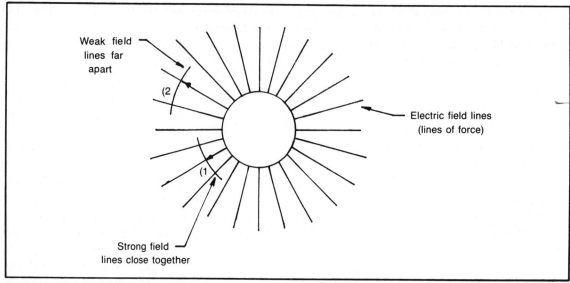

Fig. 4-1. An electric field around a charged object.

trate the concept of an electric charge. The circle represents a pith ball that has been charged by one of the above-mentioned rods. The lines radiating outwards from the circle represent the electric field around the charged pith ball. As shown, the lines diverge as they spread out from the pith ball. The strength of the electric field, at any distance, is determined by the number of lines per unit area. At the radius marked r_1, for instance, the charge created by the electric field will be greater than it is at r_2. The radius r_1 is closer to the pith ball and it will have more lines per unit area. The value of the field strength is equal to the electric charge divided by the distance from that charge. In equation form, the field strength at any distance can be calculated by:

$F(s) = (K \times Q)/R^2$

Where

$F(s)$ = the field strength in newtons/coulomb.

  K = A value that depends upon the units of measurement.

  Q = the electric charge in coulombs.

  R = the distance from the pith ball in meters.

  In Fig. 4-1, suppose that the pith ball has re-

ceived a charge of one coulomb. If the radius (r_1) is equal to one meter, then the field strength is equal to:

$$F(s) = 9.07 \times (1)/(1)^2$$
$$= 9.07 \text{ newtons/coulomb.}$$

A similar calculation at a radius of two meters (r_2) would show that the corresponding field strength is:

$$F(s) = 9.07 \times (1)/(2)^2$$
$$= 2.28 \text{ newtons/coulomb}$$

This equation is important in electrostatics because it is used to calculate the field strength at any radius from a charged object. In addition to the electric field, a charged object has another characteristic that is important. If a magnet is placed near a piece of steel, there is a force of attraction between the magnet and the steel. In a similar fashion, if a charged object is placed near a second object, there will also be a force of attraction. In this case, the force is created by the electric field.

Force Created by an Electric Field

In Chapter 2, the magnetic field around a magnet produced a force of attraction or repulsion. This same principle is also true of the electric field around a charged object. The force is a function of both the field strength and the electric charge. The value of this force can be calculated by:

$$F = F(s) \times Q$$

Where

F = the force in newtons.
F(s) = the field strength in newtons/coulomb.
Q = the electrical charge in coulombs.

In the previous example, the field strength at r_1 was equal to 9.07 newtons/coulomb. Inserting this value into the force equation indicates that there will be a force of attraction that is equal to:

$$F = 9.07 \times (1)$$
$$= 9.07 \text{ newtons}$$

At a radius equal to r_2 the field strength is 2.28 newtons/coulomb and the resulting force will be equal to:

$$F = 2.28 \times (1)$$
$$= 2.28 \text{ newtons}$$

Although a force in newtons is understood by the people in the scientific fields, it has little meaning to the average audio amateur. However, if each of the above values is multiplied by 0.248, the force will be in pounds. At a radius of one meter (which is equal to r_1), the force is 2.28 pounds. At two meters, (radius r_2), the force is reduced to 0.58 pounds. The above analysis has indicated that the force around a charged object is related to both the field strength and the electric charge. So far, this discussion has covered the characteristics of a single charged object. In electrostatic speakers, and in many other things, there are usually two charged objects.

The laws which govern the relationship between two charged objects are similar to the ones used for a single charged object. They were established by the French scientist Charles Coulomb. Coulomb's Law states that the force between any two charged objects can be determined by dividing the product of their magnitudes by the square

of the distance between them. This is written in equation form as:

$$F = k(Q_1 \times Q_2)/R^2$$

Where F = the force in newtons.
k = a constant used to make the units come out right.
Q_1 = the charge on one object in coulombs.
Q_2 = the charge on the other object in coulombs.
R = the distance between the objects in meters.

To indicate the use of this equation, suppose that two pith balls are placed one meter apart. One of the balls receives a positive charge from the glass rod, while the other ball receives a negative charge from the rubber rod. The force being exerted on each ball by its adjacent partner is:

$$F = ((9.07 \times (1) \times (1))/(1)^2$$
$$= 9.07 \text{ newtons.}$$
$$= 2.25 \text{ pounds.}$$

If the two pith balls were located two meters apart, the force would decrease to:

$$F = (9.07)/(2)^2$$
$$= 2.27 \text{ newtons}$$
$$= 0.562 \text{ pounds}$$

These calculations indicate the amount of force that will exist between two charged objects. The one factor that is missing from the calculations is the direction of the force.

Forces of Attraction and Repulsion

The lines between the two balls shown in Fig. 4-2 represent the electric field between two oppositely charged bodies. Because unlike charges attract each other, the force on the two balls is one of attraction. The two balls will move towards each other. If the two balls were touched by the same rod, then the same force would exist on each ball. In Fig. 4-3, the lines represent the electric field between two bodies with the same charge. Because the force is now an opposing one, the two balls will repel each other. They will move away from each

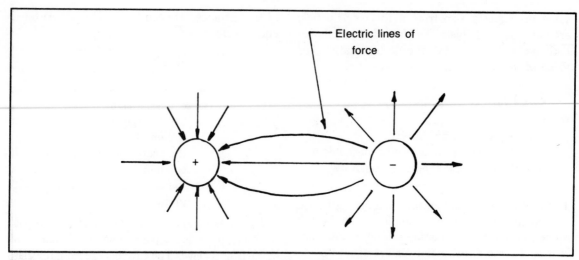

Fig. 4-2. Electric lines of force between two charged objects that have the opposite polarity.

other. Figure 4-4 shows the direction the polarity and the resulting force on each ball.

It is this principle of attraction and repulsion by an electric charge that is the basis of how an elec-trostatic speaker functions. In a simplistic view of this type of speaker, one of the pith balls is replaced by a conductive plate and the other ball is replaced by a moveable conductive diaphragm.

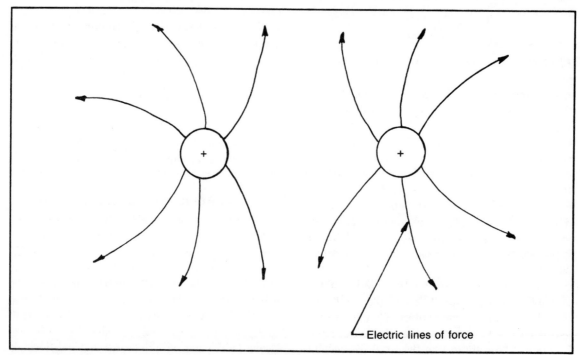

Fig. 4-3. Electric lines of force between two charged objects that have the same polarity.

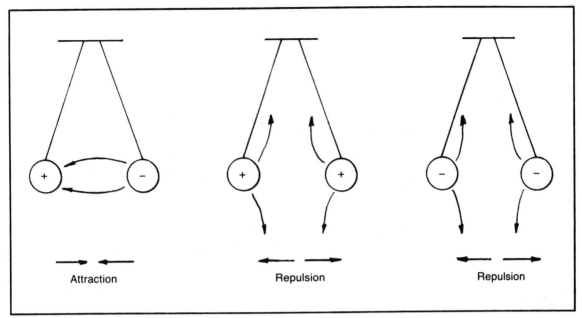

Fig. 4-4. The direction of the force between two charged objects.

ELEMENTARY ELECTROSTATIC SPEAKERS

Before going into the details about the factors that affect the performance of an electrostatic speaker, it is appropriate to find out how an electrostatic speaker can be built.

There are two types of electrostatic speakers. The first type is a single-ended speaker. In addition to the mounting structure, the speaker consists of a rigid plate with holes to let the sound out, some spacers (which are used to separate the plate from the diaphragm) and a moveable diaphragm. Figure 4-5A is a pictorial diagram of the components needed to make this type of speaker. For the diaphragm, most electrostatic speakers use mylar or some other plastic film. During construction, the diaphragm is fastened to the spacers. To create an electric charge, the plate and the diaphragm are connected to an external dc power supply. The voltage from the power supply will cause the plate and the diaphragm to have opposite charges. This will make the force one of attraction. One major difference between the electrostatic speaker and the pith balls is that both balls are free to move but in a single-ended speaker, only the diaphragm can

move. This, as will be shown later, can produce some undesirable effects.

The second type of an electrostatic speaker is a symmetrical or push-pull speaker. This speaker is the one that is most often built. It was developed because of the technical problems of the single ended speaker. The pictorial diagram of Fig. 4-5B indicates the configuration of a symmetrical or push-pull speaker.

Essentially, this type of speaker is made like a sandwich. On the outside, the speaker has two rigid plates. They are separated from the inner diaphragm by a set of spacers. The speaker is symmetrical because the distance and capacity (to be described) between each of the plates and the diaphragm is exactly the same. The speaker is also push-pull. When it is operating, one of the plates will become positive with respect to the diaphragm, while the other one will be negative. The positive plate pulls the diaphragm towards it. At the same time, the negative plate pushes the diaphragm away from it. This assumes that the diaphragm has a negative charge. The push-pull action is produced by the audio signal. Although most electrostatic

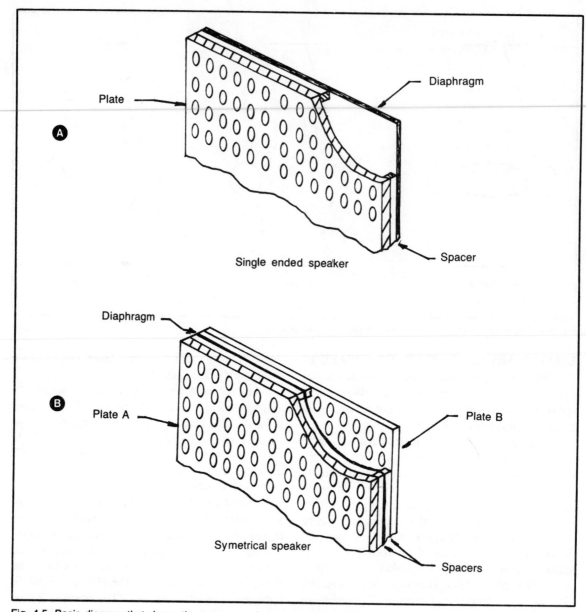

Fig. 4-5. Basic diagram that shows the two types of electrostatic speakers.

speakers are of the push-pull type, a detailed explanation will be given of each type.

SINGLE-ENDED ELECTROSTATIC SPEAKERS

As already indicated, a single ended elec-

trostatic speaker consists of a rigid plate and a moveable diaphragm. This is shown, without any supporting structure, in the diagram of Fig. 4-6A. The two conductive surfaces are separated by an air gap. If a voltage source is connected between the two surfaces, as shown in Fig. 4-6B, they will acquire charges of opposite polarity. Initially, when

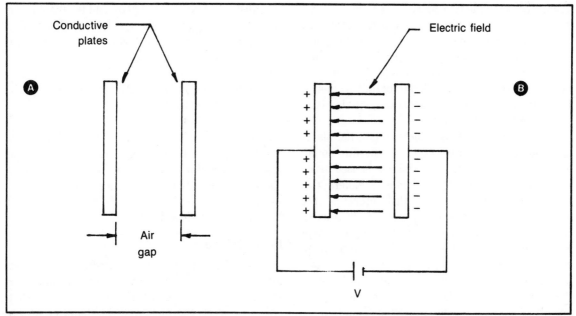

Fig. 4-6. The component parts of a single ended electrostatic speaker.

the two conductive surfaces are connected to the power supply, the electric field and the force are both zero. After some period of time, the voltage difference between the two conductive surfaces will equal the voltage from the power supply. At this instant, the electric field and the force will have reached their maximum static value.

For an ideal speaker, if the voltage source is removed, the electric field and the force will still exist. This indicates that some of the energy has been transferred from the voltage source to the electric field. In electronics, a device that stores energy in an electric field is a capacitor. The stored energy is called potential energy (PE) and its value can be calculated by:

$$PE = 1/2(Q \times V)$$

Where PE = the amount of stored potential energy (Joules).

Q = the charge in coulombs.

V = the difference in potential between the two plates.

In an electrostatic speaker, this energy is stored in the electric field between the plate and the movea-

ble diaphragm. If the stored energy is momentarily increased or decreased, it will cause the diaphragm to move. The addition or subtraction of energy changes the potential energy to kinetic energy. If the diaphragm movement occurs within the audible range, a sound will be heard.

Electrostatic Speaker Capacity

Not all capacitors or electrostatic speakers store the same amount of energy. Because an electrostatic speaker has air between the plate and the diaphragm, the storage capability is determined by both its physical size and the plate to diaphragm separation.

When a speaker is first connected to a power supply, the electric charge on the plates is zero. As the charge between the two surfaces increases, the electrons located between the two plates will begin to move. Electrons that are near the negative surface will be repelled by its increasing charge. In a similar fashion, the surface with the increasing positive charge will attract the electrons. This movement of electrons, from the negative plate to the positive one, does not happen instantly. If the voltage between the two plates causes one coulomb of charge to be transferred in one second, then the speaker has a storage capacity of one farad. In electronics, a farad is usually too coarse of a measurement unit. The capacity is most often measured in microfarads or picofarads. A microfarad is equal to 10^{-6} farads while a picofarad equals 10^{-6} microfarads or 10^{-12} farads.

The capacity between the two parallel plates is a function of several factors. As already noted, one factor is the type of material that is used in the space between the plates. For most speakers, this material is air. Another factor that determines the speaker capacity is the area of the parallel plates. If two speakers had all other factors equal except the size of the plates, the one with the larger plate area would also have more capacity. The last factor that affects the capacity is the distance between the two plates. For this factor, the capacity is inversely proportional to the separation. That is, making the plates twice as far apart will produce a capacity that is one-half of the initial value. The capacity between two plates can be calculated according to the following formula.

$$
\begin{aligned}
C &= (K \times A)/d \\
&= ((8.85 \times 10^{-12}) \times A)/d
\end{aligned}
$$

Where C = the storage capacity of the speaker or capacitor in farads.

    K = 8.85×10^{-12} and is a constant that takes care of the first factor.

    A = the area of the plate in meters^2

    d = the distance between the plates in meters.

As an example, suppose that an electrostatic speaker is made with a plate and a diaphragm that are six inches square. They are also separated from each other by an air space of 0.01 inches. To determine the capacity, these dimensions must be multiplied by 2.54×10^{-2} to convert them into meters. The results are:

$$
\begin{aligned}
\text{Plate Area} &= (6 \times 2.54 \times 10^{-2})^2 \\
&= (0.1524)^2 \\
&= 0.0232 \text{ meters}^2
\end{aligned}
$$

The distance between the plate and the diaphragm in meters, is equal to $0.01 \times (2.54 \times 10^{-2})$, and this multiplication equals to 2.54×10^{-4} meters. The storage capacity of this speaker is:

$$
\begin{aligned}
C &= ((8.85 \times 10^{-12}) \times (2.32 \times 10^{-2}))/(2.54 \times 10^{-4}) \\
&= 808.3 \times 10^{-12} \text{ farads} \\
&= 808.3 \text{ picofarads}
\end{aligned}
$$

For an electrostatic speaker, this value is the load for the audio amplifier. The amount can affect the amplifier's ability to produce a constant voltage across the speaker terminals. More details will be presented a little later.

Field Strength

In addition to its capacity, another factor that affects the performance of an electrostatic speaker is the strength of the electric field. The field that exists between the plate and the diaphragm of a speaker is the same as the electric field that existed between the two pith balls. The strength, in volts/mil, can be calculated by:

$$ E = V/d $$

Where E = the field strength in volts/mil.

    V = the voltage between the plate and the diaphragm.

    d = the distance between the plate and the diaphragm in mils (a mil equals 0.001 inches).

If the speaker in the above example was connected to a dc voltage of 100 volts, the field strength is equal to 100/10 or 10 volts/mil. This is not a very large quantity and commercial electrostatic speakers have values between 50 and 70 volts/mil.

Field Strength Limits

People who have witnessed electrical storms have seen what happens when the field strength limit is exceeded. The lightning is produced when two charged bodies are near each other with a field strength so great that the air layer between them breaks down. This is the upper limit on the value of the field strength.

For an electrostatic speaker, the maximum value is determined by the air gap. If enough voltage is applied across the plate and the diaphragm, the air between them will break down. When this happens, a spark will jump from one surface to the other one. The strength of the air gap or dielectric, as it is usually called, is its ability to prevent an electrical discharge. The value is specified in volts/mil. The dielectric strength of air is 75 volts/mil or 75 kilovolts/inch. Normally, the voltage between the plate and the diaphragm cannot exceed this limitation. One manufacturer, however, overcame this problem by placing the speaker inside a pressurized bag. See the section on the Dayton-Wright speaker in Chapter 1.

FORCE BETWEEN THE PLATE AND THE DIAPHRAGM

At the beginning of this chapter, it was shown that the force between two charged objects was a function of the charge and the distance between them. For a speaker with a six inch diaphragm and a plate separation of 0.01 inches, the force that is exerted is:

$$F = (9.07 \times Q)/d^2$$
$$= (9.07 \times Q)/(2.54 \times 10^{-4})^2$$

The charge "Q" in coulombs is equal to the capacity between the parallel surfaces multiplied by the difference in voltage. That is:

$$Q = (C \times V)$$

Where Q = the charge in coulombs.
      C = the capacity in farads.
      V = the potential difference in volts.

If the voltage between the two six inch plates is 100 volts, then the value of Q is:

$$Q = (8.09 \times 10^{-10}) \times 100$$
$$= 8.09 \times 10^{-8}$$

Inserting this value into the force equation provides the following result.

$$F = ((9.07) \times (8.08 \times 10^{-8}))/(6.45 \times 10^{-8})$$
$$= 11.4 \text{ newtons}$$
$$= 2.84 \text{ pounds}$$

The significance of this value is indicated by the following example. Suppose a speaker is to be built according to the dimensions defined in the above example. That is, the plate and the diaphragm are each 6 inches square and they are to be separated by an air gap of 0.01 inches. However, during construction an error is made in the separation. Instead of having "d" equal to 0.01 inches it becomes 0.005 inches.

This error will have several effects on the performance of the speaker. The first will be an increase in the capacity from 808 picofarads to 1616 picofarads. While this increase may not appear to be a significant factor, it can have some serious effects on the overall system performance. One effect is to create an oscillation in the amplifier. This happens because the speaker capacity alters the amplifier internal feedback. A simple solution to this problem is to place a small resistor between the amplifier output and the capacity load. Do not make this value too large because it will limit the high frequency response of the speaker.

Even if there isn't an oscillation, the increased capacity puts an additional load on the amplifier. When this happens, the amplifier may not be able to deliver the required amount of power and there will be a loss in the high frequency response of the speaker. At low listening levels, the power supply and the amplifier may be able to deliver enough energy to charge and discharge the speaker capacity. This may not be true at higher listening levels. A simple test for this condition is to run a frequency response of both the amplifier and the speaker at full output. To eliminate the undesirable acoustic effects of this test, the high voltage power supply should be turned off.

Diaphragm Tension

If two objects have a force of attraction, and there is no other restraining force, they will move towards each other until they touch. In an electromagnetic speaker, the force is applied so that the cone can move either forwards or backwards. The total movement is restricted by the suspension system. When the input signal is zero, there is no current in the voice coil and this produces no cone movement.

The electrostatic speaker differs from its electromagnetic counter part. Even without an audio input signal, the electrostatic speaker will have a force between the plate and the diaphragm. As already explained, this force is due to the electric field created by the two charged surfaces.

If a single-ended speaker is built and no tension is applied to the diaphragm, it will move toward the plate until they touch. Depending upon the speakers construction this contact can have different results. One effect can occur just as the two surfaces are approaching each other. There is still a difference in potential between the plate and the diaphragm. As the separation becomes smaller, this potential difference can exceed the dielectric strength of the air and the speaker will begin to arc. While this may not destroy the speaker, it probably will stop operating when the two surfaces contact each other.

Another effect can occur if the diaphragm has some tension, but not the required amount. In this case, the moment the diaphragm touches the plate, the potential difference is zero and so is the electric field. If the tension is large enough, then the diaphragm may be able to pull away from contact with the plate. The instant that this happens, the force of attraction will be restored and the diaphragm will be pulled back to the plate. This process of the diaphragm making and breaking contact with the plate will produce a flapping sound. This will continue until the speaker is either destroyed or the force of attraction is removed.

The diaphragm in Fig. 4-7 shows a plate and a diaphragm of a single-ended speaker. When the voltage V is applied, the two charged surfaces will be attracted to each other. If the diaphragm and the plate are to be prevented from touching, a force must be applied to restrict the diaphragm movement. Ideally, the additional forces should be opposite to the one created by the plate. In a

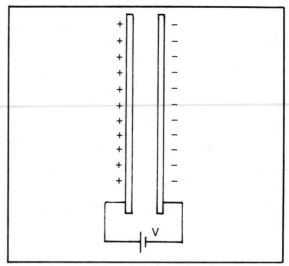

Fig. 4-7. The electric charge on the plate and the diaphragm of a single ended electrostatic speaker.

single-ended speaker, there is no way this can be done. To overcome this limitation, the tension must be applied at right angles to the force created by the electric field, that is, the force that must be created by stretching the diaphragm. This will make the diaphragm behave like a stretched spring.

As an example, Fig. 4-8A shows a spring connected to a weight. If the weight is moved from its rest position to the point marked "A," the spring will be stretched. When the weight is released, the force contained in the stretched spring will make the weight return to its rest position. The same principle will happen if the weight is moved to position "B." In this case the spring will be compressed. Releasing the weight will cause it again to return to its rest position.

The amount of force required to stretch or compress the spring is determined by a factor called the spring rate. The spring rate is equal to the force required to change the spring's dimension divided by the change in the spring's length. This is written as:

Spring rate = k = Force/distance.
Where   k = the spring rate.
           F = the force required to stretch or compress the spring.

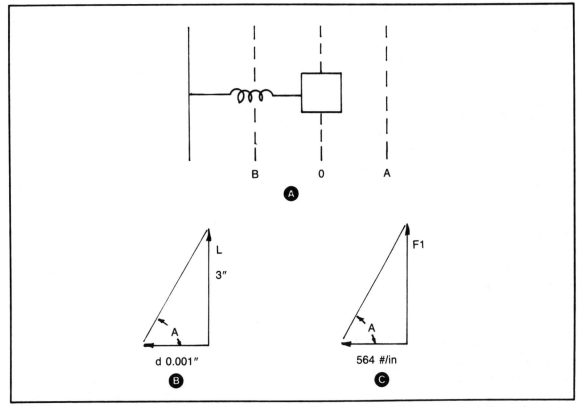

Fig. 4-8. A pictorial representation of the spring rate and how it can be calculated for an electrostatic speaker.

d = the amount that the spring is
stretched or compressed.

In an electrostatic speaker, there is no restoring force and the spring rate is equal to the applied force divided by the distance that the diaphragm can move. In the example of the six inch speaker, the force between the plate and the diaphragm is 2.84 pounds. The total movement is limited by the speaker's construction to 0.01 inches. For this condition, the spring rate is equal to:

$$k = 2.84/0.01$$
$$= 284 \text{ pounds/inch.}$$

To prevent the diaphragm from touching the plate, the external force must be applied so that it limits the diaphragm movement to some value less than 0.01 inches. As a starting point, suppose the

movement is limited to 50% of the total distance. For this spacing, this is equal to 0.005 inches, and this makes the spring rate equal to:

$$k = 2.82/0.005$$
$$= 564 \text{ pounds/inch.}$$

As indicated, the external force on a single-ended speaker can only be applied at right angles to the diaphragm. At this point, a vector diagram and some trigonometry must be used to calculate the tension that must be placed on the diaphragm. For the six inch speaker, the vector diaphragm is shown in Fig. 4-8B. The value of the angle "A" is equal to the arc-tangent of (L/d). That is:

Angle (A) = $\tan^{-1}$ (L/d)
Where   L = 1/2 of the diaphragm's diameter.
         d = the distance.

69

For the six inch speaker, this is:

$$= 3/0.005$$
$$= 89.90 \text{ degrees.}$$

Figure 4-8C shows the same diagram, but instead of using the speakers dimensions, the vectors now represent the forces that must exist in each direction. The value of F_1 is the tension required to make the spring rate equal to 564 pounds/inch. The value can be calculated by:

$$F_1 = \tan(A) \times 564$$
$$= \tan(89.90) \times 564$$
$$= 600.0 \times 564$$
$$= 3.384 \times 10^5 \text{ pounds/inch}$$

The value of F_1 is the spring rate that must be placed on the diaphragm in order to limit the movement to 50% of the total distance between the plate and the diaphragm. The amount of force that is required to achieve this value can be obtained from the equation for the spring rate.

$$\text{Force} = k \times \text{distance}$$
$$= (3.384 \times 10^5) \times 3$$
$$= 1.015 \times 10^6 \text{ pounds}$$

This last calculation shows that a force of 1.015×10^6 pounds must be applied to the outside edge of the diaphragm to limit the total movement to 0.005 inches.

There are several problems associated with obtaining such a large number. First, it is difficult to make a fixture that has enough strength to generate this type of force. Second, the force between the diagonal corners of the speaker will exceed the tear strength of the material. With this in mind, and to explain some additional characteristics of this type of speaker, the spacing will be changed from 0.01 inches to 0.03 inches.

Dynamic Characteristics, Single-Ended Speakers

In the above discussion, the diaphragm was offset by the static force created by the bias voltage.

In this section, attention will be given to the effect of making the diaphragm move. For the new spacing, the value of the applied voltage is maintained at 100 volts. The force produced by a spacing of 0.03 inches will be reduced to 0.42 pounds. This will make the diaphragm spring constant equal to:

$$k = 0.42/.03$$
$$= 14 \text{ pounds/inch.}$$

The value of angle(A) is:

$$\text{Angle(A)} = \tan^{-1}(3/.03)$$
$$= 89.427 \text{ degrees.}$$

To make the diaphragm stable, the static movement must again be limited to 50% of the total value. This makes the spring rate equal to:

$$k = 0.42/0.015$$
$$= 28 \text{ pounds/inch.}$$

When the value of angle(A) is 89.43 degrees, the spring tension on the diaphragm is equal to:

$$F_1 = \tan(A) \times 28$$
$$= 2800 \text{ pounds/inch.}$$

When this tension is placed on the diaphragm and the electric field is applied, the diaphragm will move toward the plate according to the following calculation.

$$d = 3/\tan(A)$$

The tan(A) is equal to spring rate applied to the diaphragm divided by the force created by the electric field. That is:

$$\text{Angle(A)} = \tan^{-1}(2800/14)$$
$$= \tan^{-1}(200)$$
$$= 89.713 \text{ degrees}$$

Plugging this value into the equation for "d" makes

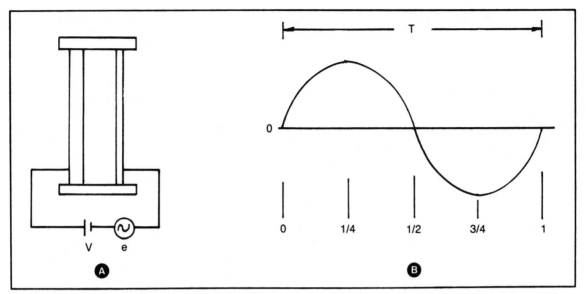

Fig. 4-9. (A) shows how the bias supply and the alternating ac voltage are connected to a single ended electrostatic speaker. (B) is the time relationship of the ac voltage.

the diaphragm movement equal to:

$$d = 3/\tan(89.713)$$
$$= 3/200$$
$$= 0.015 \text{ inches}$$

This verifies the previous calculations, and it is the static position for the diaphragm shown in Fig. 4-9A. In addition to the bias voltage shown in Fig. 4-9A, an ac voltage has been connected so that the two voltages are in series. The waveform for this voltage is shown in Fig. 4-9B, and it is similar to the current waveform of Fig. 2-13B. In this case, the voltage is zero at $T = 0, 1/2$ and 1. It achieves the greatest positive voltage at $T = 1/4$ and its greatest negative value at $T = 3/4$.

Because the two voltages are in series, when the waveform is at $T = 1/4$, the diaphragm voltage will be at its minimum value. If the peak of the ac waveform is equal to 10 volts then the diaphragm voltage is equal to:

$$V\text{diaphragm} = V_{dc} + V_{signal}$$
$$= -100 + 10$$
$$= -90 \text{ volts}$$

With the diaphragm at 90 volts, the force is equal to 0.379 pounds. The horizontal spring rate is equal to 12.6 pounds/inch. Using this value, plus the vertical spring rate on the diaphragm, makes the value of the angle(A) equal to 89.74 degrees. When the three inch dimension is divided by the tan of the angle(A) the results indicate that the diaphragm movement will be 13.5×10^{-3} inches. This is a dynamic displacement of 1.46×10^{-4} inches.

When the elapsed time is equal to the 3/4 point, the voltage waveform corresponds a value of -10 volts. The total diaphragm voltage now equals 110 volts. The force now equals 0.463 pounds. The horizontal spring rate is now 15.45 pounds/inch. The corresponding value of angle(A) is 89.684 degrees. For this angle, the movement of the diaphragm corresponds to 16.55×10^{-3} and the dynamic displacement is equal to 1.55×10^{-4} inches. The total diaphragm movement is equal to the sum of the dynamic displacements and this value is 3.01×10^{-3} inches.

Problems with Single-Ended Speakers

In addition to the problems created by the force

71

of the electric field, the sound output from the speaker will not be an exact duplicate of the input. In other words, it will be distorted. The distortion is created because the diaphragm excursion is not centered around its static position. The distortion content can be calculated by:

% distortion = (max. value − min. value)/max value

Where

max. value = the displacement when the input waveform is at T = 1/4.

min. value = the displacement when the input waveform is at T = 3/4.

Max value = corresponds to the maximum numerical value either positive or negative.

For the indicated diaphragm movement, the distortion value is equal to:

%distortion = $((1.55 \times 10^{-3} − 1.46 \times 10^{-3})/1.55 \times 10^{-3}) \times 100$
= $((9.0 \times 10^{-5})/(1.55 \times 10^{-3})) \times 100$

= $(0.058) \times 100$
= 5.8%

This is a significantly large value and is one more reasons why this type of speaker is not used. Details of this analysis will be found in Professor Hunt's book "Electro-acoustics." The book explains why the symmetrical speaker with its uniform electrostatic field will eliminate most of the problems found in the single-ended speaker.

SYMMETRICAL ELECTROSTATIC SPEAKERS

Early electrostatic speaker designers changed to the symmetrical configuration at a very early stage. As noted in the section on "Elementary Electrostatic Speakers," the symmetrical speaker is made like a sandwich.

In this type of speaker, the diaphragm is centered between two rigid plates. This is shown in Fig. 4-10A. If the electrical connections of Fig. 4-10B are applied, the charges on the plate and the

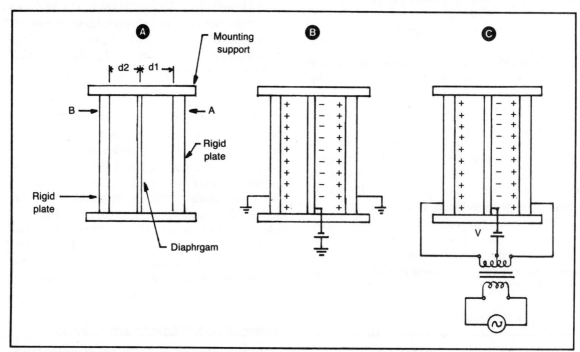

Fig. 4-10. Pictorial diagram of a symetrical electrostatic loudspeaker and how the bias and ac voltages are connected to the speaker.

diaphragm will be as shown. In this type of speaker, the distance d_1 (from plate "A" to the diaphragm) is equal to d_2 (the distance between the diaphragm and plate "B.") The electrostatic charge that will exist between the plates and the diaphragm will be uniform and this will keep the distortion low. Ideally, the plates exert an equal and opposite amount of force. This should cause the diaphragm to remain centered. Any tension that needs to be applied will be small because it will only be necessary to make up for tolerance variations between d_1 and d_2.

CAPACITY OF A SYMMETRICAL SPEAKER

The capacity between each of the plates and the diaphragm, of Fig. 4-10A will also be equal. That is the capacity between the diaphragm and plate "A" will be equal to the capacity between the diaphragm and plate "B." The total capacity between the two plates will be equal to:

$$C_{total} = (C_1 \times C_2)/(C_1 + C_2)$$

Where C_{total} = the total capacity between the plates.

C_1 = the capacity between the diaphragm and plate "A."

C_2 = the capacity between the diaphragm and plate "B."

In effect, the two capacitors are in series and this will make the total capacity smaller then either C_1 or C_2. The value of either capacity can be calculated by the same formula that was used for the single-ended speaker.

As an example, suppose that a symmetrical speaker is made with a set of plates that measure six inches by six inches. The separation between either plate and the diaphragm is 0.01 inches. These are the same dimensions used in the single-ended speaker. The capacity between either plate and the diaphragm is 803 picofarads.

The total speaker capacity consists of two 803 picofarad capacitors in series. The value can be calculated according to the previous equation. That is:

$$C_{total} = (803 \times 10^{-12} \times 803 \times 10^{-12})/(803 \times 10^{-12} + 803 \times 10^{-12})$$

$$= 401.5 \times 10^{-12}$$
$$= 401.5 \text{ picofarads.}$$

This is one half of the capacity between a plate and the diaphragm. As long as the speaker is made symmetrical, this will always be true.

Diaphragm Stability

In the diagram for the single-ended speaker, it was shown that the force on the diaphragm had to be offset by the tension. Because the tension could only be applied at right angles, the spring rate of the diaphragm had to be considerable larger than the force created by the electric field. In a symmetrical, or push-pull, speaker the tension will be much less. In fact if everything was perfect, the actual value would be zero. To show that this is true, consider the following formula, which computes the force on a diaphragm of a symmetrical speaker.

$$F = ((k(C_1 \times V)/d1) - ((k(C_2 \times V)/d2)$$

Suppose that the symmetrical speaker with the six inch plates, has a separation of 0.01 inches. The bias voltage between either plate and the diaphragm is 100 volts. Under these conditions the force is:

$$F = ((9.07 \times (8.09 \times 10^{-8})/(6.45 \times 10^{-8})) - ((9.07 \times (8.09 \times 10^{-8})/(6.45 \times 10^{-8}))$$
$$= ((7.34 \times 10^{-7})/(6.45 \times 10^{-8})) - ((7.34 \times 10^{-7})/(6.45 \times 10^{-8}))$$
$$= 0.0$$

The variation in the spacing of a symmetrical speaker is largely due to two factors. The first is the variation that can occur in the material thickness that is used for the spacers. This value can be in the order of one to ten percent. If both the front and rear spacers are made from the same stock, then this variation will be so small that it no longer is a problem.

The other problem is created by the plates not being parallel to the diaphragm. If the width and length of the plates are small, and some care is taken in assembling the speaker, the variation will

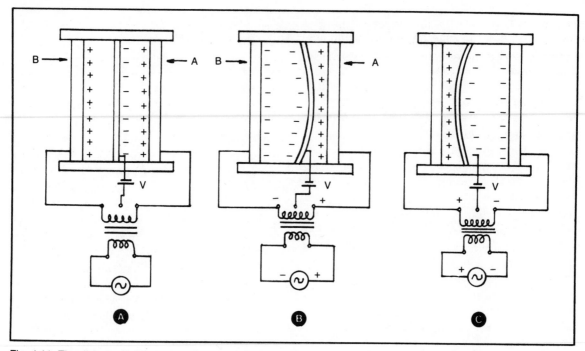

Fig. 4-11. The diagram in (A) shows how an ac signal is connected to a symetrical electrostatic speaker. Diagrams (B) and (C) indicate the polarity of the charges on the plates and the diaphragm as a function of the ac voltage.

be so small that it will not be a problem. Even with the 24 inch speaker described in Chapter 6, the variation was so small that the spring rate on the diaphragm was only 0.125 pounds/inch.

Diaphragm Tension vs. Shape

The resonant frequency of a stretched membrane is a function of the tension. This is the same principle that is used in tuning a stretched string. As the tension on the string is increased, the fundamental frequency also increases.

For an electrostatic speaker, the three most significant configurations for the plate and the diaphragm are: circular, square and rectangular. The diaphragm tension can be determined from one of the following equations, and a measurement of the speaker resonant frequency. For a circular membrane the tension is:

$$T = M((f \times r)^2/(0.146))$$

For a square membrane the tension is:

$$T = M((f \times a)^2/(0.497))$$

and for the rectangular diaphragm, the tension is:

$$T = M((f \times a \times b)^2/(0.6273)).$$

Where
M = the mass in grams.
f = the resonant frequency.
T = the tension in dynes/cm.
r = the radius of a circular membrane in cm.
a = the length of one side of a square membrane in cm.
a,b = the length of each side of a rectangular membrane in cm.

Diaphragm Movement

In a push-pull speaker, the diaphragm is forced to move by changing the electrostatic charge between the plates and the diaphragm. If one plate

74

has a positive potential with respect to the diaphragm and the other plate is negative, the forces of attraction and repulsion will cause the diaphragm to move toward the positive plate.

The diagram of Fig. 4-11A depicts how an ac signal can be applied to the plates of a symmetrical speaker. Because the transformer winding has almost no resistance, the dc polarizing voltage between the diaphragm and either plate will be equal to the value of "V."

Figure 4-11B shows an ac signal that is connected to the speaker through a transformer. The polarity of this signal, for both the source and the secondary winding of the transformer, is also shown. When the transformer winding makes plate "A" positive, with respect to the diaphragm, it also makes "B" negative. If the value of "V" is 100 volts and the ac voltage across the entire secondary transformer winding is 20 volts, then the voltage on Plate "A" will be – 90 volts. Plate "B" will have a voltage of – 110 volts. The diaphragm force created by plate "A" will be one of attraction and it will be equal to 2.54 pounds. Similarly, the force on plate "B" will be one of repulsion and will be equal to 3.1 pounds. These forces are based on a plate-to-diaphragm spacing of 0.01 inches. When the polarity of the ac voltage reverses itself as shown in Fig. 4-11C, the forces will also reverse themselves and this will cause the diaphragm to move in the opposite direction.

The back and forth motion of the diaphragm compresses and rarifies the air molecules next to the diaphragm. Since the plates are made acoustically transparent, the sound created by the motion of the molecules will be heard as coming from the speaker.

Spacing vs Bias Voltage

One other factor that can affect the performance of an electrostatic speaker is the amount of dc bias voltage that is applied between the plates and the diaphragm.

This voltage directly affects the sound pressure that can be obtained by the speaker. For the full range speaker described in this book, the sound

pressure below a bias voltage of 2000 volts would double for each doubling of the dc voltage. This is equal to an increase of 6 db per octave. Above the 2000 volt point, the sound pressure level was essentially constant and changed by only a couple of dB for a doubling of the voltage. This relationship is shown in the graph of Fig. 4-12.

Although the graph only indicates the sound pressure output for a 100 Hz. tone, it was found that a 4 kHz tone had an identical curve. This indicates that the curve is not frequency sensitive. It may (and this was not checked), however, be related to the separation between the plates and the diaphragm. If the spacing is closer then the 0.125 inches used for the speaker described in Chapter 6, it should be anticipated that the curve will level off at a lower voltage.

Most articles that have been written about electrostatics indicate that the bias voltage should be as high as possible. At a first glance, the graph seems to contradict this view point. However, increasing the dc voltage above the knee of the curve affects the distortion level. In addition, the humidity affects the amount of bias voltage. To compensate for changes in voltage and to keep the distortion level low, it is a good idea to keep the voltage as high as possible. The maximum limit is imposed by the breakdown voltage of air.

Factors that Affect the Performance of a Symmetrical Speaker

Even though electrostatic and electromagnetic speakers have some similarity in the way they create sound, there are also some significant differences. To reproduce low frequency sounds, more air must be moved. In a conventional speaker, this is achieved by making the cone larger or by making the voice coil longer. When the voice coil is longer, the cone can move a greater distance. Frequently both methods are used. In a push-pull electrostatic speaker, the diaphragm is centered between the two plates and this limits the amount of movement that can be achieved by the diaphragm. Because of this limitation, any increase in the bass response of this type of speaker is

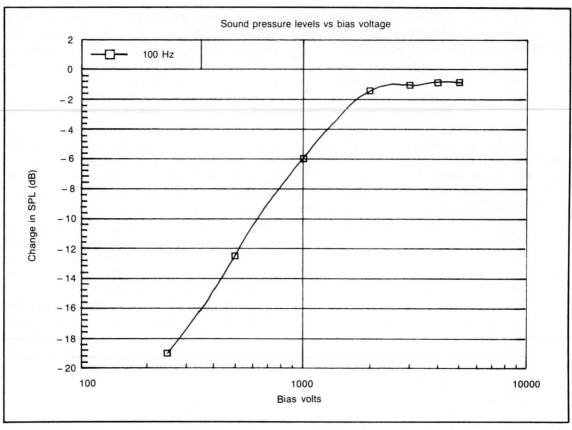

Fig. 4-12. A graph that relates the acoustic output of an electrostatic speaker to the bias voltage that is applied to the diaphragm.

usually achieved by making the speaker larger. An electrostatic speaker has an advantage over its electromagnetic counterpart because the driving force is applied over the entire surface instead of only at the center of the cone.

Directivity

As a speaker is made larger, it creates other problems. One of the aspects of sound reproduction is the relationship between the size of the speaker and the highest frequency that it must reproduce. As indicated in Chapter 2, a speaker becomes directional above the point where ka = 2 (see Graph 2-18). To solve this problem, a conventional speaker manufacturer resorts to one of two methods. To maintain a large angle of radiation, either multiple speakers with an appropriate cross-

over network, or a single speaker with a mechanical crossover must be used. The result is that the dispersion angle is maintained relatively constant with an increase in frequency. This concept can present some interesting problems to the designer of a conventional speaker system. Because of size limitations, the usual solution to solving the dispersion problem, is to use speakers in an array. With this method, the individual speakers are angled outward so that the array covers a large area.

In an electrostatic speaker, it is relatively easy to create a speaker with a variable area. Typically this speaker does not have a minimum size. For instance, suppose that it is desired to radiate a 20 kHz signal over an angle of at least 90 degrees. Using the point where ka = 2 and solve for the radius "r," the speaker must have a radius that does not exceed 0.214 inches. This is about 1/3 the wavelength of a 20 kHz tone. The wavelength itself can be calculated by:

$$\text{Wavelength} = \text{(speed of sound)/frequency.}$$
$$= 13440 \text{ inches}/20000$$
$$= 0.672 \text{ inches.}$$

To manufacture an electromagnetic speaker with a diameter of 0.214 inches is a significant task. Besides the size problem, there is an additional concern about how much power can be produced by such a small speaker.

An electrostatic speaker can be not only this small, but even smaller. For instance, some electrostatic speakers have used wire for plates. With this technique, the minimum size is determined by the diameter of the wire. The radiated power, on the other hand, is a function of the area. The power in an electrostatic speaker can be increased by making the plates longer.

Impedance

One factor that has not been mentioned is the impedance of the speaker and how it changes with frequency. In Chapter 3, Fig. 3-3 indicates how the impedance of an electromagnetic speaker varies as a function of the frequency. Above cone resonance, the impedance rises with increasing frequency. This effect is caused by the speaker voice coil.

An electrostatic speaker, on the other hand, is a capacitor. This device has the opposite characteristic to that of a coil. As frequency is increased, the impedance will decrease.

For a symmetrical speaker with six inch plates, the capacity was 401.5 picofarads. The impedance of this speaker can be calculated by:

$$X_c = (1.59 \times 10^{-1})/(f \times C)$$
Where X_c = the speaker's impedance in ohms.
   f = the frequency.
   C = the capacity of the speaker.

At a frequency of 1000 Hz the speaker impedance is:

$$X_c = (1.59 \times 10^{-1})/(1000 \times 401.5 \times 10^{-12})$$
$$= 396,509 \text{ ohms.}$$

This value is a linear function of the frequency and is inversely proportional to the capacity. If the frequency increases by a factor of 10, the speakers impedance will decrease by the same amount. At 10,000 Hz the impedance of the speaker will be 39,651 ohms. Similarly, at 100 Hz, a reduction in the frequency by a factor of 10, the impedance will increase to a value of 3,965,087 ohms. An impedance curve for an electrostatic speaker is shown in Fig. 4-13.

Most amplifiers are rated for impedances values between 4 and 16 ohms. The above calculations are considerably larger and they would produce some significant limitations if the speaker was directly connected to the amplifier. The diagrams shown in Fig. 4-11 all have a transformer between the signal source and the speaker. The purpose of the transformer is to change the voltage from the amplifier to a value that will be compatible with the speaker. The transformer also changes the speaker impedance to a value that is compatible with the requirements of the amplifier. More details about the transformer will be found in Chapter 12.

Constant Charge

Another factor in speaker performance is the method for charging the capacity. Professor Hunt indicates in his book, that if the diaphragm excursion is large, there may be a considerable amount of distortion. This is caused by a variation in the capacity on each side of the diaphragm. If the variation can be limited to less then 8%, then the distortion will be less then 1%. Professor Hunt shows that when the charging time constant is much greater than the half period of the lowest signal frequency, the effect of the unbalance is reduced. This charging time constant is made up of a resistor in series with the speaker capacity and the dc bias voltage. This is shown in Fig. 4-14.

If the lowest frequency to be reproduced is 30 Hz, then the half period is equal to 66.6 milliseconds. To be considerably larger, the charging time constant should be about 10 times greater. This would be 666 milliseconds. If a speaker has a capacity of 401.5 picofarads then the value of the resistance can be calculated by:

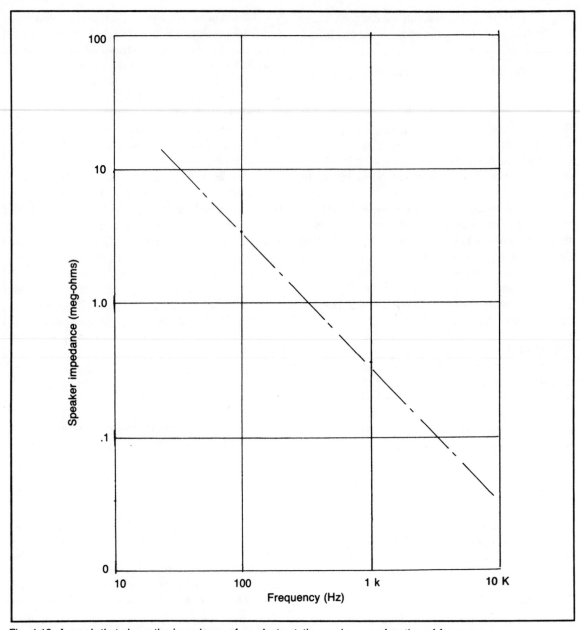

Fig. 4-13. A graph that shows the impedance of an electrostatic speaker as a function of frequency.

$$T = R \times C$$

Where T = the half period charging time constant.

R = the value of the series resistance.

C = the speaker capacity.

For the indicated parameters, the value of R is:

$$R = T/C$$
$$= (6.66 \times 10^{-1})/(4.015 \times 10^{-10})$$
$$= 1.66 \times 10^{9} \text{ ohms}$$

This resistance value is extremely large and very difficult to obtain. Because the six inch speaker will not produce a response to 30 Hz, the value can be made considerably smaller. A reasonable value might be 50 megohms. This would make the charging time constant equal to 20 milliseconds, and this would produce the desired effect down to a frequency of 500 Hz.

Humidity

Another factor that can affect the speaker performance is the humidity. The voltage being supplied to the diaphragm is usually high (1 to 6 kilovolts). It is also supplied through a large series resistance. Normally, the resistance of the air between the plate and the diaphragm, is much greater than the resistance. Under this condition, most of the voltage will appear across the space between the plate and the diaphragm. This is shown in Fig. 4-15A. As an example, suppose the air resistance between the plate and the diaphragm is 200 megohms. If the bias voltage is 1 kilovolt, the actual voltage that will appear between the plate and the diaphragm (Fig. 4-15B), can be calculated by the following formula.

$$V_{\text{(plate to diaphragm)}} = (R_1/(R_1 + R_2)) \times V$$

$$\text{Where } R_1 = \text{insulation resistance between the plate and the diaphragm.}$$

$$R_2 = \text{the resistance in series with the speaker capacity.}$$

$$= (2.0 \times 10^8)/(2.2 \times 10^8) \times 1000$$

$$= 909 \text{ volts.}$$

This value is approximately 90% of the available supply voltage.

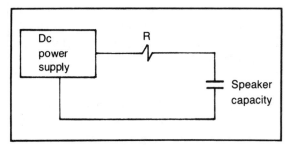

Fig. 4-14. A diagram that shows a method for producing a constant charge on the diaphragm of an electrostatic speaker.

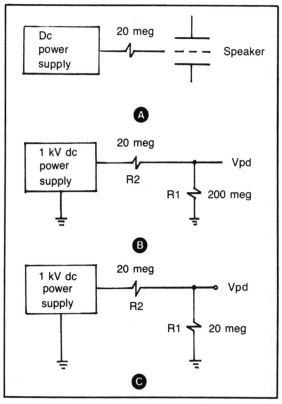

Fig. 4-15. Indicates the relationship between the bias voltage and the air resistance.

When the humidity increases, the air resistance decreases. Figure 4-15C depicts the condition where the air resistance has decreased to the value of the series resistance. The voltage that will appear across the plate and the diaphragm is equal to half of the supply voltage. The other half will be dropped across the 20 megohm resistor. If the speaker bias voltage is above the knee of the curve in Fig. 4-12, then the voltage drop may only have a small affect on the acoustic output level. On the other hand, if the bias voltage is set at or near the knee of the curve, the change in voltage will cause the volume to change by 50%.

At this point, you should have some understanding of how an electrostatic speaker functions. Based on this knowledge, it is time to start considering how to build such a speaker. The next chapter will begin by describing how to build a full range electrostatic speaker.

Chapter 5

Building a Full-Range Electrostatic Speaker

The techniques to be described in the following chapters can be applied to tweeters, mid-range, woofers, and full-range speakers. The type of speaker is determined by its size and by the distance between the plates and the diaphragm. The technique that will be described can be used to build individual electrostatic speakers for any frequency range. The procedure will describe how to build a speaker that uses a single diaphragm to cover the entire audio range. When all of the indicated steps are completed, the finished full range speaker will be 24 by 48 inches.

Each of the chapters will address a particular aspect in the speaker construction. This chapter, for instance, will begin with a description of the materials that will be needed for the speaker. After this section, information will be given about the plates and the possible material choices. Because the plates of the speaker described in this book, are plastic, the following section will describe how such a material can be used to make a plate. Also included in this chapter are the steps that are required to make the plastic plate conductive.

MATERIAL SELECTION

From a construction standpoint, a symmetrical electrostatic speaker consists of four parts. The first three are; the plate and diaphragm material (which create the electrostatic field), the ribs (used for structural support of the plates), and the frame (which holds everything together). In addition to these items, the fourth component is a set of spacers that are used to separate the plates from the diaphragm.

The construction materials for an electrostatic speaker can be divided into two groups. The first group consists of the materials that are used to make the plates. They can be made from metal, masonite, or plastic. The advantages and some of the disadvantages of each of these will be presented.

The second group is used to make the plate supporting structure. There are many choices in this area but the selected material was wood. It is easy to work with and is readily available. In addition to this, most "do-it-yourselfers" will have most of the necessary tools to make the parts. The type of wood for the frames and the ribs does not have to be the best. The wood is being used as a support structure and not as a cabinet. Lumber companies and many hardware stores carry a suitable grade of pine. It doesn't make much difference if the wood has some knots. They can be removed when the pieces are cut to size. It is a good idea, however, to try to keep the number of knots to a minimum.

Before actually starting construction, a decision should be made about the material that will be used for the plates. There are at least three possible choices. Each has advantages as well as some disadvantages. If a plastic material is chosen for the plates, fabrication can be done in parallel with the work on the rest of the speaker.

PLATE MATERIAL

In building a large electrostatic speaker, the plates must perform two functions. First they must be conductive so that an electrical charge can be dispersed evenly over the entire surface area. Second, they must be rigid. The plate, when it is mounted in the frame, must be flat and unmovable.

Extruded Aluminum

The principle advantage of extruded aluminum is that it is readily available and has a moderate cost. One disadvantage is that the material does not lend itself to being easily fastened to a wood frame. Also one of the sides has a sharp edge. Care must be taken to ensure that this side is away from the diaphragm. Failure to do this may cause arcing when the high voltage is applied. Another disadvantage is due to the size of the aluminum sheets. As explained in Chapter 2, the speaker width and the highest frequency that it must reproduce are directly related. As indicated in the noted chapter, the speaker width must be less then 1/3 of the wavelength of its highest frequency. If the width dimensions exceeds this value, then the speaker will become directional.

While it is possible to cut the perforated aluminum sheets into smaller sizes, and thereby decrease the width, several problems are created by this method. First the cutting operation will pro-

duce sharp edges. In addition to this, a method for mounting each of the individual sections must be designed. A further problem will be encountered when trying to build a tweeter to the above width requirement. A tweeter panel, that is less then 1/3 the wavelength of a 20 kHz frequency, will have a width that is less then 0.22 inches. The wavelength of a 20 kilohertz signal is 0.67 inches. Making a strip this size is not very difficult. Holding it flat and parallel to the diaphragm over the entire length *is* a problem.

Masonite

The problems associated with the aluminum plate can be eliminated by using a material that is non-conductive. However, it must have a perforated pattern. One possible choice that fulfills this requirement is perforated Masonite. Sheets of this material can be purchased from local building supply stores where it is frequently sold as a material for room dividers.

Using Masonite for a plate material provides several advantages over the extruded aluminum. First, it is an easy material to cut and drill. Second, by applying a coating of conductive paint, the Masonite can be made selectively conductive.

The disadvantages to this material are that it not only has sharp edges but it also has a rough and a smooth side. If this material is chosen, you must make sure that both the rough surface and the sharp edges are facing away from the diaphragm. One other drawback is the effect produced by changes in the weather. Masonite is a paper product and, as such, it absorbs water. When the humidity changes, the water absorption will affect the efficiency of the speaker. Most of the time, the change will only produce a slight variation in the acoustic level and it may not be noticeable. The effect is also fairly long term. Its presence is indicated by a need to change the volume level on the amplifier. The volume setting may have to be changed to maintain the same audio level that you had on the previous day.

Plastic Plates

Plastic plates do not have many of the previous problems. The exception is the sharp edges. However, because the material is plastic, the sharp edges can be removed with either a file or a sharp knife. The biggest drawback to the plastic material is the cost. The material required to build a pair of 2 by 4 foot speakers is about $40.00. At first, this may not appear to be a significant amount. It should be noted that this is a solid piece of plastic without any holes.

PERFORATING

To obtain a hole pattern, the 4 foot by 8 foot sheets of plastic must be perforated. This will make them acoustically transparent. The best place to locate a company that does this type of operation is in the local phone book. There are a number of headings that can be checked. Besides looking under perforating, be sure to check perforators as well as perforated metals and plastic, etc. After finding one or two companies that will perforate plastic, it is a good idea to pay them a visit. Besides the cost of perforating, be sure to find out if there are any additional charges for set-up. Do not be surprised if the set-up charge is more than the cost of perforating.

In addition, you should also find out if there are any special requirements. One possible item is the size of the material that can be accommodated in the press during the perforating operation. If the press is limited to a two foot width, then you will need to cut the 4 by 8 foot sheet into four pieces. You will also need to discuss how the pattern should be orientated on each of the four pieces. Make sure that the 2 by 4 foot plate is divided in half and that the perforating operation produces two identical sections. Each section should not only be the same size, but they all should be mirror images of each other. The diagram shown in Fig. 5-1 indicates how and where the pattern should be located. One other important factor is to indicate to the perforators, that the smooth side of the plates must be free from any burrs or sharp edges. If they use sharp punches, this should not be a problem. The diagram shown in Fig. 5-2 is a detailed drawing of one plate and shows the required pattern.

Before going ahead with the perforating, you might find out if any of your friends are interested in building a set of speakers. There is usually a cost advantage if you all get together, buy the material, and then have it perforated. Not only will you get a slightly lower material cost, but the one-time set-up charge for the perforating operation can be spread out among all of you. While the plates are being perforated, you can skip to the next chapter and start making the frame and the rib assemblies.

PLATE PREPARATION

After the plates have been perforated, there are three additional steps needed before they can be used as plates for the speakers. First, the plates must be masked. Then, the second step consists of applying a conductive coating. This will be done to specific areas of the speaker. The third step is to apply an insulating paint to the assembly.

If you look at the plate material you will see there is a smooth side and a rough side. When the entire assembly is put together, the smooth side must have the conductive coating. When the speaker is assembled, the two conductive surfaces will face each other and they will be on the inside of the speaker. In some instances, the rear side of the plate may have burrs and other residue that was produced by the perforating operation. This material will have to be cleaned off.

If the plates were perforated in 2 by 4 foot sections, then the first step is to cut them apart. To do this, take a rule and divide the four foot length in half. This should produce a line that is exactly halfway between the two patterns. Next, place the plastic plate on your table saw and cut the plate along the line that was just drawn. Be sure to keep the blade centered on the line. After the plates are separated, mark on the rear side of the plates a designation that will indicate which ones are matching mirror-image pairs. One convenient indication is to use a letter of the alphabet. Mark one plate with the letter "A." On the other half of the pair, mark an "AA." After the second plate is separated, mark one plate with a "B" and the other half with "BB." After you have separated one pair of plates,

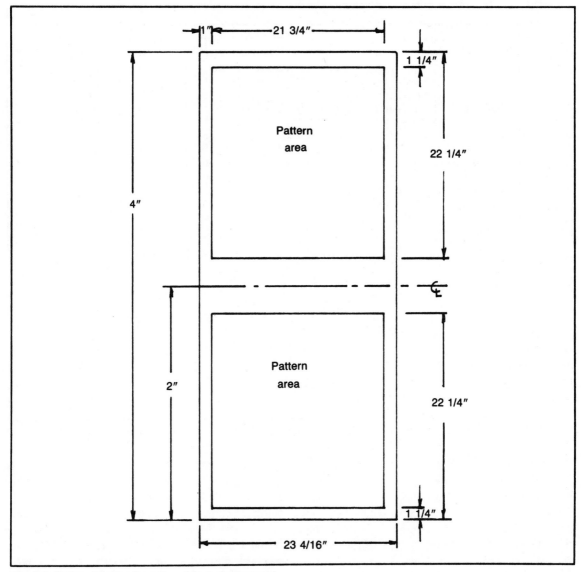

Fig. 5-1. Pattern location for a 2 × 4 foot plastic panel.

continue and do the same thing with the other plates. When you are finished you should have sixteen plates.

Once the plates have all been separated, you can proceed to deburr them. Most of the burrs can be eliminated by lightly sanding the back of the plate with 100 grit sandpaper after mounting the sandpaper on a block of wood.

After this last operation is completed, any slivers of plastic can be removed with a 1/4 inch rattail file. An alternate method would be to lightly scrap the edge of the holes with a sharp hobby knife. Be sure you do this operation from the rear side. You do not want to scratch the smooth front surface.

After the plate has been deburred, the next step

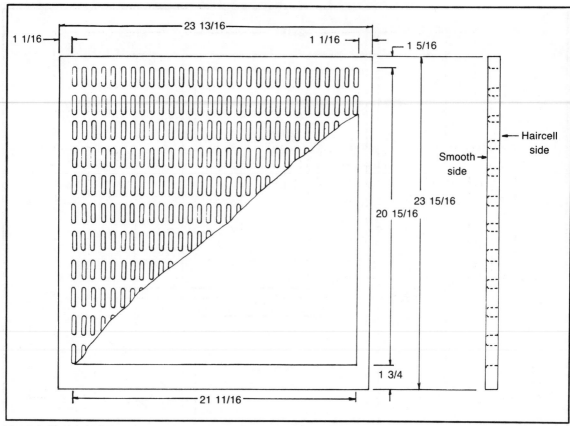

Fig. 5-2. Mechanical dimensions for the hole pattern on one 2 × 2 foot plastic speaker panel.

is to lay one plate of a pair on top of its counterpart. After aligning the sides, check the hole pattern. The holes should all align. Note there is a difference in spacing between the holes at the top edge and those at the bottom edge. Be sure that these two spacings correspond and that the smooth surfaces are facing each other.

The next step is to drill the holes that will be used to make the connections to the conductive portion of the plate. See Fig. 5-3 for the location of the holes in one plastic plate and Fig. 5-4 for the holes in the other plate. Separate the pairs into two groups (single letters in one group and double letters in the other group). Use a 9/64 bit and drill 8 holes in each plate that has a single letter. Use Fig. 5-3 for a pattern. Next, drill the same holes in the doubled lettered plates. Use Fig. 5-4 as a pattern.

To check the drilling operation, take the two corresponding pairs and place the plates opposite each other with the smooth side inwards. If everything is correct, the drill holes should be opposite each other. If they are not, be sure to correct the problem before continuing to the next step. Be sure to check all of the pairs. After checking the hole location, countersink the holes so that the head of a 6/32 screw is flush with the surface. If you use a drill press, set the depth stop to the required value. It is a good idea to check the depth of the countersink. The screw head must be flush or slightly below the surface. It must not protrude above the edge of the surface because this will create a sharp edge and the speaker may arc when the high voltage is applied.

Be sure the edges of the screw holes have no

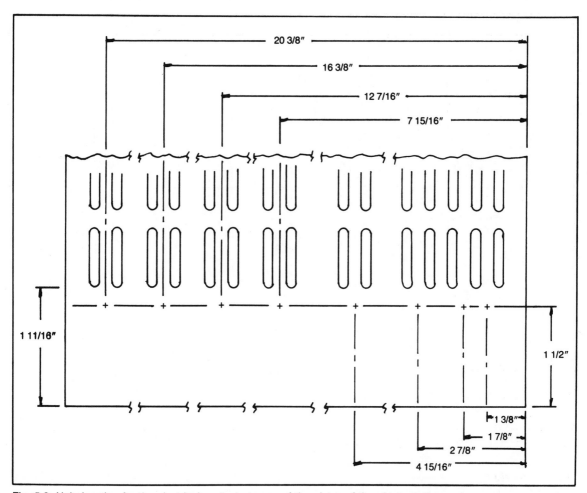

Fig. 5-3. Hole location for the electrical contacts to one of the plates of the electrostatic speaker.

burrs. Normally the countersink will do this but, when you are finished, rub your hands over the surface to make sure there are no sharp edges. If you find some, use a 1/2 inch drill and rotate it by hand in the hole. This should remove any extra material.

Before the plate can be made conductive, the smooth side of the plate must be cleaned. Use a soft lint free cloth and dip it in lacquer thinner. Lightly go over the surface and remove any grease or other marks that may be there. When you do this, make sure that the lacquer thinner does not attack the plastic material and make the surface rough. Once the surface is clean, try not to touch it. When you pick up the plate, do it by the edges.

CONDUCTIVE COATING

After you have cleaned the front surface of all the plates, the next step is to mask each one of the plates so that the conductive coating can be applied. The coating is applied to the smooth surface. Photographs of the required patterns are shown in Fig. 5-5. The upper photograph is for the plates with a single letter while the lower photo is the pattern for plates with a double letter.

Look at Fig. 5-6. On the right side, there are four small dark areas separated by a small area of white. These small white spaces are where the masking tape is placed. Also, notice that some of the white spaces are wider than others. When

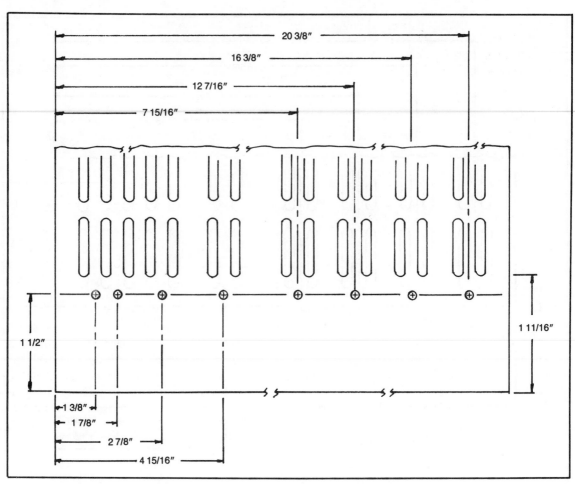

Fig. 5-4. Hole location for the electrical contacts to the opposite plate of the electrostatic speaker.

masking, try to avoid placing the masking tape at the edge or only partly across a hole. Such a procedure will produce an excess of conductive bridges. More on this will follow. To mask the wide areas, use 1/2 inch masking tape. Lay a strip from the top of the plate to bottom. The smaller areas use 1/4 inch masking tape. Proceed across the surface of the plate and mask the areas between the conductive strips. After all the inside masking strips have been installed, the next step is to mask the outside edges of the plates. To do this, use 2 inch masking tape and place it between the edge of the pattern and the outside edge of the plate.

After all the masking tape is in place, it must be rolled so that it is flat and tight against the sur-

face of the plate. If a good, tight seal is not obtained between the masking tape and the surface of the plate, the conductive paint will seep under the masking tape. When this happens, it may form a bridge between the two conductive sections. The procedure for removing the bridge is very slow and tedious. It is suggested that you spend a little extra effort to ensure a good fit between the tape and the plate. Partial bridges can be seen on both photos of Fig. 5-5. Although they do not actually form a bridge from one conductive area to the next, they must be removed. To properly flatten the tape edges, place the plate on a solid flat surface. The masking tape should be face up. Take a small wooden roller and go over every inch of the tape, especially at the edges. It is also best to go over the masking tape several times.

When you have finished masking and rolling the two plates, place them on top of each other. The conductive patterns should face each other. Be sure that the screws for the electrical connections are also opposite each other. If you look down between the plates, the patterns should align so that each plate is a mirror image of the other. If this is what you see, then proceed to the next step. If the two plates are not mirror images, one of the plates has been incorrectly masked or you have it upside down. In either case, the problem will have to be corrected. Refer to Fig. 5-5 to determine where the error is and make the correction before proceeding.

Now that the first pair of plates has been correctly masked, use the same procedure and mask the remaining plates. Be sure to check each one for the mirror image. After all the plates have been masked, you are ready to coat the plates with a conductive coating. Put some newspapers down on your work surface. Place some long wood strips on top of the paper. The strips should run the same direction as the pattern. Lay a plate on top of the wood strip with the masked side up.

When rolling the conductive paint, do it in the same direction as the pattern. The roller should be a small cloth type that has a width of 3 or 4 inches. Pour some conductive paint in a tray. Place the roller in the conductive paint. Be sure to roll the excess paint from the roller before applying it to the plate. If this isn't done, the coating will run down into the holes and possibly form a bridge across the rear surface. After you have applied the first coating, set this plate aside and then coat the next one. Be sure the first plate is flat. You do not want the coating to run. When all of the plates have had one coat, go back and apply a second coating. Continue until the entire surface has a nice even coating. All of the plates will need to have at least two or three conductive coatings. When all areas have a nice even coat and the paint has dried, the masking tape can be removed. Next, the plates will need to be cleaned. You cannot, however, use any type of solvent.

The part that needs to be cleaned is the un-painted strips. If there are any conductive bridges, they must be removed. This usually can be done by lightly scraping the surface with a sharp hobby knife. Also, if any coating material has run down through the holes, be sure to remove it. A little overlap at the front edges is okay. However, if the coating has run all the way to the back, it should be removed with a file. Any coating that is on the back can be left until later.

Next, insert the 6/32 flathead screws into the screw holes. Secure the screws on the back side with a flat washer, lock washer, and a nut. Make sure that the nut is tight. When the other connections and nuts are installed, you do not want this screw to turn. When the first panel is completed, install the screws in all the remaining panels. After the screws have been installed, lay one of the plates back on your work surface. Take a small artist brush and cover the screw head with the conductive paint. This needs to be a nice even coating that flows into the coating that was put on with the roller. After the paint has dried, you should not be able to see the metallic material of the screws. When this plate is finished lay it aside. Be sure it is flat so that the coating on the screws doesn't run. After coating one panel continue and coat all of the screws on all of the other panels.

Now that the painting is complete, place a plate back on your work surface. Before proceeding to the next operation, the plates will need to be re-masked. Take the two inch masking tape and again mask the outside edge of the plate. Place the masking tape about 1/16 of an inch farther out (toward the outside edge of the plate) than the conductive coating. This will ensure that all of the conductive coating is covered. Do not mask between the areas that are covered with a conductive coating. After the first plate has been masked, lay it aside. Take another plate and mask it in the same fashion. Continue with this procedure and mask all of the remaining plates.

INSULATING COATING

Once all the plates have been masked, you are ready to apply the high voltage insulating paint.

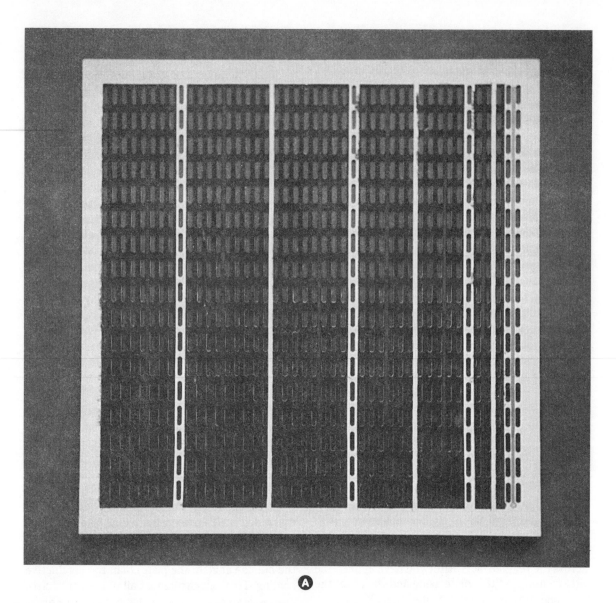

Fig. 5-5. Two photos of the plates of the electrostatic speaker.

This paint is made by General Cement and is called Red "X" corona dope. It comes in either a spray can or in one gallon containers. The larger size is intended for use with a roller. Because of the spacing between the plate and the diaphragm, it is important to have an even coating without any runs.

The corona dope must also overlap the edges of all the holes. The best method for doing this is to stand the plate upright with the screws for the electrical connections at the bottom. Start spraying at the top left corner and sweep back and forth across the plate. Each sweep should be slightly lower than the preceding one.

The spray can should be about 6 to 12 inches from the plate during the spray operation. It should also be tilted slightly downwards. You will need to

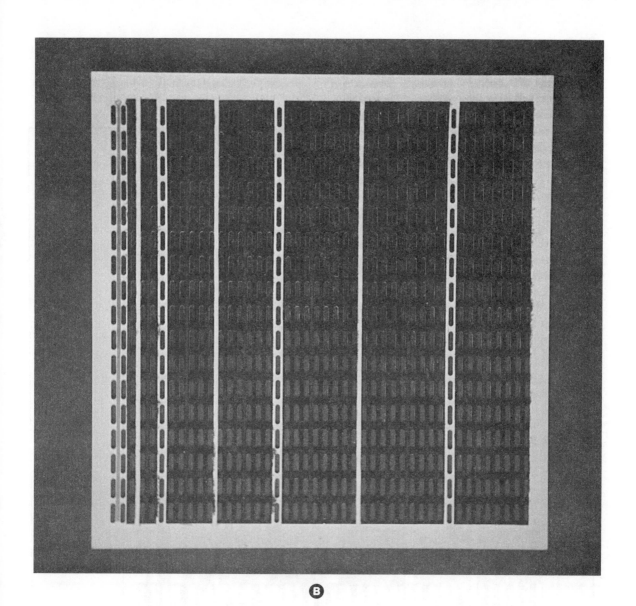

B

find the position that provides an even coating without any runs. When you have finished spraying the first plate, place it to one side. Do not turn it. It must be placed exactly as it was when you sprayed it. To prevent runs, however, it should be laid flat. Now take another plate, orient it like the first one and proceed to coat it in the exact same fashion. When you have finished the second plate, lay it

down next to the first plate. The two plates should have the same orientation. Continue with this coating procedure until all of the plates have had one coating. After you have finished the first coating and the paint has dried, it is time to apply the second coating. Take the first panel and rotate it 90 degrees from the position you used in the first spraying. The slots should now be horizontal and the electrical connections should be on your right. Spray the plate using the same procedure that was used for the first coating. When you have finished this coating, set the plate aside. Keep the plate in the same orientation. Continue to spray the rest of the plates in the same manner.

After the second coating has dried, take the first plate and again rotate it another 90 degrees.

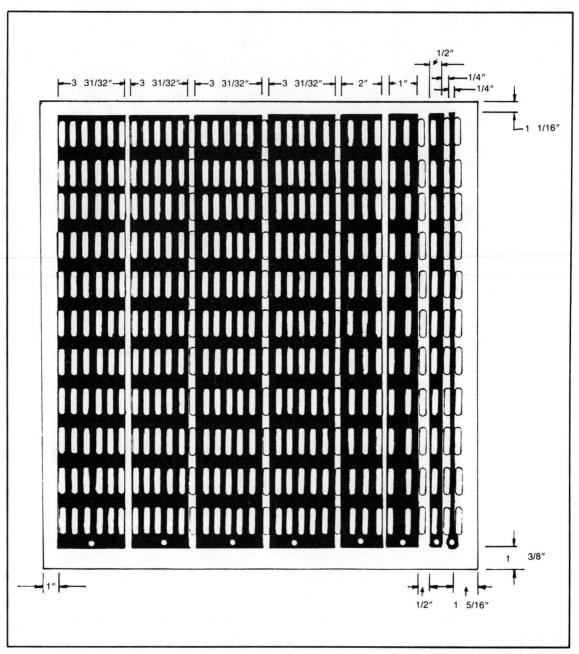

Fig. 5-6. Conductive coating pattern for one 2 × 2 foot plastic speaker panel.

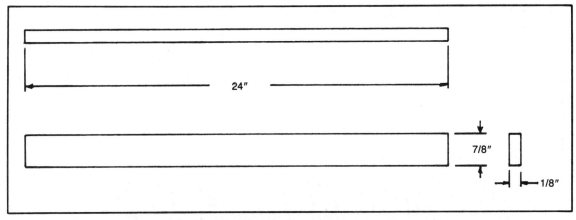

Fig. 5-7. Cutting diagram for the spacers for the electrostatic speaker.

The plate should now be orientated exactly as it was in the first step except that it is upside down. The holes for the electrical connections should now be at the top. Spray this plate and set it aside. Again, be sure that the orientation is the same. After spraying the first plate, continue to do the rest of the plates.

By this time, there should be enough corona dope on the plate so that the conductive coating is no longer visible. Before applying the last coat, lightly sand the surface with fine sandpaper. Use approximately 240 grit paper. Do not sand through the insulating coating. After sanding, wipe off the dust with a damp rag. Repeat this sanding and wiping operation for all of the plates. Take the first plate and rotate it another 90 degrees. The slots should be horizontal but the electrical connections should be on your left. Spray this plate. Repeat this last spraying procedure for all the remaining plates.

If you look at the plate, it should not only be a solid red color but it should also be perfectly smooth. After the paint has dried, look over the plates for run spots. If there are any, go over them with fine sandpaper and then apply another coating of insulating paint. Be careful when sanding to not go through the insulating coating because you may damage the conductive coating. After the paint has dried on the final coating or after any touch up the masking tape can be removed. This completes the operation on the plates and they can be laid aside.

SPACERS

Although the spacers will not be required until the assembly operation, they can be cut to size at this point. If you are using plastic plates, then use the same material for the spacers. The physical dimensions of the spacer are shown in Fig. 5-7. You will need a total of 32 for the two 4 foot speakers. Cut 32 pieces according to the size shown in Fig. 5-7. After they all have been cut to size, lightly sand or file the edges so there are no burrs. Place some tape around the spacers and lay them aside.

Chapter 6

Frames and Ribs

Not all electrostatic speakers require a separate frame and rib assembly. Their necessity is based on two factors. They are thickness of the plate material and the size of the plates. For a given plate thickness, the amount of bracing increases as the plate gets larger. On the full range speakers that are described in this book, they are an absolute necessity.

The purpose of this chapter is to provide a procedure for making the frame and the ribs. In making the parts, it is important to remember that the cutting and drilling operations must be done accurately. To help in this area, the following motto should be placed on the wall over your work area.

```
* * * * * * * * * * * * * * * * * * * * * * * * * * * * * * * * * * * * * * * * *
```

MEASURE TWICE SO THAT YOU WILL ONLY CUT ONCE

```
* * * * * * * * * * * * * * * * * * * * * * * * * * * * * *
```

To help you remember this motto, additional steps have been added to check various operations. Do not attempt any shortcuts unless you thoroughly understand the operation. Deviations will not only affect the ease of assembly but they can also create problems with the speaker performance.

TOOLS

When making measurements, accuracy is important. Turning the measurements and materials into a speaker requires the right tools. With the exception of a drill press and a radial saw, the average person should have most of the required tools. A minimum tool list will be found in Appendix.

If you do not have a table or a radial saw, there are a couple of alternate approaches available. One possibility is to borrow one from a friend. If the friend wants to do the work, make sure that he does it accurately. If you don't know anyone with a table or radial arm saw, check with your local lumber company. Most of them are willing to cut purchases to the required size. Another possibility is to contact a local cabinet shop. They may cost a little more then the lumber yard, but they work with closer tolerances.

The best tool for drilling all of the required holes is a drill press. If one is not available, an electric hand drill can be used. In this instance, more care must be taken in the alignment and drilling procedure. To make sure that all of the holes are straight, you will need a doweling fixture. Another required item is a stop block. This block is used to limit the drill penetration. The exact block size must be determined by the length of the drill and the depth of the hole.

It is also a good idea to place a piece of aluminum on top of the wood block. Without the metal plate, the drill chuck will make a groove around the top of the block. The next time a hole is drilled, it will be a little deeper. The drill chuck will again make the groove a little deeper. This process will continue each time a hole is drilled. By the time the last hole is drilled its depth may be significantly different then the first hole.

FRAME

The frame and the ribs are the supporting structure for the plates that were discussed in Chapter 5. It is essential that all of the pieces fit correctly. If this isn't done, then the final assembly will not be straight.

The frame consists of four pieces. These are the left and right sides, plus the top and bottom pieces. To build a stereo pair, like the ones described in this book, you will need a total of 32 pieces. A diagram of the frame and its parts is shown in Fig. 6-1.

Each of the following steps describe one operation for making the parts of the frame. The bracket in front of each step, can be used to check off the completion of that step.

☐ Take a 1 by 12 inch board, at least 8 feet long, and divide it into three 24 inch long sections.

All three pieces must be the same length, and one method for doing this is to use a stop block on the saw. This block should be clamped to the saw table so that there is exactly 24 inches between it

and the blade. This is shown in Fig. 6-2. For those readers with a table saw, another extremely useful tool is the miter gauge holddown clamp. This tool prevents the board from moving while a cut is being made. If you have a radial saw, the wood can be clamped directly to the saw table.

☐ After setting the stop block in the required position, place the board on your saw table and butt it against the block.
☐ Clamp the board in place with the miter gauge hold down clamp.
☐ Turn the saw on and cut the board to size.
☐ At this point, it is a good idea to measure the length of the board.

It should be exactly 24 inches. If it is not, then check the position of the stop block. Correct the positioning problem before going to the next step. If the board that was just cut is a little short, it can be used to make the ribs.

☐ After cutting one board to the 24 inch length, proceed to cut two more boards to the same length. Note, if your wood has a lot of knots, you may need more than three boards.

After completing the above steps, measure the length of each board. If all pieces are 24 inches long, then the next step is to cut the end overlap.

☐ Take each of the 24 inch boards and place a mark 3/4 of an inch from each end (See Fig. 6-3).
☐ With a square, draw a line across the face of each board.

To cut the overlap, a set of dado blades should be installed on the saw. If the 3/4 inch cut can not be obtained, then set the dado blades for a 3/8 inch cut.

After the blades are installed, the next step is to set the depth of the cut. The depth should be 1/2 of the board thickness, and this should be approximately 3/8 of an inch. Before making any cuts, you should measure the actual thickness and then set the blade height to 1/2 of this value.

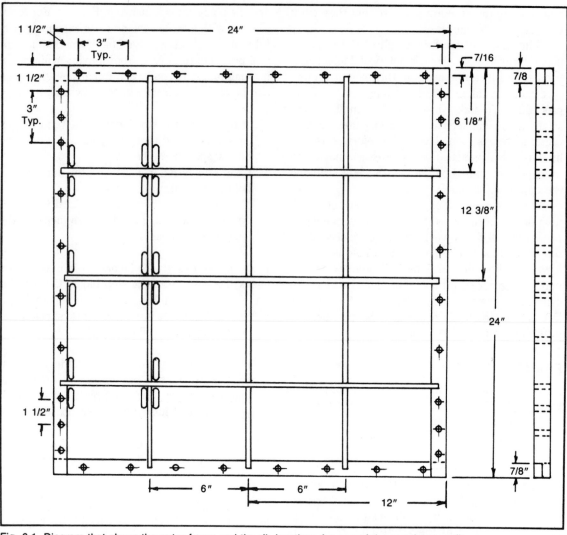

Fig. 6-1. Diagram that shows the outer frame and the rib locations for one of the speaker panels.

☐ With the blade set to 1/2 of the board thickness, make a test cut on a piece of scrap wood.

☐ After the cut is made, check its depth to insure that it is 1/2 of the board thickness.

When you have the correct depth, you are ready to continue and cut the end lap.

☐ Take one of the 24 inch boards and align the edge of the board with the edge of the dado blade.

☐ Use the miter gauge holddown clamp to hold the board in position.

☐ Turn the saw on and make the cut.

If you are doing a 3/4 inch cut, then skip the next step.

☐ For those making a 3/8 inch cut, the board will have to be moved over the width of the blade.

When this is done, one edge of the blade should

94

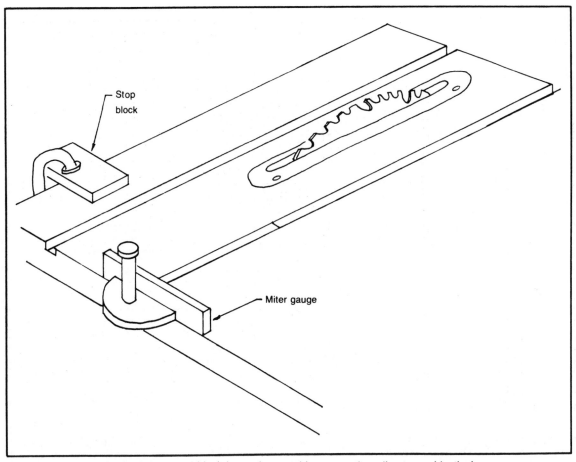

Fig. 6-2. Diagram indicates how a stop block is used on a table saw so that all cuts are identical.

align with the line drawn across the face of the board. It is important to make sure that the overlaps aren't too wide. One way this can be done is to use a stop block. Take a piece of scrap and make some test cuts. When the required width is achieved, put the stop block in place. This step should be done accurately so that all of the other boards will have the same width.

☐ When the correct width is obtained, cut the overlap in all of the boards.

After completing the above steps, you should have three boards that look like the drawing shown in Fig. 6-3. Before continuing, recheck the end laps to make sure that they are all 3/4 of an inch.

In the next series of steps, the 24 inch boards will be cut into strips that are 7/8 inch wide. For this series of steps, you will need to install your regular saw blade.

☐ If you are using a table saw, set the fence to a width of 7/8 inch. Be sure to measure both ends so that the fence is parallel to the blade. Adjust the saw blade for the correct cutting height.

☐ Take a piece of scrap wood and place it against the fence and cut a strip.

☐ Check the piece that was just cut. If it is 7/8 of an inch, go on to the next step. If the dimension is incorrect, go back and reset the fence to the correct dimension.

☐ Take one of the 1 by 12 by 24 inch boards and

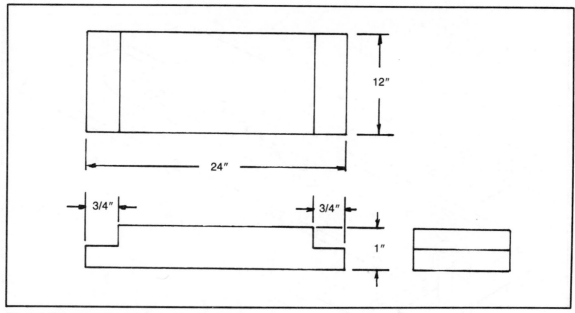

Fig. 6-3. The beginning part for making the frame.

lay it so that the 24 inch dimension is parallel to the blade and against the fence.

☐ Turn the saw on and cut a strip.
☐ Now cut a second strip.
☐ Take the two pieces and lay them so that their end laps fit together. The two boards should be at right angles to each other.
☐ Check the fit. There should be no overlaps. See Fig. 6-4.

If an overlap exists, adjust the fence until there is no overlap. Once you have obtained the correct amount of overlap, you are ready to cut the remaining pieces.

☐ Continue the cutting process until you have cut all three 24 inch boards into 7/8 inch wide strips.

When you have completed the above steps, you should have a minimum of 32 pieces. Each piece should measure 7/8 by 1 by 24 inches. It is also advisable to have six or seven extra pieces. Later on, you may make a mistake and need another piece to take its place.

☐ After you have all the strips cut, divide them into two separate groups. Each of the groups must have at least 16 pieces.

To take care of any errors, it is a good idea to have a couple of extra pieces in each group.

☐ One group will be the top and bottom frames. Take a piece of masking tape and wrap it around this group.
☐ Take a marking pen and label the masking tape "top and bottom frames."
☐ Temporarily lay this group aside.

The remaining 16 pieces will be used to make the right and left side pieces.

Left and Right Frame Members

The groove dimensions for the right and left frames are shown in Fig. 6-5. To cut the grooves, you will need to reinstall your dado blade.

☐ After installing the dado blade, set the blade height to 1/2 the wood thickness.

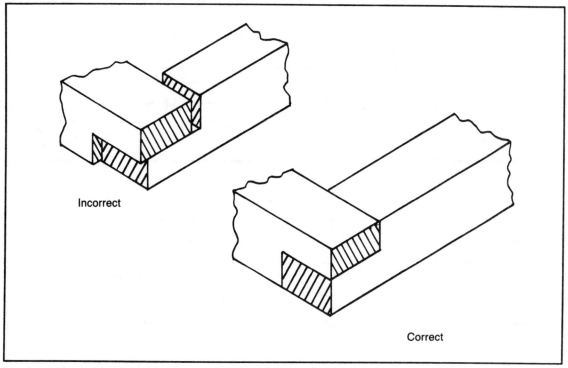

Fig. 6-4. A diagram that shows the correct way to have the end laps fit.

☐ Next, take a piece of scrap and make a test cut.
☐ Check the depth of the cut.

If the blade is at the correct height, continue to the next step. Otherwise, go back and reset the blade height and then make another test cut.

Because this operation is repetitive, it is a good idea to use a stop block. In this way, all the pieces will have the grooves in the same location. This is a very important requirement. In Fig. 6-5, notice that both the right and left sides have a groove 6-1/8 inches in from the end.

☐ Measure over from the saw blade the required distance and clamp the stop block to the table saw.
☐ Next, use a piece of scrap and the miter hold-down clamp to make a test cut.
☐ On the piece that was just cut, measure the actual distance from the edge of the board to the groove.

If this dimension equals the amount specified in the drawing, no further adjustment is necessary. If the groove on the test cut is not the correct distance, adjust the stop block and make another test cut.

☐ Once the correct dimension is achieved, divide the frame members into two groups.

There must be a minimum of 8 pieces in each of the groups. As already noted, it is also a good idea to have a couple of extra pieces.

☐ Lay one group aside. These will be the left sides.
☐ Take one of the remaining eight pieces and place it on the saw table with the end laps facing away from you.
☐ Use the miter holddown clamp to secure it in position.
☐ Now cut the groove.
☐ After the first piece has been cut, take the next piece and place it on your saw exactly like the

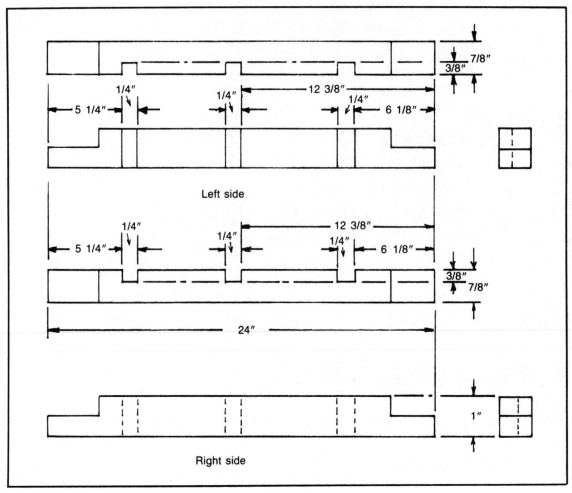

Fig. 6-5. Dimensions for the right and left side frame pieces.

first one. Again use the miter hold down clamp and then cut the grooves in this piece.
□ Repeat this operation for all the remaining pieces.
□ Place a strip of masking tape around these pieces. Mark the tape "right side" and lay these pieces aside.
□ Next get the group of left side pieces that had been set aside.

Because this group is the left side; the orientation, during the cutting operation, will be opposite to the one used to cut the right side.

□ To cut the left side, place one of the pieces on your saw table with the end laps facing you.
□ Use the miter gauge hold down and proceed to cut all of the pieces for the left frame member.

After you have completed the previous step, you should be able to place a right and left side frame side by side. With the end laps facing down, the grooves should be aligned so that they are opposite each other. See Fig. 6-6.

In the next operation, a similar set of grooves will be cut in the opposite end of the right and left frame members.

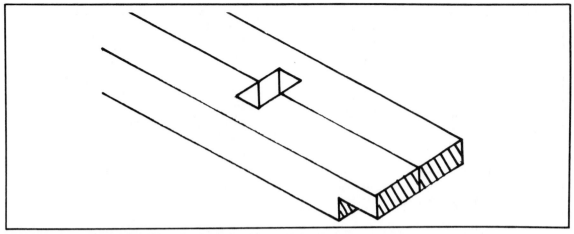

Fig. 6-6. A diagram that shows how to check the right and left side frame pieces for the correct dimensions.

☐ Set the stop block so that it is 5-1/4 inch from the blade.
☐ Check the position of this groove by making a test cut on a piece of scrap.

As noted, this process of checking and recheck-ing will reduce the possibility of making an error. If the dimensions of the last test cut are correct, then continue to the next step. If not, go back and reset the stop block and then make another test cut.

The last series of cuts was made on the frames for the left side. When cutting this next groove, the process will begin with this group and finish on the right side frame.

☐ Place the end lap of one of the left side frames so that it is facing toward you. The groove that was cut in the previous step should be on your left.
☐ Use the miter holddown to clamp the piece in position against the stop block.
☐ Turn the saw on and cut the groove in this piece.
☐ Be sure to check the dimensions of the cut against those of the drawing.

At this point, the dimensions should match the drawing and you should be able to continue to the next step. However, if there is an error, determine the cause and correct it.

☐ Continue cutting grooves in all of the remain-ing left side pieces.

After completing the above step, the same groove must now be cut in the right side frame.

☐ Wrap some tape around the left side frames and lay them aside.
☐ Get the right side frames.
☐ Take one of the right side pieces and place it on your saw with the end lap away from you.

The last groove that was cut in this piece should be on the left side. Follow the same procedure for cutting this groove as you did for the left side frames.

☐ Cut the groove in all of the right side frames.
☐ To check the position of the grooves in the left and right frame pieces place them side by side.

With the end laps facing down, the two sets of grooves should align and be facing each other.

The last groove that will be cut in both the left and right sides will be the center groove.

☐ Set the stop block so that it is 12 3/8 inches from the saw blade.
☐ On a piece of scrap, make a test cut to insure the correct position.

☐ Check the position of the cut. If it is correct, continue to the next step. If it isn't, then reset the stop block.
☐ Next take a right side piece and place it on the saw table.

The end lap should be facing away from you. Use the miter clamp.

☐ Turn the saw on and cut the center groove.
☐ Recheck the position of the cut to make sure that it is in the correct location.

If the drawing and the dimensions of the cut do not agree determine the cause of the problem and correct it before going on.

☐ If the dimensional location is correct, then proceed to cut all of the remaining right side frames.
☐ Put some masking tape around this group. Mark

it "right side" and lay them aside.
☐ Get the group that was marked "left side" frames.
☐ Place one of the pieces on the saw table with the end laps facing towards you.
☐ Use the miter holddown clamp to hold it in place.
☐ Turn the saw on and then cut the center groove.
☐ Check the location of this groove. It should correspond to the value shown in Fig. 6-5.
☐ If the above dimension is correct, then continue and cut the center groove in the remaining left side pieces.

If the dimension check is incorrect, locate and correct the source of error. You should also make sure that the grooves for the right side are correct.

☐ After completing this last step, the right and left side frame pieces should look like Fig. 6-7. Lay the two pieces side by side and check the locations of the end laps and the groove positions.

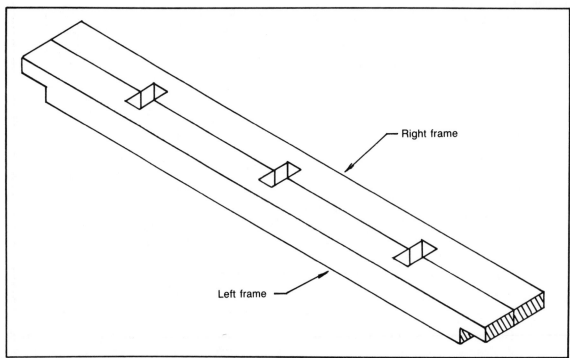

Right frame

Left frame

Fig. 6-7. A check of the dimensional locations associated with the right and left side frame.

☐ This completes the cutting of the left and right frames. Take some masking tape and wrap a piece around the left side frames.

☐ With a marking pen label this group "left side" and then lay them with the right side frames.

Top and Bottom Frames

In the following steps, a similar set of grooves will be cut in both the top and bottom frames. The procedure for cutting the grooves in these two parts is exactly the same as the one followed in making the left and right sides.

☐ Get the remaining group of frames that was previously marked top and bottom.

As shown in Fig. 6-8, the two outside grooves are the same distance from either end. Because of this, only one setup will be needed for cutting the grooves at the outside edge.

☐ To begin this series of steps, set the stop block to a dimension of 5 7/8 inches.

☐ As usual, make a test cut on a scrap piece of wood.

☐ Check the location of the groove against the value shown in the drawing.

If the groove location is the correct, then continue to the next step. Otherwise go back and reset the stop block. Then make another test cut.

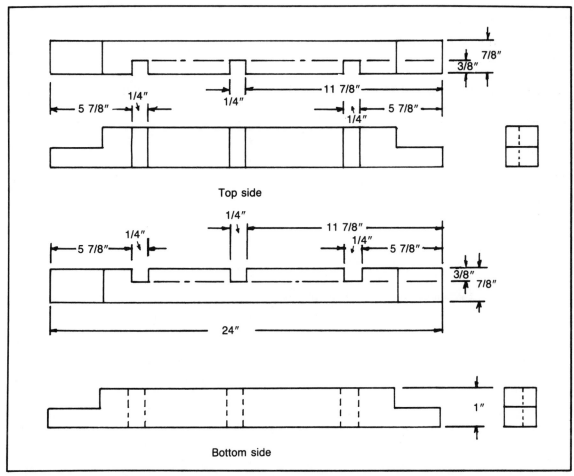

Fig. 6-8. Dimensional values for the top and bottom frame pieces.

- ☐ Once the groove has been properly located, place one of the top or bottom frame members on your saw.
- ☐ Clamp it in place with the miter holddown. The end laps should be facing away from you.
- ☐ Now turn on the saw and cut the outside groove.
- ☐ Before continuing, recheck the position of the groove.

If the position is correct, then continue to the next step. Otherwise, go back and locate the source of the error and correct it.

- ☐ After completing the above cut, turn the piece end for end. The groove that you just cut should now be on the left side.
- ☐ With the end laps still facing you, clamp the piece in the miter holddown.
- ☐ Cut the groove in this end of the frame.
- ☐ Repeat the above procedure for all of the remaining top and bottom pieces.
- ☐ After cutting the two end grooves, the next step is to cut the one in the center.
- ☐ Set the stop block so that it is now 11-7/8 inches from the blade.
- ☐ Take a piece of scrap and again make a test cut.

If the groove location is correct, then proceed to the next step. If not, go back and reset the stop block.

- ☐ Place one of the top or bottom frame pieces in the miter holddown. The end laps should be facing away from you.
- ☐ Proceed to cut the center groove in this piece.
- ☐ Recheck the position of this cut against the dimensions of Fig. 6-8.

If they are correct, continue to the next step. Otherwise, go back and correct the cause of the error.

- ☐ Repeat the cutting procedure for all of the remaining top and bottom pieces.
- ☐ Take one each of the top and bottom frame members and lay them with the end laps facing up. The grooves should be facing each other and

both the grooves and the end laps should be aligned. See Fig. 6-9.
- ☐ Next, take these two pieces and place them 23-1/2" apart (still parallel to each other). The end laps should still be facing up.
- ☐ Take one left and one right frame and place them between the top and bottom pieces. The end laps should be facing down.

The end laps of the top and bottom pieces should fit under the end laps of the right and left side.

- ☐ After placing the four pieces together, they should form a square frame. See Fig. 6-10.
- ☐ Check to make sure that all the pieces fit and that all of the grooves are aligned opposite their related part.

If this last test produces the required result, then continue to the next step. If you do not have a square or the grooves are not opposite each other, then correct the problem before continuing.

- ☐ Return the left and right sides as well as the top and bottom pieces to their respective piles.
- ☐ Next get the group that you have marked as the left frame.
- ☐ Divide this group in half. Each half must have at least four pieces.
- ☐ Wrap each group with a piece of masking tape.
- ☐ Mark one group "front" and the other as "rear."
- ☐ Repeat these last two steps for the right frame pieces.
- ☐ After you have completed the above operation, place the left and right frame pieces aside.
- ☐ Next, take the group marked top and bottom and divide them in half.

Because the top and bottom pieces were not previously separated, they should each contain a total of 16 pieces. The separation will produce 8 front and rear pieces respectively.

- ☐ Tape and mark each group with their correct designation.

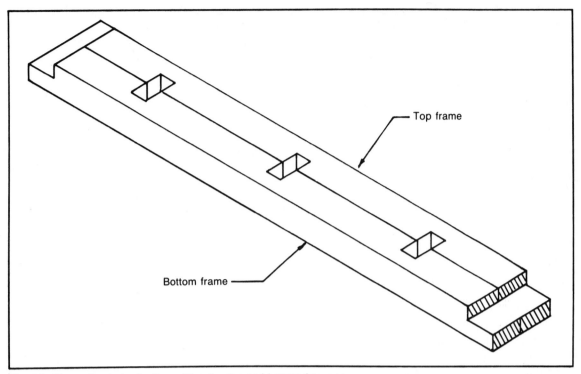

Fig. 6-9. Dimensional check after cutting the top and bottom frame pieces.

Drilling the Mounting Holes

In the following steps, a set of holes must be drilled in all of the rear frame pieces. The holes will be used for mounting the "T" nuts. When finished, the "T" nuts will hold the two speaker frames together.

☐ First, get the pieces marked "left rear."
☐ Place them on your work surface with the end laps face up.
☐ Measure the width of the board and place a mark at the inside edge of the end lap. The mark is to be one half of the frame width.
☐ Repeat this procedure on the other end of this same piece.
☐ Next draw a line down the center of this piece. The line should connect the two end marks. See Fig. 6-11.

It is essential that this line is in the center. One method to achieve this is to use a combination square with the blade set to one half of the width. With this method, you will be able to place duplicate marks at each end. As a guide, the mark should be about 7/16 of an inch from either side.

☐ Measure the width of the frame and set the blade of the square to 1/2 of the measured value.
☐ Lay the square against the frame piece.

The head of the square must butt against the side of the wood piece. The blade should lay across the face of the piece.

☐ Position the square so that the blade is just inside the start of the end lap.
☐ Use a scribe or a sharp pencil and place a mark on the frame at this position.
☐ Repeat this procedure for the other end of this same piece.
☐ Take a sharp pencil and a straight edge and draw a line connecting the two end marks.

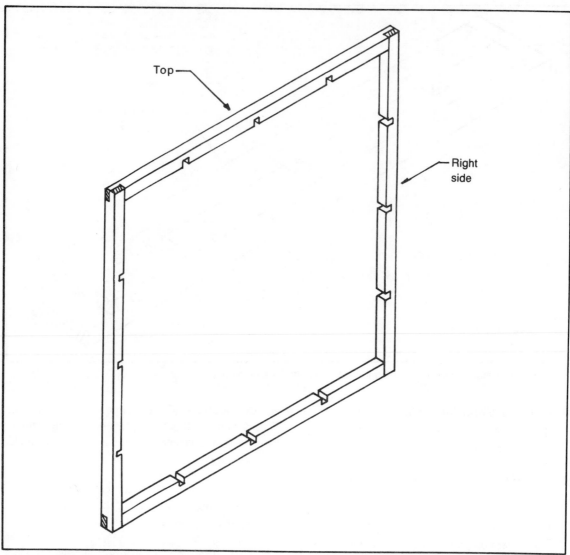

Fig. 6-10. Dimensional check of a completed frame.

This line should be in the center and should run down the length of the piece between the two end laps. Refer to Fig. 6-11.

The next step in the process is to mark the position where the holes are to be drilled.

☐ Begin by measuring in from each end 1-1/2 inches.
☐ Place a mark on the center line at this point.
☐ Next, start at one end, at the 1-1/2 inch mark,

and continue toward the other end. Place a mark on the center line every 3 inches.

At this point, it is advantageous to have a drill press. However, with some care, a hand drill can be used. One of the other advantages of a drill press is the ability to make and use a drill fixture. In this way, you will not need to mark every board before it is drilled.

If you are using a hand drill, a doweling fixture

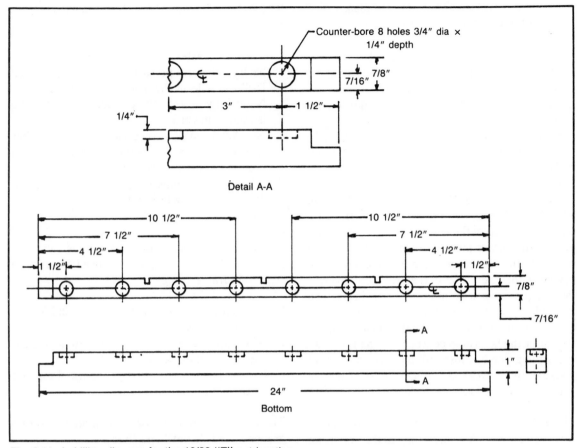

Fig. 6-11. A drilling diagram for the 10/32 "T" nut location.

can be used to locate the first set of holes. Instead of drilling the hole to size, make a small guide hole at each location. When this is completed, it can be clamped to the other frame pieces and the guide holes can be drilled in all of the other pieces. After all the pieces have guide holes, a stop block and the correct drill size can be used to make the final hole size.

For those who are using a drill press, the frame piece that was just marked will become the master. It will be used as a guide for locating and drilling all the holes in the other frame pieces.

☐ Before starting, take a piece of masking tape and place it on one of the end laps of the master piece. In this way, you will not lose track of which one is the master guide.

☐ Next, install a 3/4 inch wood bit in the chuck of the drill press.

☐ Take the master piece and align the center of the 3/4 inch wood bit with one of the first hole marks.

☐ With the bit in contact with the mark, lock the drill press in this position.

☐ Take a piece of scrap wood and clamp it along the backside of the master strip. See Fig. 6-12. This piece should be as long as the master piece and parallel to it.

☐ Next clamp another block of scrap at right angles to the master piece. This piece should be butted against the end of the master piece. The two clamped pieces should make an "L" shape with each other.

☐ After the two blocks have been installed, release

105

the drill press lock and remove the master piece from the drill table.

☐ To check the block location, place the master piece back on the drill press and butt it against both the end and the rear stop blocks.
☐ Bring down the drill bit until it again touches the wood.
☐ Check to make sure that the center of the bit aligns with the center line of the hole that is to be drilled.

If the center line and the bit are not aligned, then lock the drill press into position so that the bit is on the center line of the hole. Adjust the stop blocks against the master piece. Repeat the above procedure until the master piece can be removed and replaced so that the center of the drill bit aligns with the center of the hole. A little extra time in this step, will help insure that all of the holes will be in the correct position when the speaker is assembled.

After the bit is aligned, the next thing is to set the drilling depth. Most drill presses have an adjustable stop that can be set in order to control the depth of penetration.

☐ Set the depth stop on the drill press so that the drill will bore a hole according to the dimension shown in Fig. 6-11 (about 1/4″ deep).
☐ After the depth has been set, use a piece of scrap wood and drill a test hole.
☐ Measure the depth of the hole.

If it is approximately 1/4 of an inch, then continue to the next step. If it is not, then adjust the depth stops and then drill another test hole.

☐ Once the hole depth is correct, place the master piece in position on the drill press. Be sure to hold it firmly against both stop blocks.
☐ Bring the bit down and check alignment.
☐ Assuming that everything is okay, turn on the drill press and drill the hole.

The hole position at the opposite end of the master piece has the same spacing as the one that you just drilled.

☐ Turn the master piece end for end and place it back on the drill press against the stop blocks.
☐ Drill the hole in this end of the master piece. Note: Be sure that the previously drilled hole is facing upwards.
☐ Now lay the master piece aside and take another rear left piece and repeat the previous drilling procedure for the two end holes.
☐ When you have finished this piece, continue and drill the same hole in the rest of the rear left pieces.

Because the hole pattern is symmetrical, the present drill press setup can be used to drill the right side frame pieces.

☐ Drill both end holes exactly like you did for the left side pieces.
☐ After drilling the holes in the left and right pieces, lay them aside.
☐ Get the frame pieces that you marked top and bottom.

The top and bottom pieces were divided into two groups called "front" and "rear."

☐ Take those pieces marked "top and bottom rear" and drill holes 1-1/2 inches in from each edge.

Use the same setup that was used for the left and right pieces. In this case, however, the end laps must be facing down.

☐ Return the top and bottom pieces to their respective piles.
☐ Next, get both of the groups marked "rear left and right."
☐ On the drill press, remove the board that was clamped as the end stop.

However, do not move the piece that was clamped along the back side.

☐ Take the master piece and place it on the drill press so that the drill bit aligns with the center mark of the second hole.

☐ When you have the drill correctly aligned with the center mark of the hole, lock the drill in place.

☐ Take the stop block and position it against the end of the master piece. It should again form an "L" with the rear stop block.

☐ Clamp the stop block in this position.

☐ Remove the master piece from the drill press, and proceed to check the alignment by reinserting the piece back against the stop blocks. Use the same procedure to check the drill center alignment.

☐ When the drill bit and the center line of the master piece align after each insertion, you are ready to drill the hole.

☐ Place the master piece in position and drill the second hole.

☐ Again, turn the piece end for end and drill the corresponding hole at the other end of the master piece.

☐ After you have completed drilling the two holes in the master piece, continue and drill the same holes in the rest of the rear left and right sides.

☐ When this last step is completed, lay the left and right pieces aside.

☐ Get the pieces that were marked "top and bottom rear."

☐ Drill the same hole in the rear top and bottom pieces.

Each of the rear frame pieces should now have four holes. There are four more holes that must be drilled in each of the rear pieces. Follow the same procedure for drilling these holes, that you used on the last four holes.

☐ Drill the remaining holes in all the rear pieces.

Now that all the holes have been drilled, your pieces should look like the drawing of Fig. 6-11. The top and bottom rear pieces should be the same except the holes will be in the opposite side from those of the left and right pieces.

☐ Return all of the rear pieces to their respective piles.

In the following step, two more holes must be drilled, but they will be located on the front left and right sides. See Fig. 6-12 and 6-13. The screws that will be located in these holes will later become the electrical connections to the diaphragm.

☐ Get the front frame pieces.

☐ Take one piece, either left or right, and measure in 3 inches from the end.

☐ Draw a line across the board at this point.

Use a combination square and locate the center of this piece (approximately 7/16 of an inch).

☐ Place a mark on this piece that intersects the line at the 3 inch point.

☐ Place the frame piece against the backstop on the drill press.

☐ Bring the bit down and align the center of the bit with the intersection of the two lines that were drawn on this piece.

☐ Lock the drill in this position.

☐ Mount the stop block used as an end stop, against this piece and clamp it in position.

☐ Remove the piece that is to be drilled and then place it back in position against the stop blocks.

☐ Check to make sure the drill bit and the center mark are in the correct position.

☐ If the alignment is correct, turn on drill press and drill the hole.

☐ Remove this piece and turn it end for end.

☐ Place it back in the same position on the drill press, and drill the hole at the other end.

☐ Repeat this drilling process for all the front left and right sides.

This completes all of the cutting and drilling operations for the frame members.

☐ Before putting them aside, check to be sure that each group is correctly identified.

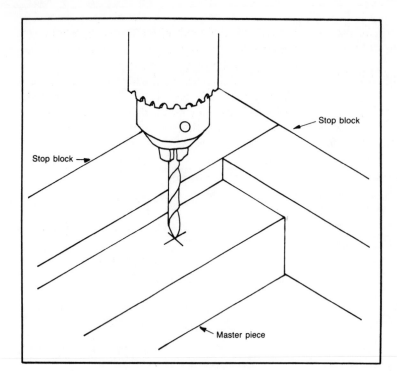

Fig. 6-12. A drill fixture for locating the "T" nuts.

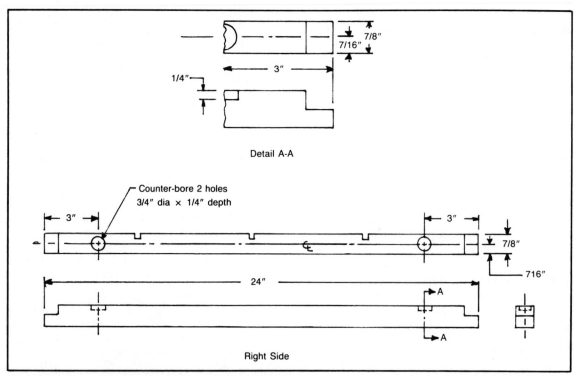

Detail A-A

Counter-bore 2 holes
3/4″ dia × 1/4″ depth

3″

7/8″

716″

24″

A

A

Right Side

Fig. 6-13. "T" nut locations for the connection to the diaphragm.

This will help when they must be retrieved for the assembly operation.

☐ Also check the number of pieces in each group.

If you do not have enough pieces, you should make whatever additional pieces you need at this time. You should be able to use one of the completed pieces as a pattern.

RIBS

After all of the frames have been made, the next step is to make the parts that will be used for the ribs. The preliminary procedure for cutting the ribs is the same as the one used for cutting the frame.

☐ Take a 1 × 12 inch board and cut it 23-1/4 inches long.

From this piece, you should be able to get approximately 30 ribs. For each 2 by 2 foot speaker that you are building, you will need 12 ribs. If you are building two of the 2 by 4 foot speakers, you will need a total of 48 ribs. In this case you will need to have two 1 by 12 inch boards that are to 23 1/4 inches long.

☐ After you have cut the two boards to size, lay one of them aside.

Look at the rib detail shown in Fig. 6-14. To simplify the process of making all of the slots, they will be cut into the board before it is cut into ribs. To cut the slots, you will need to install your dado blades.

☐ Begin by installing enough dado blades so that the width of the cut is equal to 1/4 of an inch.
☐ Next, measure the thickness of the wood.
☐ Set the height of the dado blade to 1/2 of the thickness.

As a guide, this should be approximately 3/8 of an inch.

☐ Make a test cut on a piece of scrap.
☐ Measure the depth of the cut.

It is okay if the depth of the cut is slightly more then the thickness of the wood. It must not be less. Otherwise the ribs will not fit in the frame.

It doesn't make any difference which one of the ribs is cut first. Because both outside slots of the horizontal ribs are the same distance from the end, it will be simpler to begin with these pieces.

☐ Measure over from the saw blade 5 5/8 inches.
☐ Clamp a stop block at this position.
☐ Take a piece of scrap and butt it against the stop block.
☐ Clamp it in position with the miter holddown clamp.
☐ Turn on the saw and make a test cut.
☐ Check the location and the depth of the cut.

If they are correct, go on to the next step. If not, reset the stop block and then make another test cut.

☐ Assuming that the test cut is correct, place one of the 23 1/4 inch boards on your table saw.
☐ Clamp it in position against the stop block. Use the miter holddown clamp.
☐ Turn on the saw and cut a groove across the flat portion of the board.
☐ Check the position of the groove to insure the correct location.

If everything is correct, continue to the next step. Otherwise, go back and correct the problem.

☐ Now turn the piece end for end and cut a similar slot in the other end of this board.

After cutting the two slots, be sure to check their position on the board. If, for some reason, they are not in the correct location, go back to the beginning of the rib section and start over.

☐ To cut the center slot measure in from the end 11 7/8 inches.
☐ Place a mark on the edge of the board at this position.
☐ Place the board on your saw table and align the mark with the saw blade.

□ Clamp the board in this position with the miter hold down clamp.
□ Now cut the center groove.

After cutting this last slot, you should have a board that is 1 by 12 by 23 1/4 inches long with 3 slots across the face. The position of the slots should correspond to the slot location shown in Fig. 6-14.

□ Lay this board aside. If you need 48 ribs, repeat the above procedure for another 1 × 12 × 24 1/4 inch board. Then, lay them aside.
□ Take one of the other boards that you set aside and use the same procedure to cut a similar set of slots.

Use the vertical rib diagram of Fig. 6-14. There are several things that should be noted about the vertical ribs. First, the two outside slots are not the same distance from the ends. Second, in addition to the three lower slots, there are also two additional slots on the reverse side of these pieces.

□ Cut the three slots according to the locations shown in Fig. 6-14.
□ To make the last two slots on the reverse side, measure in 7/16 of an inch from the edge of the board.

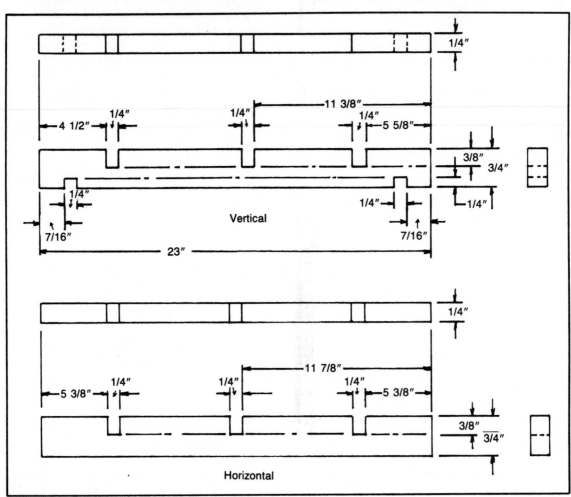

Fig. 6-14. Dimensions and cutting details for the ribs.

□ Place a mark at this location.
□ Place the board on the saw table and align the mark with the edge of the saw blade. Use a stop block for a locating point.
□ Set the height of the blade to 1/4 of an inch. This dimension is not too critical.
□ Turn the saw on and cut this slot.
□ Turn the board end for end and repeat this procedure for the slot that is located on the other end of the board.

After all of the slots in both boards have been cut, the next step is to cut them into ribs. To do this, install your standard saw blade.

□ Set the fence on the saw to the rib thickness shown in Fig. 6-14. Be sure to check both ends of the fence to be sure that it is parallel with the saw blade.
□ Place one of the boards against the fence and cut one rib.

□ Take this piece and fit it into one of the slots of the frame.

If it is too loose or too tight, adjust the fence. A proper fit will allow the rib to slide into the slot easily, but if you let go, it will not fall out.

□ Once you have achieved the proper fit, you can then cut the rest of the ribs.
□ When you have finished cutting one of the sets, wrap it with masking tape and mark it for identification.
□ Take the other board and cut it into ribs.
□ When you have finished this last step, wrap and mark this group of ribs.

At this point, you have completed all of the cutting and drilling operations for both the frames and the ribs. The next set of steps will begin to assemble these parts into a speaker.

Chapter 7

Preliminary Assembly

Now that all of the parts have been made, they can be put together to form the basic speaker assemblies. This chapter indicates how to make the frame, rib, and plate assemblies.

RIB ASSEMBLY

To assemble the rib section, a frame should be used as a guide. A temporary frame can be made by using four miter vise clamps. See Fig. 7-1. Place a corner clamp on the outside edge of each corner. The inside edge is the side that will face the diaphragm. If you are using the rear frame, the holes for the "T" nuts will be on the outside. If you are using the front frames, the holes for the diaphragm connection will be on the outside.

Because the frame and the ribs support the plates, it is essential that they have one side that is flat. Therefore, one assembly requirement is to have a large flat area to assemble the various components. A work surface that is very useful for this purpose is the top of the table saw. This area is usually a machined surface and it is therefore more

than adequate for this requirement. The ability to use this surface is determined by the size of your saw. If your saw table is not large enough, then you will need to find an alternate area that is at least 24 inches square. It also should be a surface where each assembly can be left until the glue dries. If this type of surface cannot be obtained, there may be some problems in getting the speaker to provide trouble-free performance. If you are using the saw table, first retract the saw blade. Before doing any gluing, it is also a good idea to check the depth of the slots that are located in each of the ribs.

☐ First, take three of the vertical ribs and place them on the saw table. The side that has the two slots, at each end, should be face down.
☐ Next take three of the horizontal ribs and place them into the slots of the vertical ribs. These are the slots that are facing up.

The depth of the cut in the slots is correct if the front and rear edges of the horizontal and vertical ribs are flush with each other. If this condi-

112

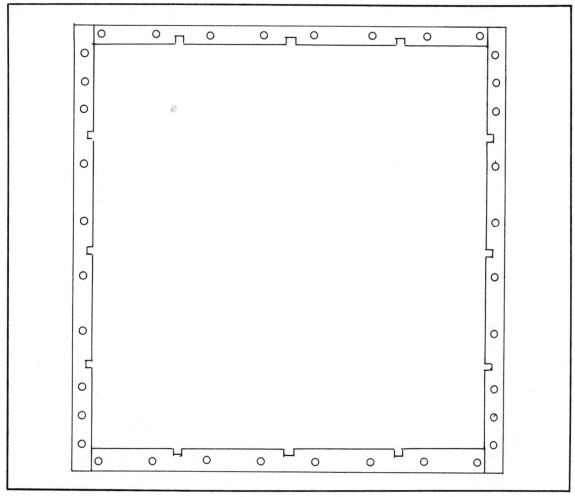

Fig. 7-1. Temporary frame assembly for assembling the ribs.

tion does not exist, then the slots will have to be made deeper. For small differences, a 1/4 inch square file can be used to file each slot a little deeper. If there is a large difference, you should use the table saw. Before cutting, however, be sure to measure the distance between the two rib edges. Now install the dado blades on your saw and adjust the blade height for 1/2 of the difference between the two rib edges. Cut both the horizontal and vertical slots so that the edges are flush. Because all of the slots were done at the same time, you will probably need to cut the slots in the rest of the ribs a little deeper. When you have achieved

the condition where the rib edges are flush with each other you are ready to assemble the ribs together.

□ If you haven't already done so, retract the saw blade.
□ Place the temporary frame assembly on your saw table. The corner clamps should be resting on your work surface.
□ Take the vertical ribs and insert them into the slots of the top and bottom frame.
□ Take the horizontal ribs and insert them into the

113

slots of both the left and right frames and in the slots of the vertical ribs.

☐ At this point, check to make sure that the entire assembly is flat. To do this, turn the entire assembly upside down and place it back on your work surface. The ribs and the frame should lie flat against the work surface.

If the assembly has a slight bow, this may be okay. A weight can be placed on top of the ribs to force them flat against the surface of the table saw. The bowing can be checked by placing some books on top of the rib assembly. If this makes the entire assembly lie flat, then you can proceed to the next step. If it is not flat, then determine the problem and fix it before proceeding.

☐ Assuming that the ribs are flat, remove one of the horizontal ribs.
☐ Put some white glue in each of the rib slots. Do not put any glue on the ends of the ribs or in the slots of the frame.
☐ When all three slots have glue in them, place this rib back in its slot in the assembly.
☐ Now remove the next rib and repeat the procedure.
☐ After the second horizontal rib has been installed in the assembly, take the last rib and perform the same gluing operation.
☐ Remove any excess glue that may have run out of the slots.
☐ Before placing a weight on top of the ribs, put some wax paper over the rib assembly.
☐ Now place the heavy weight on top of the wax paper.

The weight should cover the junctions of all the ribs. One good source for weights is several books of an encyclopedia. They can be stacked on top of each other to get the required weight.

☐ After the glue has dried, remove the weights and the wax paper.
☐ Remove the rib assembly from the frame.

All of the ribs should be firmly held in place and

the assembly should look like the one shown in Fig. 7-2.

☐ Lay the rib assembly back on the table saw. Check the ribs to make sure that they lie flat against the table surface.
☐ Place a mark on the assembly so that you will know which side is flat. Then lay the assembly aside.
☐ Take another set of vertical and horizontal ribs and repeat the assembly and gluing operation.
☐ After the second assembly has dried, and you have checked it for flatness, continue the assembly and gluing process until all of the ribs have been assembled.

When the above steps have been completed, you should have 8 rib assemblies.

☐ Put the rib assemblies aside and get the parts for the frame.

FRAME ASSEMBLY

Now that the rib assembly is completed, you are ready to assemble the frame. One frame has already been temporarily assembled. This was the one that was used as a guide in assembling the rib sections. If one of the sides is removed from the clamps, glue can be applied to the exposed end laps.

☐ Take the assembled frame and loosen two of the corner clamps.
☐ Remove the frame piece that is free.
☐ Put some glue on each of the end laps.

Do this on the part that is free as well as the two end laps that are still in the clamps. Try to get an even coat on each surface, but do not use too much glue.

☐ Now place the frame that was removed back into the frame assembly and tighten the corner clamps.
☐ Wipe off any excess glue that runs out from between the two frame pieces.
☐ Next remove the two clamps from the other side of the frame and coat the end laps with glue.

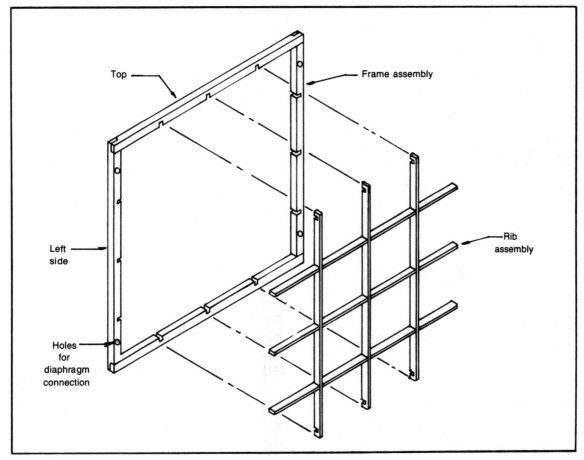

Fig. 7-2. Front frame and rib assembly.

Again, get an even coat and do not use too much glue.

☐ Place this piece back in the frame and tighten the clamps.

☐ Wipe off any excess glue.

☐ Place the frame assembly on top of the saw table. The frame should lie flat against the surface of the table.

If the frame is not flat against the table, you will need to find the cause before the glue dries. If it is not something simple, take the frame apart and wipe off the glue. After the remaining film has dried, you can temporarily put the frame back together, and then locate the cause of the problem.

☐ When the frame is flat and glued together, you

can proceed to the next step.

☐ After the glue has dried, remove the books and the clamps.

☐ Check the assembly for flatness.

☐ Assuming that it is flat, place a mark on it that indicates the flat side. Later this side will be glued to the plate.

☐ Set this assembly aside.

☐ Take another set of top, bottom, left and right pieces and clamp them together.

☐ Place them on the saw table and check to see that they are flat.

☐ If so, proceed to glue them together.

If they are not flat, locate and correct the problem before continuing.

115

- [ ] After the glue has dried, remove the weights and the clamps.
- [ ] Recheck the frame for flatness.
- [ ] Continue with this procedure until all the frame pieces from this group are glued together.
- [ ] When all of these frames are glued together, set them aside and begin gluing the other set of frames.
- [ ] Follow the same gluing process to assemble the second set of frame pieces.

When you have finished this last operation, you should have four front and four rear frame assemblies.

RIB AND FRAME ASSEMBLY

After the individual frames and ribs have been assembled, the two sections can be glued to each other.

- [ ] To start this process, take one of the frame assemblies and again lay it on the saw table.
- [ ] Place the flat side face down on your work surface.
- [ ] Take one of the rib assemblies and place it in the slots of the frame assembly. Be sure that the mark indicating the flat side is also face down.
- [ ] Check to make sure that everything fits.

If, for some reason, there is a problem, locate and correct it before going to the next step.

- [ ] Assuming that everything fits, remove the rib assembly.
- [ ] Take the frame assembly and put some glue into each of the rib slots. Place it back on the saw table. Again, be sure that the flat side is face down.
- [ ] Apply some glue to the ends of the ribs. Again, do not use too much.
- [ ] Reinsert the rib assembly into the slots of the frame.
- [ ] Wipe off any excess glue that seeps out.
- [ ] Cover the entire assembly with wax paper.
- [ ] Place the weights on both the ribs and the frames. They must be firmly pushed against the saw table.
- [ ] After the glue has dried, remove the weights and the wax paper.
- [ ] Inspect the assembly. It should lie flat against the surface of the saw table.
- [ ] Lay this assembly aside.
- [ ] Take another frame and rib assembly and follow the same procedure to glue these two assemblies together.
- [ ] After the glue has dried, check it for flatness and then lay it aside.
- [ ] Follow the same procedure for all the other frame and rib assemblies.

When you have all of the assemblies glued together, there is one final check that you should make. Take a front and rear assembly and place them together so that the flat marks are opposite each other. The two assemblies should now be flat against each other.

FRAME AND PLATE ASSEMBLY

You are now ready to fasten the plates to the frames. Notice that one side of the plate is red and one is white. The frame will be glued on the white side.

- [ ] The first step in gluing the plate to the frame is to lay the plate face down on your work surface.
- [ ] Next take some sandpaper and remove any of the conductive coating that may have run onto the back side.
- [ ] Now take one of the frames and lay it over the plate with the counterbored holes up.
- [ ] Align the plate and the frame so that their sides are parallel.

Try to align the vertical ribs so that they do not cover any holes. Also make sure the frame is correctly orientated on the plate. Remember the horizontal rib spacing is smaller at one end. This should be where the electrical connections are located.

☐ Take a colored pencil and mark on the rear (white side) of the plate the position that will be occupied by the frame and the ribs. Make the marks as close to the frame and ribs as you can.

☐ Remove the frame assembly from the plate.

☐ Coat the side of the frame that was laying on the plate with contact cement.

☐ Coat the back side of the plate, between the colored pencil marks, with the same cement. Try to cover all the areas with an even coating.

☐ After you have coated the plate with glue, in the proper areas, lay it down on your work surface so that it is face down.

☐ Cover the plate with some wax paper.

☐ Lay the frame on top of the plate. Make sure that the plate and frame do not touch each other except on the wax paper.

☐ Align the frame as you did before the glue was applied.

☐ When you are satisfied that the alignment is correct hold the frame and the plate on one side and remove the wax paper.

Make sure that the frame and plate do not move relative to each other. Once the two glue surfaces touch, it becomes almost impossible to separate them. Be careful and do it right.

☐ Once you have the frame and the plate glued together, turn the entire assembly over.

☐ Take the small wooden roller and roll it over the plate surface where it contacts the frame.

Note when rolling over the plate, press hard on the roller.

☐ Now lay the plate back on the saw table and put some weights back on the frame.

Make sure that the frame and the plates are firmly pushed against the surface of the saw table.

☐ When the glue has dried on this assembly, take the entire unit and lay it aside.

☐ After you have completed the first plate, go on and glue the remaining plates and frames.

SPACER ASSEMBLY

The next step in the process of building an electrostatic speaker is to glue the spacers onto the plates. The spacers fit around the outside edge of the plate and are located on the opposite side from the frame.

☐ Take a plate and lay it face up on your work surface.

☐ Take four spacers and lay them on top of the plates. Place them along the outside edges. In this area, there should be no corona dope.

☐ Two of the spacers will be too large. Mark each one so that they can be cut to size.

☐ Cut the spacers to size and then put them back on the plate.

☐ When everything fits, mark on the plate the location of the spacers.

☐ After the plate is completely marked, remove the spacers.

☐ Apply a coat of contact cement to the area between the pen line and the outside edge of the plate. When the spacers were made, one side was beveled. Put the glue on the opposite side.

☐ When all of the spacers have been coated, place them on the plate in their respective positions.

☐ Be careful when doing this. Make sure that the spacer is correctly aligned before it touches the plate.

If necessary, use wax paper between the two surfaces so that they can be positioned. Then, carefully slide the wax paper from between the plate and the spacer. Make sure that the spacer doesn't move.

☐ After the spacers have been glued into position, use a wooden roller and roll the spacer against the plate.

☐ Repeat these procedures for all the remaining spacers and plates.

You now have completed all the subassemblies. Before starting the final assembly, a test should be done on the insulating coating. This will be described in the next chapter.

Chapter 8

Preliminary Speaker Testing

An important step in building an electrostatic speaker is to make sure that the coating used for insulation is effective. Most builders of electrostatic speakers do not check the coating until after the final assembly. At that point, if the speaker arcs, there are two alternatives.

First, the speaker can be operated at a lower voltage. In Chapter 4, Fig. 4-12 showed there was a relationship between the acoustic output and the amount of high voltage on the diaphragm. If the voltage is decreased so that the speaker does not arc, then the acoustic output may also decrease. This is true if the voltage is less than the knee of the curve. The other alternative to the arcing problem, is to take the speaker assembly apart. Locate and repair the section that arcs and then reassemble the speaker. The problem with this technique is that the speaker may arc at different points and at different voltages. After one problem is fixed and the speaker is reassembled, another area may arc at the same voltage or at a slightly higher voltage.

This will again necessitate taking the speaker apart. Each time the speaker is disassembled, it destroys all of the work that was done in coating and stretching the diaphragm. This is also a time consuming job, and it wastes a lot of diaphragm material.

This problem can be eliminated by testing the speaker before the final assembly step. In the following steps, no diaphragm is used between the plates. Therefore the diaphragm material will not be wasted. The time that would be spent stretching and coating the diaphragm is completely eliminated. The only drawback to this procedure is the amount of voltage that will be required. Without the diaphragm, the high voltage must be twice the amount that will be used for an operational speaker.

High Voltage Power Supply

At this point, a word of caution is required. The voltages that you will be applying to the speaker are very high. The large series resistor limits the amount of current that can be supplied by the power supply. If, while testing, your body completes the circuit and provides a path for the current, you will probably get a good shock. Except under some unusual circumstances, the voltage and the current are not fatal. However, as an added safety precaution, always remember to:

* *

TURN OFF THE HIGH VOLTAGE SUPPLY
BEFORE DOING ANY WORK ON THE SPEAKER.

* *

The first step in the preliminary testing operation is to assemble the high voltage power supply. The components used for this purpose are a variable voltage transformer, two of the speaker high voltage transformers, two diodes, two capacitors, and one resistor. The schematic is shown in Fig. 8-1.

- ☐ Mount the step up transformers, high voltage diodes, and capacitors on a scrap block of wood. Use a terminal block to mount the diodes and capacitors.
- ☐ Wire the components together according to the schematic diagram.
- ☐ After you have assembled and wired this temporary high voltage power supply, go over the wiring to make sure that you have not made any mistakes.

- ☐ When you are certain that the circuit is wired correctly, connect the primary of the step up transformer to the variable transformer.
- ☐ Turn the knob on the variable transformer down so that its output voltage is zero.
- ☐ Take a high voltage dc probe and connect it across the output of the power supply. This is between the points marked "A" and "B" in the diagram of Fig. 8-1.
- ☐ Connect the probe to a dc voltmeter and set the meter to the proper range.
- ☐ Turn on the variable transformer and slowly increase the output voltage. The dc meter reading should follow this increase.

If it does not, turn the variable transformer back to zero and then turn the power off. Allow a few minutes to pass so that any charge on the capacitors will be drained off.

- ☐ Check the output voltage by reading the value indicated on the voltmeter.
- ☐ When the voltage is zero, disconnect the circuit from the variable transformer.
- ☐ Go over your wiring until you find the cause of the problem. Correct it before continuing.

Once you have located and corrected the problem, connect the circuit to the variable transformer.

- ☐ Again connect the high voltage probe to the output of the power supply (Between points A and B).

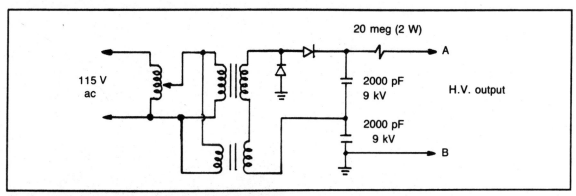

Fig. 8-1. High voltage power supply for testing the speaker.

☐ Turn on the variable transformer and again increase its output voltage.

If the dc output voltage of the power supply follows the increasing input voltage, continue to raise the voltage until the voltmeter reads twice the speakers normal operating voltage. For the speakers described in this book, this value is approximately 10 kilovolts.

CAUTION
* *

TO AVOID ELECTRICAL SHOCK BE SURE THAT YOU DO NOT TOUCH ANY PART OF THE HIGH VOLTAGE POWER SUPPLY WHILE THE HIGH VOLTAGE IS ON!!!!!!!

* *

☐ After determining that the high voltage power supply can be adjusted to twice the required value, turn the variable transformer back to zero.
☐ Again allow several minutes for the capacitors to discharge before continuing.
☐ Check to make sure that the output voltage is zero by reading the value indicated on the dc voltmeter.

SPEAKER TESTING
From the speaker panels that were assembled in Chapter 7, select a matching front and rear set. To test the speaker, the front and rear panels must be fastened together, but this does not have to be a permanent type of assembly.

☐ Place the two panels so that their insulated coatings are facing inwards.
☐ Now place "C" clamps around the edges. One clamp on each side is usually enough. Make sure there is a tight fit between the spacers. If the fit isn't tight, use more clamps.
☐ Next connect all the speaker terminals on the

front side together. This can be done with clip leads or with pieces of wire.
☐ After you have finished the front side, repeat the process for the terminals on the rear side.
☐ Now set the speaker upright so that you can see both the front and rear panels.

You may have to lean it against something for support. *Be sure that the support is non-conductive.*

☐ Make sure your high voltage power supply is turned off and the capacitors are discharged. You can check this with the dc voltmeter.
☐ Connect the output of your high voltage power supply (terminals A and B) to the two terminals of the speaker. Use high voltage wire for this purpose.
☐ Plug in the variable transformer.
☐ Slowly increase the output voltage while monitoring the value with the dc voltmeter. The voltage should again follow the increasing dial of the variable transformer.
☐ Adjust the high voltage until the meter reads 10 kilovolts, or until the speaker starts to arc. (If arcing occurs, go to the section on arcing.)

If a value that is equal to twice the operating voltage is achieved, then let the speaker stand this way for several minutes. If no arcing occurs during this time, reduce the input voltage to zero. Be sure to wait a few minutes for the capacitors to discharge before disconnecting the speaker panels. If the speaker passed this test, then go on to the other panels and test them in the same way. When all of the speaker panels can pass this test without arcing, you are ready to proceed to the final assembly steps.

ARCING
Arcing problems are created by one of two possibilities. One cause of arcing is a sharp point. A light sanding of the plate surface and then a spraying with corona dope will usually take care of this problem. The other cause is due to an insufficient amount of corona dope. This may occur in one or

or more areas of the speaker panel. The following procedures will help identify the arcing and provide some steps that will help to eliminate the problem.

☐ When a speaker arcs, make a note of the approximate position where the arc occurs. Sometimes it helps to do this in a dark room. The points that are going to arc will have a bluish glow.
☐ After you have located an arc, reduce the power supply voltage to zero.
☐ Turn off the supply voltage and wait for the capacitors to discharge.
☐ Disconnect the wires from the high voltage supply to the speaker.
☐ Separate the two sections by removing the "C" clamps.
☐ Inspect each panel in the area where the arcing occurred.

Look for dark brown or black spots or some other signs of discoloration. Another possibility to look for is that the conductive coating was not completely covered.

☐ Even if there is no visible evidence of the arcing, lightly sand the area where the arcing occurred.
☐ Next mask the spacers at the edge of the speaker panel.

☐ Spray the corona dope in the area of the arcing.
☐ If a black or carbon spot exists where the arc occurred, it must be removed. The best way to do this is to sand the area with fine sandpaper.
☐ When all of the black area has been removed, proceed to respray the panel. Be sure to mask the spacers at the edge of the panel.
☐ After the spray has dried, reclamp the panels together.
☐ Connect the high voltage power supply.
☐ Increase the power supply voltage and again monitor the output value.
☐ When you can now reach the 10 kilovolt point, let the speaker stand for a few minutes.
☐ If arcing is still a problem, go back to the beginning of this section and repeat the procedures.
☐ If no further evidence of arcing is apparent, then reduce the power supply voltage to zero.
☐ Turn the supply voltage off and, after the capacitors have discharged, remove the connections to the speaker.
☐ Remove the "C" clamps and set these speaker panels aside.

If other panels have similar problems, repeat the procedure for each one of them. When all speaker panels can support a value that is equal to twice the operating voltage for several minutes, you are ready to proceed to the next step.

Chapter 9

Stretching Frame

After all of the panels have been tested so that they can support a voltage that is twice the normal bias voltage, the next step is to assemble the panels into a speaker.

One of the problems associated with the assembly of an electrostatic speaker is diaphragm stability. As indicated in Chapter 4, the bias voltage will exert a force on the diaphragm. In an ideal push-pull speaker, the forces are balanced and the diaphragm remains centered. In the practical world, this ideal condition does not usually exist. Slight variations, in the voltage or in the spacing, will produce a corresponding variation in the force. When this happens, the diaphragm will be pulled to the side that exerts the greatest force.

To overcome this problem, a tension is created by stretching the diaphragm. This chapter will show how to build a fixture that can be used to apply the tension. A second benefit of using this fixture is that all of the speakers will have the same tension and, therefore, they should all perform the same.

Figure 9-1 is an exploded view of the stretching frame. As shown, it consists of a base, a set of diaphragm clamps, a method for placing some tension on the diaphragm, and a method for indicating the amount of tension that has been applied. With the exception of the plywood in the base, and the tensioning system, all material is pine.

BASE CONSTRUCTION

The first step in building the stretching frame is to build the base. This consists of parts number (7) and (16) in Fig. 9-1.

For the lower part of the base, you will need to cut two pieces of one inch pine into boards that are two inches wide and 48 inches long. You will also need two shorter pieces of the same material. The shorter pieces must be 40 1/2 inches long. They will become the other two sides of the base.

☐ Install your standard saw blade.
☐ Place the fence on your saw and set it for a width of two inches.

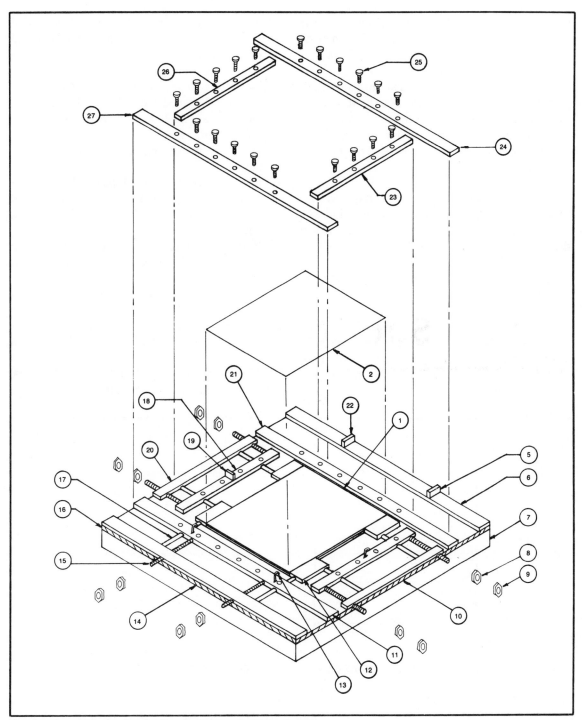

Fig. 9-1. Assembly drawing for the diaphragm stretching frame.

□ Take some 1 inch pine that is longer than the required length, and cut it into 2 inch wide strips. When you finish, you should have four pieces that are at least 48 inches long.

□ Take two of the pieces and measure their length. Mark each one for exactly 48 inches.

□ Repeat the above step for the other two pieces, but their length will be 40 1/2 inches.

□ Now that all of the parts have been marked, cut them to size.

After the pieces have been cut to the required size, they can be fastened together. As shown in Fig. 9-2, the completed base assembly should form a box that is 48 by 42 by 2 inches high.

□ Take one of the 48 inch boards and locate two 2 inch finish nails at each end.

Place the nails so that they are 3/8 of an inch from the end and 1/2 inch from each side. Drive the nails down until their points are just starting to protrude from the other side of the board. Do this on both ends of this board.

□ Repeat the last step for the other 48 inch board.

□ Now take one of the 40 1/2 inch boards and apply a coating of white glue to one of the ends. Try to get a nice even coating.

□ Place the nailed end of one of the 48 inch boards on top of the glued end and drive the nails down until they are flush. Be sure the sides and edges are aligned.

□ Wipe off any excess glue that may have seeped out.

□ Repeat these last three steps for the other end of this 40 1/2 inch board. Use the remaining 48 inch board on this side. The three boards should now form a "U."

□ When this last step is complete, take the remaining 40 1/2 inch board and apply glue to both ends.

□ Insert it between the opposite ends of the two 48 inch boards.

□ After making sure that the sides and ends are aligned, drive the nails down until they are flush.

This completes the lower part of the base. At this point, you should have a frame that is 48 ×

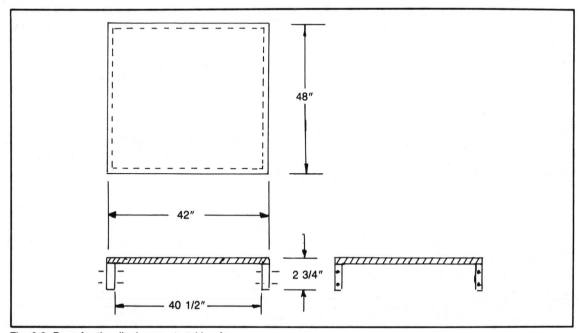

Fig. 9-2. Base for the diaphragm stretching frame.

42 × 2 inches. The next step is to cut and install the top.

☐ Take a 48 by 48 inch piece of 3/4 inch plywood and cut it so that it measures 42 by 48 inches.

Use a piece that is flat without any burrs. If necessary, sand the surface so that it is smooth. This is part number (16) in the drawing.

☐ After the plywood is cut to size and the glue on the lower base parts has dried, screw the plywood to the base. Use 1 1/2 inch #10 wood screws for this purpose. Put at least two screws on each side.
☐ For the moment, set this assembly aside.

FRONT AND REAR DIAPHRAGM CLAMPS

The following steps will be used to make the parts for the diaphragm clamps.

☐ The first step is to cut six pieces of 1 inch pine so that they are 42 inches long and 2 inches wide.

After you have all of the pieces cut to size, the next step is to locate all of the screw holes. See Fig. 9-3.

☐ Take one of the pieces that was just cut and draw a line parallel to the 42 inch side and 1/2 inch from its edge.
☐ Now measure in one inch from each end. Place a mark at this point. This mark should intersect the line that was drawn in the previous step.
☐ Start at one of the one inch marks and measure over 10 inches. Place another mark at this point.
☐ From this last mark, continue to place a mark every 10 inches until you get to the other 1 inch mark.
☐ This is part number (6), and it is shown in Fig. 9-3A. Check your layout against those shown in the drawing. If they are the same, then continue. Otherwise, locate and correct any discrepancies.
☐ Now take a #10 wood bit that also has a pilot

bit, and drill holes at each of the intersecting lines.
☐ After this last step has been completed, this piece can be screwed along a 42 inch side of the base. Whatever side is used, it will be the back of the base.
☐ Take two more 42 inch pieces and lay them parallel to each other so that their ends and sides are all aligned.
☐ Clamp them together.
☐ Measure 8-3/4 inches in from each end and draw a line across the one inch side of both pieces. See Fig. 9-3B.
☐ Measure in 7 inches, from each end, and again draw another line across the one inch dimension of both pieces.
☐ Remove the clamps.
☐ Take one of the pieces and with a pencil divide the one inch width in half. Do this on both ends, and then place a mark at that point.
☐ With a straight edge, draw a line down the center of the 1 inch width. The line should connect the two end marks together.

The line that was just drawn should also intersect the other four lines that were drawn in the previous steps. Each intersection should be centered at 1/2 of the boards' thickness.

☐ If you have a drill press and a set of wood bits with brad points, place a 1/4 inch bit in the chuck of the drill press.

If you do not have a drill press or any wood bits with brad points, skip to the section marked "Alternate Drilling."

☐ Place the piece with the center line down its length on your drill press.
☐ Align the center of the bit with one of the marks that is located at the 8 3/4 inch point.
☐ Clamp the board in place. Make sure that the center of the brad tip still aligns with the center of the 8-3/4 inch mark.
☐ Turn on the drill press and drill a hole so that it is 1/4 inch deep.

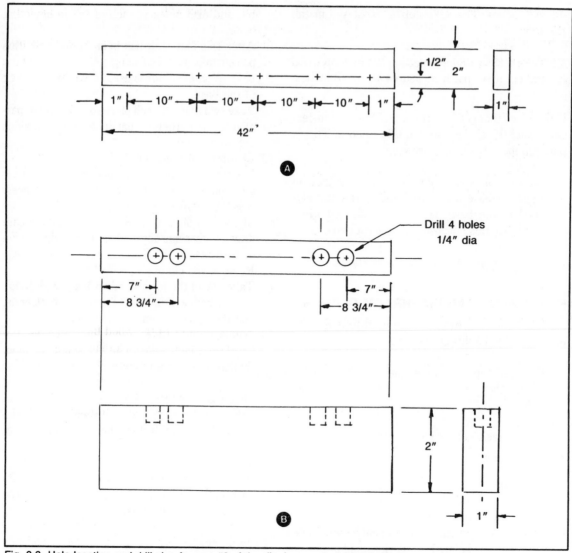

Fig. 9-3. Hole location and drill size for part #6 of the diaphragm stretching frame.

☐ Unclamp the wood and move it over until the bit is centered on the mark at the 7 inch point.
☐ Reclamp the piece.
☐ Drill this hole 1/4 inch deep.
☐ Unclamp the wood and turn the piece end for end.
☐ Repeat the drilling procedure for the two marks located on this end of the board.

After unclamping this piece, the board should be compared to the diagram shown in Fig 9-3B. If the holes are not at least 1/4 inch deep, or if they are not in the indicated position, go back and correct the problem. Do not proceed to the next step until your piece matches the drawing. When they do, skip to the section marked "Part No. 14."

Alternative Drilling

If you are using a drill press but do not have wood bits with brad points, then use the following

126

procedure. If you are using an electric hand drill, skip to the section marked "Electric Drill."

In the following steps, the purpose of the small drill bit is to help place the holes in the center of the board.

- [ ] As a beginning step, place a 1/16 inch bit in the chuck of the drill press.
- [ ] Align the center of the bit with the center line of the mark located at the 8 3/4 inch point.
- [ ] Clamp the piece of wood to the drill press table and drill the hole so that it is at least 1/4 inch deep.
- [ ] Unclamp the wood and move it over so that the center of the bit aligns with the mark at the 7 inch point.
- [ ] Clamp the wood in this position and drill another hole that is 1/4 inch deep.
- [ ] Turn the board end for end.
- [ ] Repeat the drilling procedure for the two marks on this end of the board.
- [ ] Once you have drilled all four holes, remove the 1/16 inch bit and replace it with a 1/4 inch wood boring bit.
- [ ] Clamp the board in a position so that the center of the wood bit aligns with one of the holes made by the 1/16 inch diameter bit.
- [ ] Turn on the drill press, and bore the hole so that it is 1/4 inch deep.
- [ ] Repeat this same procedure for the other three holes.

After unclamping the board, you should have a piece that has four holes. The position of each hole and the depth is shown in Fig. 9-3B. If your piece is not a duplicate of this drawing, locate and correct any problem before continuing to the next step. When your piece matches the drawing, continue to the step marked "Part No. 14."

Electric Drill

Because you are going to use an electric hand drill to make the holes, a little more care must be taken. It is important to make sure that the drill bit is at right angles to the piece you are drilling. If it is crooked, then the holes that will be bored through the piece will also be crooked. This may cause the tension adjustment to bind and this will prevent you from getting an accurate and reliable reading of the diaphragm tension.

The best way to drill the holes so that they are all in the center of the board, is with a doweling fixture. This will also insure that the holes are straight.

- [ ] Place a 1/16 inch bit in the chuck of the electric drill.
- [ ] Align the doweling fixture so that the center of the bit is opposite the center of the mark at the 8 3/4 inch point on the board.
- [ ] Drill the hole so that it is 1/4 inch deep.
- [ ] Repeat the last two steps for the marks at the other three positions on the board.
- [ ] After all four 1/16 inch diameter holes have been drilled, replace the 1/16 inch bit with a 1/4 inch wood bit.
- [ ] Align the center of the wood bit with the center of one of the 1/16 inch diameter holes.
- [ ] Make sure the drill bit is again at right angles to the piece that is being drilled.
- [ ] Drill the hole so that it is 1/4 inch deep.
- [ ] Repeat these last two procedures for the other three 1/16 diameter holes.

When this last step is complete, you should have a board with four holes. The position and depth are shown in Fig. 9-3B. If your piece matches the drawing, continue to the next step. Otherwise, locate and correct any differences between your piece and the drawing.

PART NO. (14)

The next procedure puts a set of corresponding holes in the other 2 × 42 inch boards. These holes must be exactly opposite the ones that were drilled in the first board. The best way to align the holes is with a set of 1/4 inch dowel points. You will need four of them for this purpose.

- [ ] Place one dowel point in each of the four 1/4 inch holes.
- [ ] Take the board with the dowel points and place

it on a flat surface against a rigid backstop. The dowel points should be facing away from the backstop.

☐ Place a second 2 × 42 inch board against the one with the dowel points.

☐ Align the center of the dowel points with the lines drawn across the surface of this second board.

☐ Take a hammer and tap the back side of the second board so that it is forced against the dowel pins.

☐ Remove the second board and check the position of each of the marks. They should be on the line that was drawn across the 1 inch side. They should also be in the center of the 1 inch dimension.

☐ If this is what you have, then proceed to the next step. Otherwise, locate and correct any error.

☐ With the drill press, bore the two holes at the 8-3/4 inch mark all the way through both boards. Use a 1/4 inch bit.

If you are using an electric drill, use the doweling fixture to center the bit and to make sure that it is perpendicular to the piece being drilled.

☐ After the two holes have been bored all the way through both boards, take one of the boards and bore the two holes at the 7 inch mark so that they are one inch deep. This piece is part number (14).

The next set of steps are for the holes that will be used to screw part number (14) to the base.

☐ On the two inch width, draw a line down the length of the board so that it is parallel to the 42 inch length and 1/2 inch from the edge.

☐ Now measure in one inch from each end. Place a mark at this point so that it intersects the line at the 1/2 inch point.

☐ Starting from one end, at the one inch mark, continue and place marks every 10 inches until you get to the one inch mark at the other end of this board. See Fig. 9-4.

☐ At each of the intersecting marks drill a hole with a #10 wood bit that also has a pilot bit.

Before mounting part number (14) to the base, it will need to have some shims placed on the bottom of the board. Convenient ones can be made

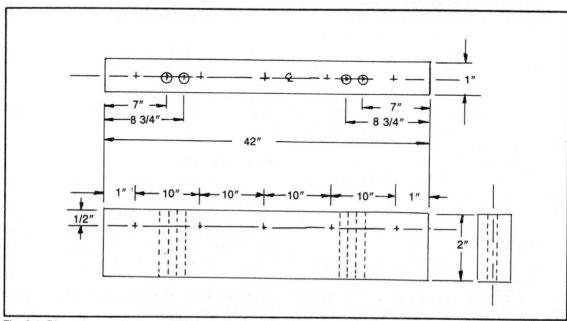

Fig. 9-4. Dimensions and hole locations for part #14 of the diaphragm stretching frame.

from the back of a cardboard writing tablet.

☐ Cut several strips of cardboard so that they will fit on the bottom of (14). Do not let any of the pieces stick out.

☐ Place the cardboard on the bottom of part (14). They can be held in place with tape or with glue.

☐ After installing the shims, part number (14) can be screwed to the top of the base with 1 1/2 inch #10 wood screws. The holes located at the 7 inch mark should be on the inside of the frame. Part (14) is located on the front edge of the base. See Fig. 9-1.

☐ Take the second 2 × 42 inch board and bore the holes at both the 7 and the 8-3/4 inch marks all the way through the board. Use a 1/4 inch bit. This piece is part number (11).

PART NO. (11) AND (27)

The following procedure will be used to make the screw holes that will hold the two sections of the diaphragm clamp together. These are part numbers (11) and (27).

☐ Take part number (11) and one of the remaining 2 × 42 inch pieces and clamp them together. This second piece should be on top of part number 11. Align the sides and the ends.

☐ Draw a line down the length so that it is parallel to the 42 inch side and 3/4 of an inch from the edge.

☐ Now measure 6 inches in from each end. Place a mark on the board so that it intersects the line at the 3/4 inch point. See Fig. 9-5.

☐ Place another pair of marks so that they are 11 inches from each end. They should also intersect the 3/4 inch line.

☐ Use the preceding step, and make another set of marks that are 16 inches from the end.

☐ If you are using a drill press, take a 1/16 inch bit and align it with the center of the line located at the 6 inch mark.

If you are using an electric hand drill, follow the same procedure but use the doweling jig to make sure that the holes are straight.

☐ Now drill a hole through both boards.

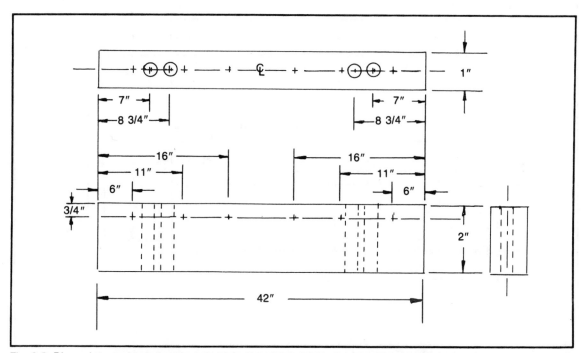

Fig. 9-5. Dimensions and hole locations for part #11 of the diaphragm stretching frame.

☐ Repeat this procedure for each of the other marks on this board.
☐ Separate the two pieces.
☐ Mark the piece with the 1/4 inch holes as part number (11). The other piece is part number (27).

PART NO. (21) AND (24)

☐ Take one of the remaining two 2 × 42 inch pieces and clamp it on top of part number (11). Make sure that all of the sides and the ends align.
☐ Take the 1/16 inch diameter bit and drill through each of the 1/16 inch holes that were already in board (11).
☐ Unclamp the two pieces.
☐ Take the second piece that was drilled and mark it as part number (21).
☐ Clamp the last 2 × 42 inch board to part number (21).

☐ After aligning the ends and sides, drill the 1/16 inch diameter holes through both boards.
☐ Unclamp the two boards and mark this last piece as part number (24).

The following steps are for the holes that will hold part number (21) to the base.

☐ On part (21), draw a line parallel to the 42 inch length and 3/4 of an inch from the edge. This line should intersect all of the 1/16 inch holes.
☐ Next measure 3 inches in from each end. Place a mark at this point so that it also intersects the 3/4 inch line. See Fig. 9-6.
☐ Start from one of the 3 inch marks and measure over every 6 inches until you get to the other 3 inch mark. Place a mark at each of these points so that they will intersect the 3/4 of an inch line. All of the marks should occur between the 1/16 inch hole locations.

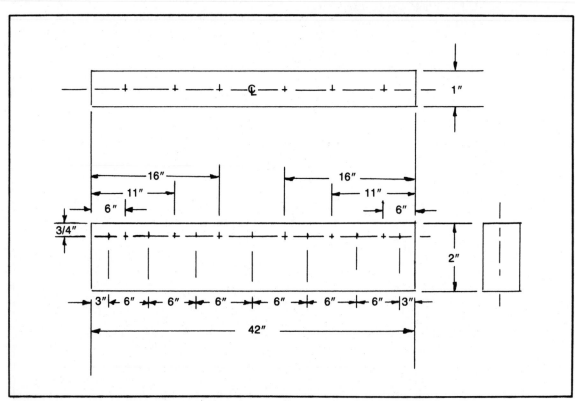

Fig. 9-6. Dimensions and hole locations for part #21 of the diaphragm stretching frame.

- [ ] To install part (21), measure 7 inches in from the rear of the frame. The rear is where part (6) is located. Place a mark on each of the outside edges of the plywood. With a straightedge, draw a line across the plywood so that it connects the two marks together. This line should be parallel to the 42 inch side of the base.
- [ ] Now take a 3/4 inch wood boring bit and countersink the bottom side of part number (21). Start with the holes located 6 inches from the ends. The bored holes should be 1/4 inch deep.
- [ ] After the holes have been bored, place part number (21) on top of the plywood. Align the back side where all the holes are located, with the line located at the 7 inch point.
- [ ] Clamp part number (21) to the top of the plywood.
- [ ] Take the 1/16 inch diameter bit and drill out the holes that start 3 inches from each end.
- [ ] When this is done, continue and drill the holes that are spaced every 6 inches from the beginning holes.
- [ ] Unclamp part number (21) from the plywood.
- [ ] Take part number (11) and use the 3/4 inch wood boring bit to counterbore the bottom side of this piece. The hole depth is the same as the one in part (21).
- [ ] Take a 1/4 inch bit and enlarge the 1/16 inch holes in the plywood base. This is where part (21) will be located.
- [ ] Enlarge the remaining 1/16 inch holes in both part (11) and (21).
- [ ] After enlarging the holes, you are ready to install the 10/32 "T" nuts. On parts (11) and (21), the "T" nuts go in the counterbored holes. On the plywood base, the "T" nuts are located on the bottom side of the plywood.
- [ ] Take part (21) and countersink the holes that start at the 3 inch point. The countersink is located on the opposite side from where the "T" nuts are located.
- [ ] Place part (21) on top of the plywood base. The rear side is again aligned with the line at the 7 inch mark.
- [ ] Install 1 1/2 inch 10/32 screws in all of the mounting holes on part (21).
- [ ] Screw part number (21) to the plywood base.

LEFT AND RIGHT DIAPHRAGM CLAMPS

The following steps are used to make the side diaphragm clamps. This includes two parts numbered (18), two pieces marked (10) and (20), as well as two more pieces marked (23) and (26).

- [ ] Begin by cutting six pieces of pine so that they are 2 by 27 by 1 inch.
- [ ] After these pieces have been cut, take four of them and clamp them together so that their sides and edges are all equal.
- [ ] Measure 5 inches in from each end and draw a line across the one inch width of all four pieces.
- [ ] Now measure 3 1/2 inches in from the end and place a similar mark at this point.
- [ ] Unclamp the four pieces.
- [ ] Take one of the pieces and divide the one inch width in half. Do this on both ends. Place a mark in each location.
- [ ] Draw a line down the center of the one inch width so that it connects the two marks together.

You are going to install dowel pins in the four holes that will be located at each of the marks on this board. The procedure for this is the same as the one used to make the holes in the front diaphragm clamp. Refer back to Fig. 9-2 and follow the indicated procedure. In this case, the holes will be at 5 and 3 1/2 inches.

- [ ] After all of the appropriate measurements have been made, drill the required 1/4 inch holes and install the dowel pins.
- [ ] Because all four pieces are identical, you can use the dowel pins to locate the center positions on each of the three other boards.
- [ ] Place the board with the dowel pins on a flat surface against a rigid backstop.
- [ ] Place each of the other boards against the one with the dowel pins and tap the edge of the board with a hammer.
- [ ] At this point, you should now have four pieces of wood. Each one should have a center point

located 3 1/2 and 5 inches in from each edge.

☐ Using a technique that is similar to the one used on parts (11) and (14), bore the two holes at the 5 inch mark all the way through the board. The holes at the 3 1/2 inch mark should then be bored so that they are 1 inch deep. Use a 1/4 inch bit for these holes. The hole location is shown in Fig. 9-7.

PART NO. (10) AND (20)

☐ Take two of the pieces and again clamp them together.

☐ Draw a line down one edge so that it is parallel to the 27 inch length and is 1/2 inch from the edge. This will be the front side of these pieces.

☐ Measure in from each end 1, 6, and 11 inches. Make a mark on the 1/2 inch line at each of the end locations.

☐ Take a 1/16 inch bit and drill through both boards.

☐ Unclamp the two pieces and mark one of the boards as part number (10) and the other as part number (20).

PART NO. (18)

☐ Take the other two boards that were marked with dowel pins, and bore out all four holes with a 1/4 inch bit. Follow the procedure that was used on the front diaphragm clamp.

☐ On one of the boards, draw a line parallel to the 27 inch sides and located 1/2 inch from the edge.

☐ Place intersecting marks at 1 3/4, 5 3/4, and 9 3/4 inches from each end.

☐ Clamp this piece to the other 27 inch board with the bored holes. Be sure the sides and the ends are aligned.

☐ Take a 1/16 inch diameter bit and drill holes at the six indicated locations. Drill through both boards.

☐ Unclamp the two boards.

☐ Mark both boards as part number (18).

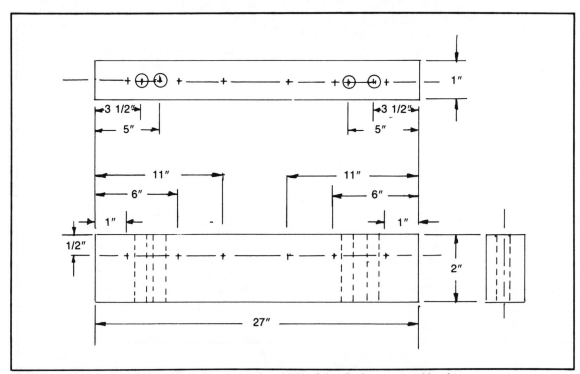

Fig. 9-7. Dimensions and hole locations for parts #10 and #20 of the diaphragm stretching frame.

PART NO. (23) AND (26)

☐ Take each of the boards without any holes, and clamp one to each of the number (18) boards. Align the sides and ends of each board.

☐ Take a 1/16 inch bit and drill a hole through both pieces.

☐ Repeat the previous step for the other two boards that are clamped together.

☐ After separating the two pieces, take one of them and mark it as part number (23). Keep it and its corresponding part number (18) together.

☐ Separate the second two boards and mark them as part number (26).

☐ On both of the number (18) boards, bore a 3/4 inch hole, 1/4 inch deep, on the bottom of the board. The hole location will correspond to the 1/16 inch diameter holes. The 3/4 inch holes are for mounting the "T" nuts.

☐ Bore the 1/16 inch holes to a 1/4 inch diameter. Drill all the way through the board. Be sure to do this on both number (18) parts.

☐ Now mount 10/32 "T" nuts in all of the coun-

terbored holes in both number (18) boards.

OTHER PARTS

☐ Cut a piece of one inch pine so that it is 2 × 22 1/2 × 1 inch.

☐ From this piece, make 4 pieces that are 5 1/2 inches long. These will become part number (12) in Fig. 9-1.

PART NO. (12)

The following steps are used to make the holes which will connect via an aluminum rod to other parts of the frame.

☐ On one end, divide the two inch width in half. Draw a line across the thickness of the wood at this point. See Fig. 9-8.

☐ Divide the thickness of the wood in half. Place a mark at this point so that it intersects the previous line.

☐ Put the piece on your drill press and align the

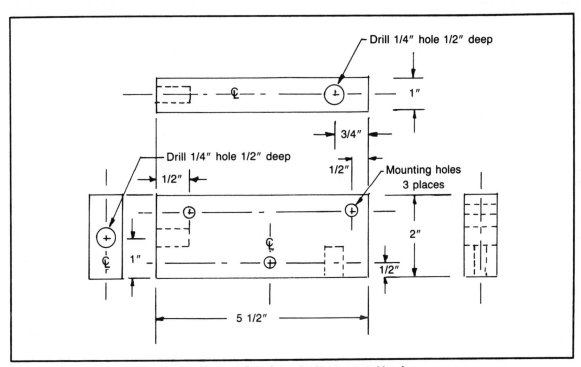

Fig. 9-8. Dimensions and hole locations for part #12 of the diaphragm stretching frame.

mark with the center of a 1/4 inch wood boring bit.

☐ Drill the hole so that it is 1/2 inch deep.

☐ On one of the 5 1/2 inch sides, measure 3/4 inch in from the end. This is the opposite end from where you just made a mark.

☐ With a square, draw a line across the 1 inch dimension.

☐ Divide the thickness of the wood in half. Place a mark at this point so that it intersects the 3/4 inch line.

☐ Place the piece on your drill press and align the bit with the mark at the 3/4 inch point.

☐ Drill this hole so that it is 1/2 inch deep.

☐ Repeat these last nine steps for the other three pieces that are part number (12).

The following steps are used to install the mounting holes for part number (12).

☐ Draw a line down the length so that it is parallel to the 5 1/2 inch side and 1/2 inch from the edge.

☐ Repeat this last step for the other edge of this board.

☐ Measure 1/2 inch in from each end and place a mark so that it intersects the 1/2 inch line. This intersection should be located on the opposite side from the hole at the 3/4 inch point.

☐ Place a mark at one half of the 5 1/2 inch length. This mark should intersect the 1/2 inch line that is located on the same side as the 3/4 inch point.

☐ Put a #10 wood bit in the chuck of your drill press and drill the holes at the three indicated locations.

☐ Repeat these last five steps for the other three pieces that are marked number (12).

☐ Start at the front right side and place one block on the plywood base so that it is six inches in from the right side and 10 1/2 inches back from the front. This assumes that you are standing in front of part (14) and facing the frame.

☐ Draw a set of lines around the outside edge of the piece. The lines should be on the plywood.

The lines will be used as guides to replace the piece

in a latter step. Final placement will be taken care of later.

☐ Take a 1/4 inch metal rod and insert it into the 1/4 inch hole located on the end of part number (12). Push it in as far as it will go.

☐ Place the block back in its position on the base with the rod on top of part number 14.

☐ Measure and mark the length of the rod so that it extends 1/4 of an inch beyond the inside edge of part number (14).

☐ Remove the rod and cut it to the measured length. Then clean off any burrs that are located on the sawed-off end.

☐ Insert one side of the rod back into the hole on part number (12).

☐ Take the other end of the rod and push it through the hole at the 7 inch point of part number (11).

☐ Now insert the end of the rod into the corresponding hole located in part (14).

☐ Take a carpenters square and place it against the inside edge of part number (14). The other blade of the square should be parallel to the rod.

☐ Move part number (12) until the rod and the square are parallel.

☐ Check the position of part number (12). It should again be 10 1/2 inches from the front of the frame and it should be located approximately in the position where you drew the lines on the plywood.

☐ If the block is at the correct dimension and the rod is parallel to the square, use an awl and make a set of marks in the plywood. They should correspond to each of the three mounting holes.

☐ Remove the entire assembly from part number (14).

☐ Take an electric hand drill and drill a 1/16 inch hole in the plywood at each of the mounting hole positions.

☐ Before placing it back in position, put a cardboard shim under part (12).

☐ Now put rod that is inserted in part (12) back into part (14). The rod should still pass through part (11).

- [ ] Align part (12) with its mounting holes. You will have to pierce the shims to do this.
- [ ] Screw it to the base.
- [ ] Repeat the above steps for the block that is located on the left side of the base. This block should be located 26 1/2 inches from the right block.
- [ ] For the block located on the right side of the base, insert a 1/4 inch rod into the hole at the 3/4 inch point.
- [ ] Slide part (10) under the edge and adjust it so that it is flush with the left edge of the base.
- [ ] Measure and mark the rod length so that it protrudes 1/4 of an inch beyond the inside of part (10).
- [ ] Repeat this last step and cut another rod to the same length.
- [ ] After removing the burrs located on the sawed-off ends, reinsert one of the pieces in part (12).
- [ ] Take part (18) and insert the rod through the hole that is located at the 3 1/2 inch dimension.
- [ ] Now place the end of the rod into the corresponding hole in part (10).
- [ ] Take a carpenters square and place it against the inside edge of part (10).
- [ ] Adjust the position of part (10) until the other blade of the square is parallel to the rod.
- [ ] Place some shims under part (10).
- [ ] Take the number (10) piece and clamp it on the top right side of the base. It should be positioned so that one end is 11 1/8 inches from the front of the base. The 1/2 inch line should then be facing towards the outside edge of the base.
- [ ] After clamping the piece in place, take a #10 wood bit with a pilot point, and drill the holes located at the 1, 6, and 11 inch marks. The drill should go all the way through the wood and into the plywood.
- [ ] Install number 10 wood screws in each of the holes and screw the piece to the base. The screws should be at least 1 1/2 inches long.
- [ ] Repeat this same procedure for the rod that is located in part (12) on the right side of the base.
- [ ] Repeat the steps for mounting the diaphragm clamp that is located on the left side of the base. This is part (20).

- [ ] On the rear end of a number (10) part, insert the other 1/4 inch rod in the hole at the 3 1/2 inch location. This rod should also pass through part (18).
- [ ] Take one of the remaining number (12) parts and cut it so that it is 3 inches long. Measure from the end that has a hole at the 3/4 inch location.
- [ ] Place one of the number (12) parts over the end of the rod that passes through part (18).
- [ ] Position this block so that part (18) moves freely back and forth.
- [ ] Put a shim under this piece and screw it into position.
- [ ] Repeat these last steps for the remaining number (12) part.

At this point, the diaphragm clamps should be in position. The next step is to insert the threaded rods into their respective holes.

- [ ] Push part (11) forward so that it is against part (14).
- [ ] Insert two 1/4 inch "T" nuts in each of the holes at the 8 3/4 inch location. The "T" nuts should be located on the inside of part (11).
- [ ] Now move part (11) so that it is back against part (12).
- [ ] Put two 1/4 inch "T" nuts on the front side of part (11).
- [ ] Use the same procedure for both number (18) parts.
- [ ] Take a 1/4 inch threaded rod and place it on top of parts (11) and (14). Be sure that part (11) is against part (12).
- [ ] Measure the length of the threaded rod so that it will protrude on both sides of (11) and (14) by 1/2 inch.
- [ ] Cut the threaded rod to length. Then clean and deburr it.
- [ ] Insert the rod through part (14).
- [ ] Thread a 1/4 inch nut on the inside end of the rod.
- [ ] Now thread the rod into part (11) until it protrudes out the back by 1/2 inch.
- [ ] On the back side of the rod, place a lock washer

and a nut. Tighten the nut against the "T" nut.

☐ Tighten the nut that is located between parts (11) and (14) against the "T" nut located on part (11).

☐ Repeat this same procedure for the threaded rod that is located on the opposite end of the front diaphragm clamp.

☐ After the two rods are in place, check to make sure that part (11) still slides freely. If it doesn't, locate and correct the problem before continuing.

☐ Now that the two rods are in place, take a large flat washer, a lock washer, and a nut. Thread them on the end of the rod that protrudes from part (14).

☐ Repeat all of the above steps for mounting the threaded rods in the side diaphragm clamps.

The last group of steps is for mounting the tension indicating devices.

☐ First take each of the scales and drill two holes through the handle of the scale. The holes should be large enough for a #6 wood screw.

☐ Take one of the scales and mount it in the center of part (26). Use a 3/4 inch #6 wood screw to hold it in place. Use a square to make sure that it is at right angles to the side of part (26).

☐ Take one of the other scales and mount it on part (6) so that it is 10 1/2 inches from the left edge. Be sure to align it so that it is at right angles to the part (6).

☐ Repeat this last step for the scale on the right side of part (6). It should be 10 1/2 inches from the adjacent side.

Now that the scales are in place, the last step is to put the hooks for the end of the chain in place.

☐ Screw a hook into the center of part (23).

☐ Screw the other two hooks into part (27). Position them so that they are in line with the center of the scales that are mounted on part (6).

This completes the work on the stretching frame. Your frame should look like the one in Fig. 9-1.

Chapter 10

Final Speaker Assembly

The final assembly steps consist of installation of the "T" nuts, stretching the diaphragm, application of the conductive coating to the diaphragm, and then bolting the two halves together so that they will form an electrostatic speaker.

Before the diaphragm can be stretched, the speaker panels will require some additional work. In Chapter 5, a designation was placed on the rear of each panel. This indication identified it and its corresponding mate.

- ☐ Separate each of your panels into their corresponding pairs.
- ☐ Take one pair and lay them on your work surface with one panel on top of the other.
- ☐ Align the two panels so that the tweeter sections are opposite each other and all of the sides are parallel.
- ☐ Take a couple of "C" clamps and clamp the two halves together. The screw side of the clamp should be on the rear side of the panel.
- ☐ Next take a 1/4 inch bit and place it in the chuck of the drill press.

If you are using an electric hand drill, you will again need the doweling fixture to ensure that the holes that will be drilled are vertical.

- ☐ Place the two panels on your drill press and align the drill bit with the center of the holes for the "T" nuts.
- ☐ When the bit and the hole center are aligned, turn on the drill press and drill out the hole.

Drill through the frame, both spacers, and the frame that is located on the other side. If your bit will not go all the way through both frames, then drill the hole as deep as you can. Make sure, however, that it penetrates the second frame.

- ☐ After you have drilled the first hole, align the bit with the center of the next hole and drill it out.
- ☐ Continue this procedure for all of the holes on the rear of the frame. This method will ensure that all of the mounting holes are aligned.

- ☐ When all the holes have been drilled, remove the clamps.

If your drill did not go through both frames, then drill out the holes in the second frame.

- ☐ Next take a countersink or a 1/2 inch drill and turn it by hand in each of the holes on the spacers.

Do this last step for both the front and rear panels. The purpose of this operation is to remove any burrs that may be on the plastic.

- ☐ After all of the burrs have been removed, set these two speaker panels aside.
- ☐ Get another pair of matching front and rear panels and clamp them together.
- ☐ On this pair of panels, follow the same drilling procedure that was used on the first speaker panel.
- ☐ After all of the holes are drilled, unclamp the two sections and remove any burrs that are on the plastic spacers.
- ☐ Set this speaker assembly next to the first one.
- ☐ Use the procedure described in the last four steps on the remaining speaker panels.
- ☐ After all of the front panels have been drilled, then take the countersink or a large drill and insert it into the chuck of the drill press.
- ☐ Turn the drill press on.
- ☐ Take each of the front speaker panels and countersink the screw holes in the frame. This is on the opposite side of the spacer. Make the countersink deep enough so that a 10/32 screw head is flush with the surface of the frame.

The front frame also has four countersunk holes for the diaphragm connection. These will have to be drilled out, but you do not want the 1/4 inch drill to penetrate the plastic of the spacer.

- ☐ Insert a 1/16 inch drill bit in the chuck of the drill press.
- ☐ Align the bit with the center of a countersunk hole located on the front speaker frame.
- ☐ Drill a pilot hole through the wood frame, through the plastic plate, and then through the spacer.
- ☐ When this first hole is completed, drill out the other diaphragm connection holes on the front panel.
- ☐ After you have finished the first panel, continue and do all of the other front panels.
- ☐ When all of the front panels have been drilled with a 1/16 inch bit, replace it with a 1/4 inch bit.
- ☐ Take one of the front panels and lay it on your drill press table with the conductive side down.
- ☐ Align the plate so that the drill bit comes down next to the edge of the plate.
- ☐ Bring down the bit until it touches the edge of the plastic plate.
- ☐ Lock the drill in this position.
- ☐ Now set the depth gauge on the drill press so that the drill bit will not go lower than this point.
- ☐ After the depth has been set, release the lock.
- ☐ Before drilling, lay the front plate on the table and bring down the bit.
- ☐ Check the depth to make sure it doesn't penetrate the plastic plate.
- ☐ When this last step checks out okay, align the bit with the center of the 1/16 inch hole.
- ☐ Turn on the drill press and drill the hole.
- ☐ After drilling the first hole, continue and drill the other three holes.
- ☐ When one plate has been finished, continue and drill the front plates of the other three panels.
- ☐ After all the 1/4 inch holes have been drilled, replace the bit with a countersink.
- ☐ Countersink the four diaphragm connection holes so that the head of a 6/32 flat head machine screw is flush with the top surface of the spacer.
- ☐ Repeat this last operation on all of the remaining plates.
- ☐ When all of the holes have been countersunk, then check the edge of each hole for burrs.
- ☐ If there are sharp edges, remove them with a small file or by scraping the edge with a hobby knife.

Now that the holes for the diaphragm connection have been drilled, the next step is to make a conductive strip on the inside of the spacer so that it connects to the two screw holes on each end.

- [ ] On the inside of the spacer, mask a strip so that it extends down the length of the side between the holes for the diaphragm and the edge of the spacer. See Fig. 10-1. Be sure to stripe the spacers on both sides of the plate.
- [ ] When one plate has been masked, continue and mask the other plates.
- [ ] After all of the plates have been masked, take a small artist brush and dip it into your container of conductive paint.
- [ ] Paint the area between the masking tape with the conductive paint. Do both sides of the plate.
- [ ] When you have finished, set the plate aside while the paint dries.

- [ ] Do all of the other front plates in a similar fashion.
- [ ] After all of the plates have been painted, take a one inch flathead 6/32 screw and insert it in the hole until it threads into the "T" nut.
- [ ] Tighten the screw.
- [ ] Repeat this procedure for the other three holes of this plate and then do all of the other plates.
- [ ] When all of the screws have been installed, take the artist brush and paint over the screw heads with the conductive paint.
- [ ] After you have finished painting each of the four screw heads, set the plate aside so that the paint can dry.
- [ ] Continue with the painting process and do all of the screws on the other plates.
- [ ] When all of the screws have been painted, go back to the first one. Take an ohmmeter and measure the resistance between the two screws.

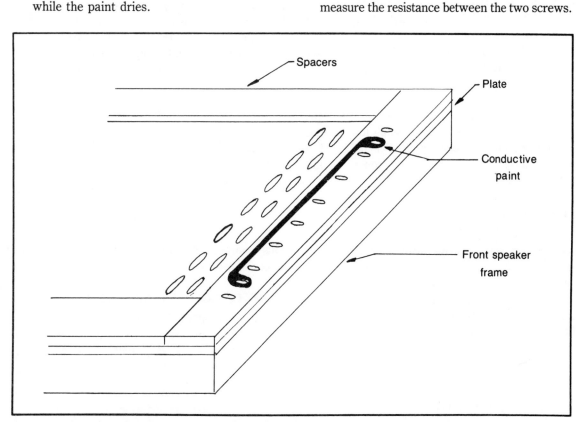

Fig. 10-1. Pictorial drawing of the diaphragm connecting strip.

There should be continuity (zero ohms) between the screws.

☐ After you have measured both sides of the first plate, go on and make the same measurement on all of the other plates. If you do not get a continuity reading between the screws, recoat the stripe with conductive paint.

☐ When you have continuity between all of the screws, you can remove the masking tape.

At this point, you are ready to install all of the "T" nuts that will hold the speaker panels together.

"T" NUT INSTALLATION

As indicated, the "T" nuts must be inserted into all of the countersunk holes on the rear frame.

☐ Take one of the rear panels of the speaker and install a 10/32 "T" nut in each of the counter bored holes.

☐ After you have completed the first speaker panel, continue to install "T" nuts on all of the other rear panels.

After all the "T" nuts have been installed, the next operation is to place some small foam pieces in the center of the speaker plate. When this is finished, foam strips must be placed around the outside of each panel.

FOAM STRIPS

The foam parts are made from a product called foam tape. It is found in hardware and building supply stores. It is used to seal cracks, as an insulation, and to reduce vibration. It comes in rolls that are 17 feet long. You will need about 1 roll for each 2 foot by 2 foot speaker. Be sure the type that you buy is called open cell. The closed cell type is too dense and it creates problems when the speaker is assembled.

☐ First, cut nine pieces of foam so that each one is 1/2 by 1/2 by 1 inch long.

☐ Peel off the tape that protects the adhesive side of the tape. Place one strip on the conductive

side of the speaker panel. Position it opposite the point where two ribs intersect.

☐ Repeat this step for each rib intersection on this panel.

☐ After this first panel has had the foam pieces installed, do all of the other panels in the same way.

Be sure to do both the front and rear panels. When you have finished, the foam pieces on one panel should be opposite a foam piece on its corresponding panel.

☐ Next, take the roll of foam and lay a strip along the outside edge next to the spacer. The foam should be on the inside of the spacer. Cut the strip to the inside length of the spacers.

☐ Peel off the adhesive coating and place the foam strip on the panel next to the spacer.

☐ Rotate the speaker by 90 degrees.

☐ Repeat the measurement and installation of the foam strip along this edge of the panel.

☐ Continue rotating the speaker and installing the foam strips until you are back to the starting side.

You should now have a speaker panel with one inch foam pieces located in the center of the panel over all of the rib intersections and four strips of foam around the outside edge of the panel.

☐ After the first panel is completed, repeat the above operation for all of the other speaker panels (both front and rear).

This completes the preliminary steps for assembling the electrostatic speaker panels.

STRETCHING THE DIAPHRAGM

Now that all of the rear speaker panels have the "T" nuts installed and the foam pieces and strips have been placed in their correct positions, you are ready to stretch the diaphragm.

☐ Take a rear panel and place it face up in the middle of the stretching frame.

☐ Next lay a piece of mylar over it.

☐ Clamp the mylar to the stretching frame. Try

to keep the mylar smooth so that it has no large wrinkles.

☐ Place a chain on the hook of the spring scale.

☐ Pull out the spring on the scale, and connect the chain to the hook located on the opposite diaphragm clamp. Do this for all three scales.

☐ Next write down the value that is indicated on each of the scales.

During the tensioning process, this initial value will be increased until each gage reads 3.0 pounds. It is important to make the tensioning adjustments in a uniform manner. Do not try to adjust a single screw for the entire 3 pounds. Start with one screw and gradually increase the tension until the scale reads about 1/2 pound. Now do this on the next screw. Follow this procedure until all of the scales indicate a tension of 1/2 pound. Then start over and repeat this process. Keep this up until each scale shows that the tension is 3.0 pounds.

☐ To increase the tension, start with one of the adjustment screws and turn it one-half turn.

☐ Now make the same adjustment on the next screw.

☐ Continue with this procedure until you have adjusted each of the tension screws 1/2 turn. You should now be back at the starting point.

☐ Go to each of the scales and compare the tension with the previous reading.

It is unlikely that this first adjustment procedure will produce a difference of 3.0 pounds. Therefore, continue on to the next step.

☐ Start again at the first screw, and increase the tension by adjusting each of the screws one full turn. If you are near the three pound mark, make several small adjustments until the indicated value is obtained.

☐ If you have not reached the required limit, continue to adjust each screw until you have returned to the starting point.

☐ After you have adjusted all of the screws, again compare the scale reading with the initial value.

If the difference is equal to 3.0 pounds then you have finished this step and you can proceed to the next one. However, if more tension is needed on any of the adjusting screws, then repeat the above steps. The final step occurs when each of the scales has increased to a value of 3.0 pounds.

☐ Now that the correct tension has been obtained, the chain for the tension gages can be removed.

Do not change the tension adjustment. Pull on the chain until you can slip it off of the hook on the diaphragm clamp. Be careful that the chain doesn't fall and hit the diaphragm. If that happens, it might put a hole in it and then you will have to start all over.

COATING THE DIAPHRAGM

Before the conductive coating is applied to the diaphragm a number of additional steps must be done.

☐ The first step is to place some double back sticky tape on top of the mylar.

The purpose of the tape is to hold the mylar to the front plate when the two panels are fastened together. This will maintain the tension on the diaphragm after the panels are removed from the stretching frame. The tape should be positioned over the screw holes located in the rear panel.

☐ For this step, use double back sticky tape. Looking down through the mylar, center the tape over the mounting holes. Do this on both the left and right sides. Make sure that the tape has no wrinkles.

☐ Repeat the above process for the top and bottom sides.

Now that the sticky tape is installed we need to prevent the diaphragm coating from getting on the tape during its application.

☐ Take a piece of 1/2 inch masking tape and gently lay it over the sticky tape.

The only place where you want the two tapes to contact is on the inside edge of the speaker. On the left and right sides, be careful that the masking tape does not cover up the section where the diaphragm contact will be located.

While many speaker builders use a powdered graphite for the conductive coating, it has several problems. First it is hard to control the application area. Ideally, you only want the coating to be on to the diaphragm and in contact with the connecting strip that is located on the front spacer. However, graphite is a powder and it has a tendency to get into and on everything. This can provide a leakage path between the diaphragm and the plate. The second problem occurs because it is hard to get a nice even coat.

To overcome both of these problems, I have found that liquid Ivory soap is an excellent substitute.

- [ ] Take the liquid soap and squirt a small amount onto the center of the diaphragm.
- [ ] Take a soft, lint free cloth and spread the soap evenly over the entire diaphragm.

After the entire surface has been coated, take another lint free cloth and gently wipe the surface.

- [ ] Start at one side of the speaker panel and wipe straight across the surface to the other side.
- [ ] Next, move over the distance of your wipe area and repeat the wiping operation.
- [ ] Keep doing this wiping action until you reach the opposite side of the diaphragm.

During the wiping operation, do not wipe along the immediate edges where the contact strip for the diaphragm will be located. It is desirable to have this area at a lower resistance than the rest of the diaphragm.

- [ ] Repeat the above wiping procedure, but instead of going in the same direction rotate the wiping action by 90 degrees.
- [ ] Keep wiping and alternating the direction until

the soap has an even appearance over the entire surface.

DIAPHRAGM RESISTANCE

In the following steps, a check is made of the diaphragm coating resistance. The resistance should be a high value and it should also be consistent.

- [ ] Take an ohmmeter and with the probes located about one inch apart measure the resistance of the coating.

The resistance value should be greater than 30 Megohms. The actual amount is not important, but it should not be too high. Optimum is about 50 to 100 megohms. If the resistance gets too high, you may find that there will not be enough high voltage on the diaphragm for correct operation.

- [ ] Move the probes around and check the coating at several different locations.

If all the values are reasonably close to each other, then you have finished coating the diaphragm and you can go to the next section.

- [ ] If large variations still exist, then wipe the mylar surface again.
- [ ] Recheck the resistance. If it is consistent, then you can proceed to the next section.
- [ ] If there are still large variations, continue the wiping and resistance checking until you obtain the same reading in all areas.

If the resistance reading gets too high, add a small amount of liquid soap. Then gently wipe the coating until it is even.

FINAL ASSEMBLY

Now all of the parts are ready to be assembled. Before the other plate can be placed on the diaphragm, the masking tape must be removed and the mylar must be pierced for the mounting holes.

- [ ] Carefully remove the masking tape from the diaphragm. Be sure not to remove the double back tape.

While an awl can be used to penetrate the diaphragm, a much better tool is a small hot soldering iron.

☐ Take whatever tool you plan to use and go around the perimeter and pierce both the double backed tape and the diaphragm over each of the mounting holes.
☐ After this is done, take the front panel and lay it on the diaphragm.
☐ Align the front and rear sections so that the tweeter panels are opposite each other.
☐ Next take four 8/32 × 2-1/2 inch flat head screws and put them through the mounting holes at each corner.

It is not necessary that you tighten them as their purpose is to align the top and bottom mounting holes.

☐ After the holes are aligned, start at one corner with 10/32 × 2 inch screws and place one in each of the holes along one side of the frame.

When you get to the end of the row, remove the two long screws that were used for alignment.

☐ After all of the two inch screws are in place, go back to the first screw and begin tightening each screw.

Be very careful when tightening the screws. If the screwdriver slips, it may puncture the diaphragm. If that happens,the diaphragm will have to be replaced.

☐ Once all the screws in the above step are tight, start down the next side of the panel and install another set of screws.
☐ When you get to the end of this row, remove the long screws used for alignment.
☐ Start at the beginning of this last row and tighten all of the screws.

☐ In a similar fashion, continue down the other two sides inserting and tightening screws until you have gone completely around the perimeter of the frame.

REMOVING THE COMPLETED SPEAKER PANEL

The above procedure completes the final assembly of the speaker panel. Before removing the panel from the stretching frame, it is a good idea to go back and make one last check on the mounting screws.

☐ Now that all the screws have been installed, go back to the first screw and go around the outside once more. Check for any screws that are not tight.
☐ If all of the screws are tight, release the mylar from the clamps by loosening the tension screws.

Before removing the panel from the stretching frame, the excess mylar can be trimmed off.

☐ Take a hot soldering iron, or a very sharp hobby knife, and go around the outside of the speaker to trim the diaphragm material to the same size as the panel.
☐ When this is done, gently lift the panel from the stretching frame.
☐ Lay it on your work surface with the front up.

DIAPHRAGM RESISTANCE CHECK

☐ Take an ohmmeter and very carefully check the resistance between the screws for the diaphragm connections and the diaphragm itself.

Adjacent to the frame, the resistance should be lower than it is in the middle of the diaphragm. Check on both sides where contact is made to the diaphragm. Do not push too hard on the probes. You do not want to puncture the diaphragm. In the middle, it should be about 50 megohms. The edge readings should be in the 10 to 20 megohm range.

☐ Now that one panel is done, go back to the beginning of this chapter and repeat all of the steps for the rest of the speaker panels.

TESTING THE
COMPLETED SPEAKER PANEL

In all of the previous steps, a considerable amount of caution was used. This was to ensure that the speaker would work when the final assembly was completed. Having assembled all of the speaker panels, it is now time to find out if our efforts have paid off.

☐ Take the variable high voltage power supply and connect the ground side to the center tap of the audio transformer. Refer to the electronics section for the complete electrical connections.
☐ Connect the lead from the 20 megohm resistor to the diaphragm.
☐ Next place a high voltage probe across the output of the power supply.
☐ After connecting the power supply to a dc voltmeter, gradually increase the voltage until a

reading of 5000 volts is obtained.

If the diaphragm pulls to one side, or oscillates back and forth, it indicates that there is not enough tension on the diaphragm and it will have to be restretched.

Another possibility is that the two panels are not parallel to each other. If one is bowed inward, the diaphragm will have a tendency to pull to that side. In some cases, it is possible to correct this by inserting some additional pieces of foam between the diaphragm and the plate. This has to be done on an experimental basis to see if the diaphragm can be centered or stopped from oscillating. To do this, turn off the high voltage and take a small piece of foam and gently push it in between the plate and the diaphragm. You will probably have to install a piece of foam on each side so that the diaphragm will stay centered. If this doesn't solve the problem, the speaker will either have to be taken apart and the diaphragm restretched or some other method will have to be found so that the plates are made parallel. One additional possibility is to place a one inch square piece of lumber across the frame

Fig. 10-2. Photo shows the terminal blocks and the equalizing resistors for the completed electrostatic speaker.

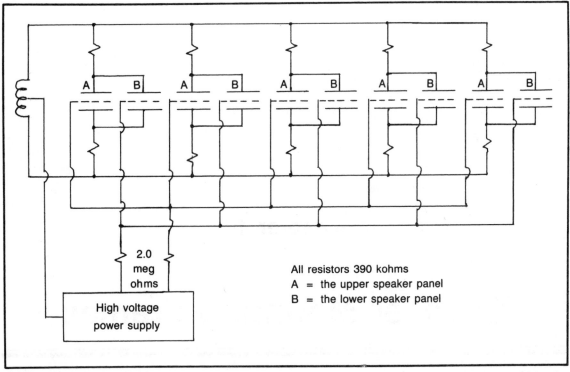

Fig. 10-3. Electrical diagram of the speaker showing the equalizing resistors and how the diaphragm is connected to the high voltage power supply.

and glue it to the ribs. An alternate method to gluing is to use nylon lacing cord. The cord can be inserted between the plate and the diaphragm and the plate can be pulled back so that it is parallel.

☐ After the first speaker panel is operational, repeat the above test process for the rest of the panels.

EQUALIZATION

Technically, this is not part of the assembly procedure. In the following steps, a series of resistors are installed on the speaker. Each resistor is in series with an element of the speaker. It, therefore, forms a low pass filter. In this way, the speaker frequency response can be adjusted.

☐ Place one speaker panel on your work surface.
☐ Install a terminal strip on each side of the

speaker as shown in Fig. 10-2. Use #6 wood screws.
☐ Take a piece of insulated wire and connect all of the four inch panels together. Do this on both sides of the speaker.
☐ Connect a 390 kohm resistor from the terminal strip to the speaker terminal connected to the four panels.
☐ Do the same thing for the panels on the reverse side of the speaker.
☐ Next, install the other two terminal strips for the other speaker strips.
☐ Connect the designated resistors between them and the panels as shown in Fig. 10-3.
☐ Repeat the above procedure for the rest of the panels.

This completes the assembly operation for the speaker panels. The next step is to make a frame to support the panels.

145

Chapter 11

Speaker Mounting Frames

In a conventional loudspeaker system, large cabinets are required to take care of the speakers rear radiation. An electrostatic speaker, because of its light diaphragm, does not need a large bulky enclosure. In fact, the use of a cabinet will often degrade the performance of the speaker. For more information on this subject, see the article in Chapter 15 by Peter Walker. Most electrostatic speaker systems are thin (typically one to two inches). The mounting system for this type of speaker consists only of a frame that is large enough to hold the required number of panels, a base to house the electronics, and some type of grill cloth.

This section will describe two frames for mounting the completed speaker panels. The first frame is a utility type that can be used to support two of the completed panels. With this frame, a check can be made of the speaker overall performance. The second frame is suitable for use in a living room.

UTILITY FRAME

A photograph of the utility frame is shown in Fig. 11-1. The frame consists of a base, two runners for support, two vertical sides separated by a spacer, and a top. There is nothing fancy about this frame and one inch pine was used as the main building material. Besides being readily available, pine is a very easy wood to work with. If you do not have the necessary tool for cutting the material to size, the suppliers will usually cut it for you.

Cutting the Parts

The diagram of Fig. 11-2 indicates the size of the frame.

☐ For those who have the necessary tools, set the rip fence on the table saw to two inches.
☐ Cut at least four boards so that they are 55 inches long to this width. These pieces are the vertical sides of the frame.
☐ Without changing the above setting, cut four other boards so that they have a minimum length of 24 inches. These are the top and center dividers.

Fig. 11-1. Photo shows a utility frame that can be used to hold and test two completed speaker panels.

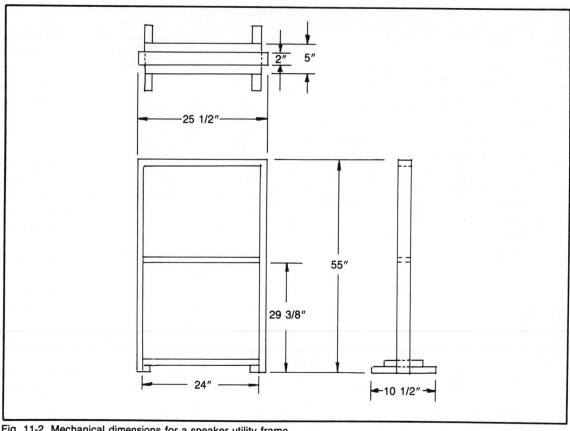

Fig. 11-2. Mechanical dimensions for a speaker utility frame.

□ Now, set the fence to five inches and cut two pieces so that they are at least 24 inches long. Each one is a base for the utility frame.

□ The next step is to measure and mark a vertical side so that it is 55 inches long.

□ After removing the fence, place one of the sides on the saw table and cut it to the required length.

□ Before cutting the next piece, measure the one that was just cut. If it is the correct size, use it as a template for the other vertical sides.

□ After marking all the vertical sides, place them on the saw table and cut each of them to size.

□ Take one of the shorter pieces and mark it so that it will have a length of 24 inches.

□ Place it on your saw and cut it to size.

□ Check your work by measuring its length. If it

is the correct size, then use it as a template for the other shorter pieces.

□ After all of the 24 inch pieces have been marked, use the saw and cut them to the required length.

□ Next, take a piece of scrap and cut four pieces so that each one is 1 × 1 × 10 1/2 inches. These are the runners that will be fastened to the underside of the base.

At this point you should have four different groups of materials. One set consists of those pieces that are 2 inches wide and 55 inches long. There should be 4 pieces in this group. Another set should consist of 4 pieces that are 2 inches wide and 24 inches long. There should also be 4 runners that are 1 inch wide and 10 1/2 inches long. The last group consists of 2 pieces that are 5 inches wide and 24 inches long.

Base

Lay all of the above pieces aside except the two that are 5 inches wide.

☐ Take one of the 5 inch boards and measure 1/2 inch in from each of the four corners. Do this from both the end and the side.

☐ Now, take a 1/16 inch bit and drill a pilot hole where the two lines intersect.

☐ Next, place the other 5 inch board under the one that was just drilled. After aligning the edges so that they are all parallel, clamp them together.

☐ Use the same bit and drill the corresponding holes in the lower 5 inch board.

☐ Separate the two boards. Take a number 8 wood bit and place it in your drill motor.

☐ At each of the four corners, drill out the 1/16 inch holes with the wood bit. Countersink one side of the board so that the head of a number 8 wood screw will be flush with the surface.

☐ Now, lay one of the 5 inch pieces aside and get two of the runners. These are the pieces that are 1 × 1 × 10 1/2 inch.

☐ On one end of the 10 1/2 inch piece measure in 2 3/4 inches.

☐ Place this under the 5 inch board so that the 2 3/4 inch line is at the edge of the board. Center the 10 1/2 inch piece under the screw holes in the 5 inch board. Be sure the 10 1/2 inch piece is at right angles to the 5 inch piece.

☐ Clamp the two boards together.

☐ Take #8 screw and screw the 5 inch board to the top of the runner.

☐ Repeat this same procedure for the runner located on the opposite edge of this base.

You should now have a 5 inch piece with two runners sticking out from each side. See the photograph shown in Fig. 11-1.

☐ If that is what you have, repeat the last five steps for the other base and its two runners.

Sides

☐ The next step is to take a vertical side and measure in from the ends 1/2 inch. Draw a line across the two inch width of the board.

☐ Next measure in from each side another 1/2 inch. The two marks should intersect the lines from the above step.

☐ At the bottom of the board, measure in from each side 1/2 inch.

☐ Draw a line down each edge so that it connects the two 1/2 inch marks together. This line should be parallel to the 55 inch length.

☐ Now measure up from the bottom end 1/2 inch. Draw a line across the two inch width at this point.

☐ Take a 1/16 inch bit and drill a guide hole at each of the intersecting lines.

☐ Using this first piece as a guide, place it on top of another side piece. Then, align all of the edges.

☐ After all of the edges are aligned, clamp the two pieces together.

☐ Using the 1/16 inch holes in the first piece as a guide, drill a similar set of holes in the second piece.

☐ Remove the second piece and take another of the side pieces and repeat these last three steps.

☐ When all of the holes have been drilled in the above board, remove it and follow same procedure for the last side piece.

At this point, you should have four sides that are 55 inches long. Each one should have a pair of 1/16 inch holes located at the end of the board.

☐ Take one of the pieces and decide which end will be the top. From this end, measure down 25 1/4 inches. Draw a line across the two inch width.

☐ At this line, measure 1/2 inch in from each edge. Place a set of marks in this position. The marks should intersect the line from the previous step.

☐ Take the 1/16 inch bit and drill holes where the marks intersect the lines.

☐ Take the piece that you just drilled and use it

as a template for drilling holes in the other three side pieces.

☐ Take one of the sides and measure down from the top 6 3/4 inches. At this point, draw a line across the width of the board.

☐ Measure down 18 3/4 inches and draw another line.

☐ Repeat this last step at both 31 3/4 and at 43 3/4 inches.

Each of the four lines should intersect the line that runs down the length of the side and is located 1/2 inch from the edge.

☐ Drill 1/16 inch holes at each line intersection.

☐ Take another side piece and place it against the first one. After making sure that the sides are aligned, clamp the two boards together.

☐ Using the first piece as a guide, drill a set of 1/16 inch holes through the second piece.

☐ Repeat this last process for the remaining two sides.

☐ Run a #8 wood bit drill through all of the holes. Countersink the holes so that the screw head will be flush with the surface.

Frame Assembly

☐ Next take a top piece and place the end against one of the side pieces. Their edges must be flush with each other.

☐ Take a #8 wood screw and screw the two boards together.

☐ Repeat this procedure for the other side piece that is the opposite part of this frame.

☐ From the top, measure down each side 24 1/16 inches. Place a mark on the edge of the side piece.

☐ Take one of the other 24 inch pieces and place it between the two vertical pieces. The top edge of this part should be flush with the line made in the previous step.

The final assembly step is to fasten the sides to the base. If the frame is going to permanently hold the speaker, then drill the required holes for mounting the step-up transformer and the high voltage assembly.

☐ Next, take one of the base pieces and place it between the two sides. Align the sides so that the end is flush with the bottom of the runner.

☐ With 1 1/4 inch #8 wood screws, fasten the side to the base. For permanent use, place some glue between the pieces before screwing them together.

☐ Repeat these last steps for the other frame.

Installing the Speakers

The utility frame is now completed and it is ready for the speaker panels. The upper speaker panel should fit between the top and the brace that was placed at 24 1/16 inches. The lower panel should fit so there is approximately 4 inches from the bottom of the lower panel to the top of the base. This should leave enough room for the transformer and high voltage power supply. See Fig. 11-1.

When the speakers are installed, be sure to orient the panels so that both of them have the tweeter sections on the same side. To connect the panels to the audio transformer and the high voltage power supply, go to the section marked "Building a High Voltage Power Supply" in Chapter 12.

DECORATIVE FRAME

Decorative frames for the electrostatic speaker panels have been built in a number of shapes and sizes. The limitations are only necessitated by the desires and skills of the individual builder.

The following steps will indicate one method to make a frame that is more decorative than the one described in the previous section. The decorative frame actually consists of two frames. There is an inner frame that holds the speaker panels, and there is an outer, decorative, frame. The completed frame with the grill cloth removed is shown in Fig. 11-3. If you have not built the utility frame for checking the speaker panels, then build the inner frame first. When finished, it can be used to test the speakers before they are mounted in the finished frame.

The inner frame uses plywood for the sides. Pine is used for the top, bottom, and center dividers. The outer frame is made from oak, but any wood can be substituted for this material.

Fig. 11-3. Photo shows a completed decorative speaker frame with the grill cloth removed.

Inner Frame

The inner frame consists of four parts. The two sides are made from 3/8 inch plywood while the top and bottom are one inch pine. The dimensions are shown in Fig. 11-4.

☐ The first step is to cut the one inch pine for the top, bottom, and center divider. Take three pieces of pine that are 50 inches long and cut them to a width of 3 inches.
☐ Next, measure the width of your speaker panels.
☐ Now, take one of the 50 inch pieces and mark the dimension that is equal to the speakers width plus 1/16 of an inch.
☐ Place the piece on your saw and cut it to size.
☐ Repeat this process for the other five pieces.
☐ Take a piece of 3/8 inch plywood that is at least 52 inches long and cut four pieces so that they are 3 inches wide.
☐ Before cutting the side pieces to length, measure the length of your speaker panels.

In the last step, be sure to measure all four frames. Take the longest one and add 1/16 of an inch to its measured value. When you have this dimension, double it, and add 3 inches. This is the required length of the inner side piece. As a check, this dimension should be approximately 51 1/8 inches.

☐ When you have the exact length, cut each of the plywood sides to this dimension.
☐ Take one of the side pieces and measure in from the end 4 inches. Place a mark at this point.
☐ Starting from this mark, continue measuring along the length and place a mark every 8 inches.
☐ Take a square and draw a line across the board at each of the above marks.
☐ Measure in 1/2 inch from the side. Place a mark at each end of the board.
☐ Repeat this last step on the other edge of this same piece.
☐ Draw a line between the two marks. This line is parallel to the length of the piece.
☐ Repeat this step for the two marks on the opposite edge of this board.

☐ Take the four side pieces and place them together. The one with the lines must be on top.
☐ Align all of the edges and then clamp them together.
☐ Take a 1/16 inch bit and drill holes at each of the marks in the top piece. Drill through all four side pieces.
☐ Use a #8 wood bit and drill out all of the 1/16 inch holes. Countersink the hole so that the screw head will be flush with the surface of the side.
☐ Separate the pieces and clean off the burrs around the holes.

When you reach this point you are ready to assemble the inner frames.

☐ Take two 1 1/2 inch finish nails and drive them into one end of a side until the point begins to protrude. Place the two nails 3/8 of an inch from the end and 3/4 of an inch from each side.
☐ Take two more nails and repeat this last step for the other end of this board. Locate these nails 1 1/8 inches from the bottom edge of the frame.
☐ When you have completed putting the nails in the first board, continue with the same procedure and put nails in all of the other side pieces.
☐ Take one of the pieces and turn it over so that you are looking at the pointed ends of the nails. Apply some white glue to this end. Spread it evenly over the protruding nails.
☐ Take a top piece and place it at the top end of the side. The two pieces should be at right angles to each other and the shorter piece should be located over the spot where the glue has been applied. Be sure that all of the sides are flush with each other.
☐ When the two pieces are aligned, drive the nails down until the heads are flush with the surface of the board.
☐ After you have completed this last step, repeat the gluing procedure for attaching the other side to this top piece.
☐ Measure up 3/4 of an inch from the bottom. Draw a line across both side pieces at this location.

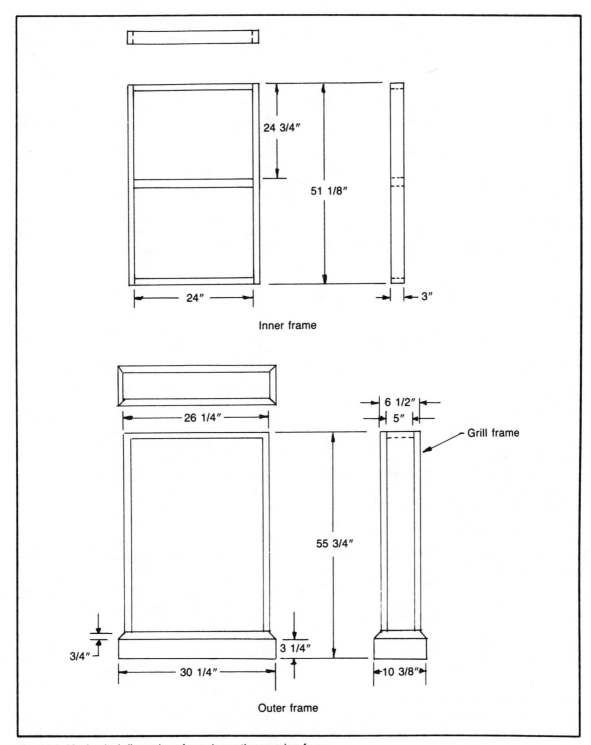

Inner frame

Grill frame

Outer frame

Fig. 11-4. Mechanical dimensions for a decorative speaker frame.

- [ ] Apply some glue over the nails protruding from the 1 1/8 inch dimension.
- [ ] Take one of the bottom pieces and align its bottom edge with the line drawn across the inside of the two side pieces.
- [ ] After aligning the pieces, drive the nails down until they are flush with the sides.

You should now have one frame nailed and glued to a pair of top and bottom pieces. The four pieces should form a box, and the sides should extend 3/4 of an inch beyond the bottom piece.

- [ ] Take the remaining two sides and two more top and bottom pieces and follow the same procedure for nailing and gluing them together.

After assembling both frames, the last step is to put the divider in place.

- [ ] Take one of the frames and lay it flat on your work surface. If that isn't large enough, then lay it on the floor.
- [ ] Next, measure the length of one of your speaker panels.
- [ ] Add 1/16 of an inch to this dimension.
- [ ] Measure the distance down the inside of the frame.
- [ ] Do this last step for the other side of this same frame.
- [ ] Repeat the procedure for the other frame.
- [ ] Take one of the remaining top/bottom pieces and place it between the two sides.
- [ ] Align the top side of this divider with the mark that was just made on each side of the frame.
- [ ] Take a pipe clamp and clamp the sides and the divider together.
- [ ] Turn the frame over and place the largest speaker panel inside the top square.
- [ ] Take one of the other speaker panels and lay it inside the lower square.

If you cannot fit both speaker panels into the frame, you will need to determine the cause and then correct it. When both panels fit, the next step is to nail the center divider in place.

- [ ] Remove the speaker panels from the frame.
- [ ] Use two 1 1/2 inch finish nails. Place them on the outside of the frame opposite the divider. Locate them 3/4 of an inch from the edge.
- [ ] Drive each nail down until the head is flush with the surface of the frame.
- [ ] Repeat this nailing procedure for the other side of this same frame.
- [ ] Take the other frame and follow the same procedure for locating the center divider.

Component Board

This board is placed on the bottom of the inner frame. It is used to mount the audio transformer and the high voltage power supply.

- [ ] Cut a piece of 1 inch pine so that it fits between the bottom edge of the two side pieces. Its width should be 5 inches.
- [ ] Before you mount this piece, place the audio transformer on one side and mark the location of its mounting holes.
- [ ] Do the same thing for the high voltage transformer, but locate it on the opposite side of this board.
- [ ] At each of the audio transformer mounting hole locations, drill a 1/16 inch hole.
- [ ] Countersink the top of the board for 10/32 "T" nuts. Do this for only the audio transformer.
- [ ] After the holes are countersunk, drill them out with a 1/4 inch bit.
- [ ] Put the "T" nuts in place in each of the mounting holes.
- [ ] Take the component board and place it between the two sides. This piece should protrude 2 inches on either side of the inner frame.
- [ ] Use 1 1/2 inch finish nails to nail the component board into its location on the bottom side of the inner frame.
- [ ] Repeat the above steps for the component board on the other frame.
- [ ] Insert each of the speaker panels into the appropriate squares of the frame. Use 3/4 inch #8 wood screws to fasten them in place.
- [ ] When you have the one set of panels in place, continue and screw the remaining speaker panels to the frame.

At this point, you should have two inner frames assembled. Each frame should also contain a pair of speaker panels. The next step is to make the outside or finished frame.

OUTER FRAME

The outer frame consists of a base, two sides, a top, and some decorative molding that goes around the base. When the frame is finished the inner frame should slide inside of the outer frame. The outer frame dimensions are shown, along with the inner frame in Fig. 11-4.

Base

The first step in building the finish frame is to build a base. The base consists of several different pieces. They can, however, be separated into two groups according to their purpose.

The drawing of Fig. 11-5 shows the basic form for the base. It is a rectangular box. After the molding is installed, it will not be visible. Because of this, it is made from 1 inch pine.

The second set of parts is made from sections of decorative moldings. This material can be purchased at your local lumber company. It comes in a variety of shapes and sizes so you can customize the look of your speaker system.

☐ To start building the base, cut four pieces of 1 inch pine so that their dimensions are 3 1/8 × 28 inches.

☐ Cut another four pieces of the same material so that there are 8 pieces 6 11/16 inches long.

☐ Take 4 of these later pieces and cut them so that their width is 2 1/4 inches.

☐ Take one of the 28 inch pieces and place a mark 3/8 of an inch from each end.

☐ Take a square and draw a set of lines across the width at the 3/8 inch mark. This line should be parallel to the end of the board.

☐ Next, place another set of marks on the end of the board. These marks should intersect the line drawn in the previous step, and should be located one inch from each side.

☐ Repeat the last steps for the other end of this same board.

☐ Measure down 9 3/4 inches from the end. Place a mark at this point.

☐ Measure down 14 3/4 inches and place a similar mark at this point.

☐ Use a square and draw a set of lines across the board at each of the marks. The lines should be at right angles to the side of the board.

☐ Measure in from the side of the board 3/8 of an inch. Do this at each end of the board.

☐ Draw a line parallel to the 28 inch length so that it connects the two marks together.

☐ Take the piece with all of the lines and clamp it to one of the other long pieces. Be sure to align all of the ends as well as the sides.

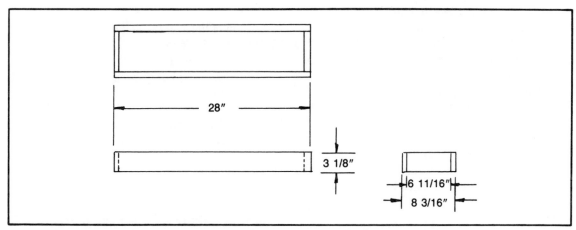

Fig. 11-5. Mechanical dimensions for the base of the decorative speaker frame.

- [ ] Take a 1/16 inch diameter bit and drill a hole at the intersection of each line. Be sure the holes are straight and that they go through both boards.
- [ ] Unclamp both boards and lay the second one aside.
- [ ] Take one of the other long boards and clamp it to the first board. Again be sure to align all of the sides and edges.
- [ ] Using the holes in the first board as a guide, drill these same set of holes in this next board.
- [ ] When you have completed this last step, unclamp the board and then repeat the last two steps for the remaining 28 inch board.

After all of the boards have 1/16 inch holes at each of the locations shown in Fig. 11-6, the next step is to drill out the holes with a wood bit.

- [ ] Take a #8 wood bit with a pilot point, and drill out the 1/16 inch holes. Countersink each hole so that the screw head will be flush or slightly below the surface.
- [ ] Lay the 28 inch pieces aside.
- [ ] Take one of the 6 11/16 inch pieces and place a mark on each end that is 1 1/8 inches from the side.
- [ ] With a straight edge, draw a line that connects the two marks together.
- [ ] Now place a pair of marks so that they are located 1 1/2 inches from each end. The marks should intersect the above lines.
- [ ] Clamp this board to another short board. Be sure the sides and end are parallel.
- [ ] Drill two 1/16 inch diameter holes at each of the 1 1/2 inch intersections.
- [ ] Remove the second board.
- [ ] Take another short board and clamp it to the first one.
- [ ] Repeat the drilling process for this board.
- [ ] Take the last short board and repeat the drilling operation for this piece.
- [ ] After all of the boards have been drilled with a 1/16 inch bit, use a #10 wood bit to enlarge the holes.

This completes all of the cutting and drilling

operations on the base. The next group of steps will assemble them into a frame.

- [ ] Take one of the long pieces and place it against the end of a short one.

The two pieces should be at right angles to each other. The short piece should be in back of the screw holes located on the end of the long piece. The countersunk holes on each board should be facing outwards.

- [ ] Clamp the two boards together.
- [ ] Take a #8 wood bit with a pilot point, and drill a guide hole into the end of the short board. The countersunk holes located on the end of the long board will be your guide.
- [ ] After drilling the two holes, unclamp the two boards.
- [ ] Apply some glue to the end of the short board.
- [ ] Screw the long board to the short one using 1 1/2 inch #8 wood screws.
- [ ] Repeat these last six steps for the short board that will be located on the other end of this same long board.

The next step is to screw the remaining long board to the other side of the two short ones. This will then make a rectangular box.

- [ ] Take one of the remaining long pieces and clamp it to the ends of the above two short pieces.
- [ ] Drill pilot holes in the end of each short board.
- [ ] Unclamp the long board and apply glue to the ends of the short board.
- [ ] Screw the long board back in place on top of the short ones.

When you have completed all of the above steps, you will have one of the base frames completed.

- [ ] Repeat all of these steps for assembling the other base frame.

The next set of steps is to make the vertical portion of the decorative frame. As already noted, these parts are made from either oak or some other wood of your choice.

☐ As shown in Fig. 11-6, cut four pieces of one inch oak so that they are 5 × 55 3/4 inches.
☐ Cut two more pieces so that they are 5 × 24 inches.

The following step places a slot down the length of the two side pieces. The slot is used to hold the wires that will be connected to the speaker panels. It is not absolutely necessary to have this groove and, if you do not have a router, you can mount the wires on the inside surface of the vertical sides.

☐ On one of the side pieces, draw a line down the inside center of the board.
☐ Next, measure in from the top end of the board and place a mark 2 inches down from the end. This mark should intersect the line in the middle of the board.
☐ Next measure down 25 3/8 inches and place another mark at this point.
☐ Measure down another 49 3/4 inches and place a mark at this point.
☐ Use a square and draw a pair of lines across the board at each of the last two marks.
☐ Repeat the last five steps for the other three side pieces.
☐ Put the edge guide and a 1/2 inch router bit in your router.

☐ Set the edge guide so that the center of the router bit aligns with the line drawn down the center of the board.
☐ Adjust the depth of the router bit for a 1/4 inch groove.
☐ After you have set the edge guide and the depth of the router bit, place one of the side pieces on your work surface.
☐ Align the center of the router bit with the center line and the mark that was made at the two inch point.
☐ Turn on the router and cut a groove all the way down the inside length of the side.
☐ When you have completed making this groove, go on and make a similar groove in each of the remaining three side pieces.
☐ Take the router and lay it on top of one of the side pieces. Place the bit in the groove and align it with the line at 25 3/8 inches.
☐ Take another board and clamp it to the side so that it butts against the router.
☐ Check the board to make sure it is at right angles to the edge of the side piece.
☐ Turn on the router and cut the groove across the board. This groove should have a length that is 1 1/2 inches on each side of center. Be sure you do not go to the edge of the board.
☐ When you have finished this first cross groove, move the router bit to the line at 49 3/4 inches.
☐ Repeat the last five steps.
☐ After cutting the cross grooves in one side piece, repeat the process for the remaining side pieces.

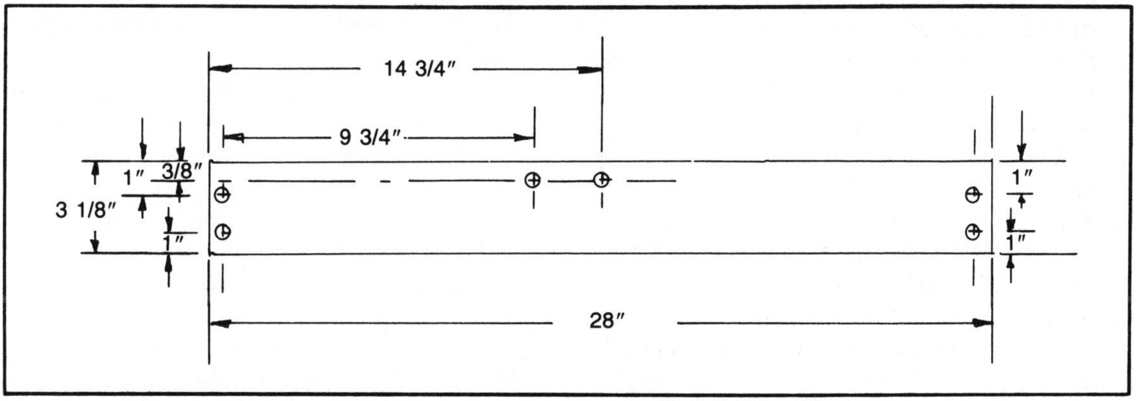

Fig. 11-6. Diagram showing the hole locations in the base of the decorative speaker frame.

In the next group of steps, the finished frame part will be assembled to the base.

☐ Take one of the base assemblies and turn it upside down.

☐ Measure and mark the width of your base. Do this on both end pieces.

☐ Take one of the sides and place a mark on the bottom end so that it is one-half of the board's width.

☐ After you have drawn the center lines on both the base and a side, place them together so that the center lines are aligned.

The vertical side piece should be on the inside of the base.

☐ Clamp the side and the base together.

☐ Take a carpenter square and place it against the side and on top edge of the base.

☐ Adjust the side so that it is at right angles to the base.

☐ Check the two center lines to make sure they are still aligned. If they are not, adjust the side until they are aligned. Then recheck the side to make sure it is still at right angles to the base.

☐ When the two lines are centered and the side is perpendicular to the base tighten the clamps.

☐ Take a #10 wood bit with a pilot drill, and drill two guide holes in the side. Use the screw holes in the sides of the base as a guide.

☐ After drilling the two pilot holes, use 1 1/4 inch #10 wood screws to fasten the side piece to the base.

☐ Repeat the last nine steps for mounting the opposite vertical side to this base.

☐ When you have the two side pieces screwed to one of the bases, repeat the required steps and fasten the other two side pieces to the remaining base.

☐ Take one of the top pieces and place it between the sides of the decorative frame. Use a large pipe clamp to hold the pieces in position.

☐ Check the top piece for fit. If everything aligns and the joints are tight, then take one of the inner frames and place it inside the decorative frame. Be sure this piece fits before going on to the next step.

☐ Remove the inner frame and the pipe clamp.

☐ Take the top piece and put some glue on each of the ends. Make a nice even coat, but do not use too much.

☐ Now place the piece between the two end pieces and after aligning it with the sides, clamp it in place.

☐ After the glue has dried, remove the clamp.

☐ Repeat the previous steps for mounting the top piece between the two side pieces of the second speaker frame.

Now that the two speaker frames have been assembled, the finished parts can be sanded.

It is not within the scope of this book to described how furniture is finished. For sanding and staining operations, the reader should consult one of the many books on furniture finishing.

After sanding the top and sides, the next step is to cut and assemble the molding that goes around the base. The molding is actually in two parts. A large 3 1/8 inch piece on the bottom and a smaller piece that is 3/4 inches on top.

☐ Take one of the wider pieces of molding and mark its length so that it is 30 1/4 inches long.

☐ After marking it, cut it to this size.

☐ Repeat these last two steps for three more pieces.

☐ Take one of the pieces of molding and place it against one of the sides of the base.

☐ Center the molding so that it protrudes the same amount on each side of the base.

☐ Mark both ends of the molding next to the edge of the base.

☐ Place the molding in a miter box. Align the saw blade so that it makes a 45 degree angle between the end of the molding and the line that was drawn on the back side.

☐ After the angle has been set, then cut the beveled edge of the molding.

☐ Take one of the other long pieces of molding, and cut the same bevel. The two pieces will be for one of the bases.

- ☐ To cut the other end of the above two pieces, turn them end for end and upside down.
- ☐ The same bevel can now be cut in the opposite ends of the two long pieces.
- ☐ Repeat the above procedure for cutting the beveled part on the moldings for the other base.
- ☐ Now take two of the long pieces of molding and place them against the base. Align the inside edge of the bevel so that it is flush with the end of the base.
- ☐ Clamp the molding in place. Be sure to put another block in front of the molding so that the clamp doesn't leave a mark on the front of the molding.
- ☐ Next, take another section of molding and cut four pieces so that each one is 10 1/2 inches long. Use your table saw for this operation. You do not want to disturb the settings on the miter saw.

Before cutting the bevels on the end of the base molding, it is a good idea to make a test cut on a scrap piece of molding.

- ☐ Take a short piece of scrap molding and cut a bevel in one end.
- ☐ Place the test cut against the base and butt the two beveled cuts together.
- ☐ They should align without any cracks at their common joint. If this is what you have, then proceed to cut bevels on one side of all four pieces.
- ☐ Next, turn the pieces end for end and cut the same bevels in the opposite ends.
- ☐ Now take one of the short pieces and place it between the two long pieces. With the back side against the base, the beveled sides should all align. If they fit, then continue to the next step. If it doesn't, then make the necessary adjustments until it does.
- ☐ After the side pieces fit, apply some glue along the back side. Do not put any glue on the bevels.
- ☐ Use a clamp to hold the molding against the base.
- ☐ Repeat the last two steps for the other three short pieces of molding.
- ☐ Take a piece of 1/8 inch masonite or plywood,

and cut it so that it is 5 7/8 × 6 11/16 inches.
- ☐ On the 5 7/8 inch side, measure in from the end one inch.
- ☐ Draw a line across the piece so that it is parallel to the 5 7/8 inch dimension.
- ☐ Now divide the 5 7/8 inch dimension in half.
- ☐ Draw a line across the piece at this dimension. This line should be parallel to the 6 3/4 inch dimension.
- ☐ Where the two lines intersect, place a mark on each side of the center line. The marks are to be located 3/8 of an inch on either side.
- ☐ At both of the marks, drill a 3/8 inch hole. These holes are for mounting the terminals for the audio connections to the transformer.
- ☐ Now glue the masonite to the sides of the two 2 1/4 × 6 11/16 inch pieces. The two boards should be parallel to the 6 11/16 inch dimension of the masonite.
- ☐ When this is done, take this assembly and glue it in place between the two long sides of the base. The two boards should align with the marks at 9 3/4 and 14 3/4 inches.
- ☐ After the audio panel is in place, take one of the long pieces of molding and apply glue along the back and on each of the beveled surfaces. Smooth the glue so there is a nice even coating.
- ☐ Put the piece of molding in place on the base. Use clamps to hold it in place while the glue dries.
- ☐ Repeat the last two steps and glue the other long pieces of molding.
- ☐ After the glue has dried, the clamps can be removed.

In the next set of steps, the remaining pieces of molding will be cut and glued together.

- ☐ Take a piece of 3/4 inch molding and cut it so that it is 28 1/2 inches long.
- ☐ Repeat this last step three times.
- ☐ Take two of these long pieces and place them in the miter box. Cut each of the corners so that they have a 45 degree angle.
- ☐ Place one of the pieces that was just cut on the top edge of the base.

It should be as long as the base and the 45 degree angle should coincide with the ends of the base.

- [ ] If this is what you have, take three small wire brads and drive them into the top of the molding. Drive them down so that the points are just protruding.
- [ ] Apply some glue to the bottom side of this piece of molding. Again smooth the glue so there is a nice even coating.
- [ ] Replace the piece on top of the base, and after aligning it, drive the nails down a little further. Do not drive them all the way down because they will be removed after the glue has dried.
- [ ] Repeat the last four steps for the other long pieces of molding.
- [ ] Take another section of this molding and cut it so that it has a length of 8 3/4 inches.
- [ ] Repeat this last step three more times.
- [ ] On each one of the short pieces, cut a 45 degree angle on each end.
- [ ] Take one of the short pieces and place it in position on the top side of the base. This part goes against the vertical side of the frame.

The two 45 degree angles on each end should butt against the corresponding angles on the long pieces. There should not be any cracks between the two pieces.

- [ ] If your piece fits properly, then drive two wire nails into the top of this molding. Again, drive it down until the nails just protrude out the bottom.
- [ ] Apply glue over the bottom surface. This is the one with the brads protruding.
- [ ] Also coat each end of the 45 degree corners and apply some glue on the back of this piece.
- [ ] Put the piece in position and drive the nails down so that they hold the piece against the base and the ends of the other two pieces of molding. Be sure to leave some of the nails sticking out so that they can be removed.
- [ ] Repeat the last six steps for the other short pieces of molding.
- [ ] When all of the glue has dried, remove all of the wire brads.

- [ ] Sand all of the moldings so that they are smooth. On those pieces that have holes from the wire brads, place a little glue in the hole before you sand. The sanding operation will fill up the holes with dust and it will no longer be visible.

At this point, you should finish the frame. Apply a stain to the vertical pieces, the top, and the molding around the base.

The next step is to put the wires in the grooves that run down the inside center of the frame.

- [ ] Cut six pieces of high voltage test lead wire so that each is 40 inches long.
- [ ] Take two of these pieces and place them in the center groove so that they come out the top cross grooves. One wire should come out each side of the cross groove. Use either a small staple or masking tape to hold the wire in place.
- [ ] Put another one of the other long pieces in the groove on the opposite side of the frame. Check your speaker panels. This wire is the connection for the diaphragm.
- [ ] Take the remaining three wires and install them in the other frame. The wire locations on this speaker should be opposite to the one that you just did.
- [ ] Cut six more pieces of this same wire so that their lengths are 10 inches each.
- [ ] Using the same principle that you did on the first group of wires, place them in the center grooves. In this case, bring them out the lower cross grooves.
- [ ] Install the single wire on the opposite side of the frame. This wire will be the high voltage connection to the lower speaker panel.
- [ ] Repeat the above two steps for the wires that will be located in the other frame.
- [ ] When all of the wires are in place, you can mount the inner frame on the inside of the decorative frame.
- [ ] Align the inner frame so that it is centered between the edges of the decorative frame.
- [ ] Use #8 sheet metal screws to hold the inner frame to the inside of the decorative frame.

The screws that hold the inner frame in place go through the holes that run down the length of the inner frame.

Electrical Connections

After the inner frame has been fastened in place, the wires can be connected to the speaker panels. The side that has the single wire is the high voltage connection for the diaphragm.

☐ Put a crimp-on lug on the end of the wire and then place it on the screw that protrudes from the frame. This screw is the high voltage connection for the diaphragm.
☐ Put both a flat and a lock washer on top of the lug and then put a 6/32 nut on the screw.
☐ Tighten down the nut. Do not over tighten, you do not want the screw to turn.
☐ Repeat the last three steps for the single protruding wire that is the connection to the lower diaphragm.
☐ When the high voltage wires have been connected the next step is to connect the audio leads. On the speaker panel, solder the wire to the terminal lug that is connected to all the equalizing resistors.

When you have finished connecting all of the audio leads, the next step is to mount the parts for the polarizing voltage and the audio transformer. Refer to the section "Building a High Voltage Power Supply" in Chapter 12 for this material. The power supply components are mounted on the component board on the bottom of the speaker.

☐ Solder two leads to the primary winding of the transformer.
☐ Mount the transformer on the bottom of the component board.
☐ Put one of the wires through each of the holes in the masonite audio board.
☐ Take two GR type terminals and place them in each of the holes in the masonite. Then solder the transformer wires to these terminals.

This completes the work on the speaker except for the grill panels that go over the front and rear

of the speaker. At this point, your speaker should be operational and should look like Fig. 11-3.

Grill

The following steps will describe a procedure for making a suitable grill to cover the front and rear sides of the speaker.

☐ Take a piece of 1 inch pine that is a least 56 inches long and cut it into 3/4 inch wide strips. You will need at least 14 strips.
☐ To make the side pieces of the grill, cut 8 pieces so that they are each 53 inches long.
☐ For the top, bottom, and middle support, cut 12 pieces so that each one is 24 7/8 inches long.
☐ Use a set of picture frame clamps to glue two long and short pieces together. They should form a rectangle that is 24 7/8 × 53 inches.
☐ Repeat these last three steps three more times.
☐ Next, measure and mark the point that is 1/2 of the length.
☐ Now, glue the center divider at this position. Use the picture frame clamps to hold the divider in position until the glue dries.
☐ Repeat this last step for the other three frames.

The following steps are used to make the mounting system for the grills.

☐ After the frame has been made, take one frame and measure down from the top six inches. Place a mark on the side of the frame at this point.
☐ Now measure in from each side two inches. Place a mark on the top side of the frame at these points.
☐ At each of the marks, measure in 3/8 of an inch and place another mark so that it intersects the first mark.
☐ Now measure down 26 inches from the top and repeat the procedure for locating the above marks.
☐ Repeat the required steps for the other three frames.
☐ When all of the above marks have been made, take another frame and clamp it to the back side

Fig. 11-7. The completed speaker and the grill cloth panels.

of this first frame. Be sure the top, bottom, and sides are all aligned.

□ Now, take a 1/16 inch bit and drill a pilot hole through both frames at the intersection of all the marks. Be sure the holes are straight.

□ Repeat the last two steps by successively clamping each of the other two frames to the first one.

□ Take one of the frames and clamp it to the front of the decorative frame. Align the top and sides of the grill frame with those of the decorative frame. The bottom of the grill should fit inside the molding that is around the base.

□ After aligning the top and sides, drill a 1/16 inch hole in the decorative frame.

□ Place a mark on the inside of the decorative frame and on the grill frame. The mark should identify the grill and the side of the decorative frame as matching pairs. Do not put the mark on the front side of the grill frame. It will be covered by the grill cloth.

□ Repeat the mounting, drilling, and identification process for the remaining three grill frames and the remaining decorative frame.

In the following steps, two slightly different size holes will be drilled in the grill frame and the decorative frame. The larger hole will be in the decorative frame. This will provide the ability to remove the decorative grill.

□ Take a 1/4 inch bit and bore the 1/16 inch holes on the inside of the grill frame until they are 1/2 inch deep.

□ Repeat this last step for all of the grill frames.

□ Now take a 17/64 inch bit and bore out the 1/16 inch holes in each of the decorative frames. These holes should also be 1/2 inch deep.

Grill Cloth

Grill cloth comes in a variety of sizes, colors and materials. Although many electronic supply houses have a limited supply of the plastic material, I have found that a visit to a fabric store can be very rewarding. When looking through the many racks of materials, keep in mind that you want a type that you can see through. There is a variety of this type of material, but you do not want it to

be too open. One technique that I found for judging the openness is to put your hand behind the material. If you can see the shadow of your hand, but cannot make out any details, then the material has about the right texture.

□ Once the material has been selected, take a piece that is larger than the speaker frame and lay it on a large flat clean work surface.

□ Lay one of the grill frames on top of it with the holes that were just bored face up.

□ Measure out from the frame 1 1/2 inches on all sides and draw a line around the edge of the frame at this point. Use a marking pen to make the lines.

□ After marking the cloth, take scissors and cut the material on the lines.

□ Replace the material on your clean work surface. Smooth out any wrinkles in the material.

□ Again lay the frame on top of the cloth. Be sure to center the frame so that you again have 1 1/2 inches of material on each side.

□ Starting at one side, fold the material over on the back side of the frame.

□ Take a stapler and staple the grill cloth to the rear of the frames.

□ When you have one side stapled, continue and do all of the other three sides.

As you work on the opposite sides from those that have been stapled, apply a little tension to the grill cloth. You do not have to pull too hard, just enough to get the wrinkles out and make the cloth tight.

□ When you have finished the first frame, use the same procedure and do the other three frames.

□ Now take the ratchet fasteners and insert one into each of the holes in the grill frame.

□ When you have all of the inserts in place, you should be able to put the grill cloth frame on the front of the decorative frame. The inserts should align with the holes in the edge of the decorative frame.

At this point, you should have finished the speaker and you can now sit back and listen to the outstanding music. The completed speaker should look like Fig. 11-7.

Chapter 12

Electronics For Electrostatic Speakers

The electronics for an electrostatic speaker is divided into three categories. These are shown in the block diagram of Fig. 12-1. For the speaker builder who is only interested in duplicating the speakers described in this book, the components of interest are the transformer and the high voltage power supply. To interface these components to the speaker, proceed to the "High Voltage Power Supply" section of this chapter.

TRANSFORMERS

A transformer for an electrostatic speaker serves two purposes. First, it takes the voltage from the output from an audio amplifier and increases its value so that it can deflect the diaphragm by the required amount. Second, it takes the high impedance of the speaker (See Chapter 4) and reduces its value to one that is compatible with the output of the amplifiers.

How it achieves these two functions will be described in the following material. With an understanding of this material, the reader should be able to select and evaluate transformers for his own speaker projects.

Turns Ratio

One of the first and most important factors needed in specifying a transformer for an electrostatic speaker is the turns ratio. A better understanding of this term will be obtained by using the diagram of Fig. 12-2 and the following explanation.

As shown in Fig. 12-2A, one winding, the primary, is connected to a source of alternating voltage. The construction of this winding is very similar to the voice coil that was explained in Chapter 2. The number of turns in the primary winding is designated as n1.

The current created by the ac source flows in the primary winding and it produces magnetic lines. The lines pass through a magnetic material, the core, and are linked to another winding, the secondary. If the two windings have an equal number of turns, then the voltage that appears across the secondary winding will be equal to the voltage on

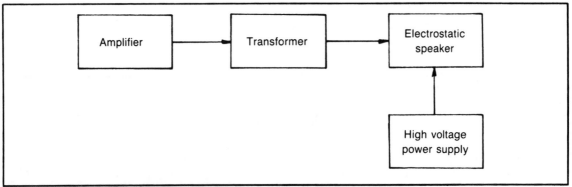

Fig. 12-1. Block diagram of the electronics for an electrostatic speaker.

the primary winding. This condition exists because most transformers are very close to 100% efficiency. The number of turns in the secondary winding is designated as n2.

A transformer can have either a greater or a lesser number of turns on the secondary winding. For an electrostatic speaker, the secondary must have more turns than the primary winding. This requirement is necessary because the output voltage from most amplifiers is significantly less than the value required by the speaker.

Usually an amplifier output voltage will not exceed 200 volts. The ac voltage needed to operate a speaker is often between 1000 and 5000 volts. The transformer must increase the amplifier voltage so that it is compatible with the requirements of the speaker. Suppose, as an example, an amplifier has a maximum output voltage of 100 volts. If the electrostatic speaker requires a maximum voltage of 5000 volts, the ratio of these two numbers will determine the required transformer turns ratio. That is:

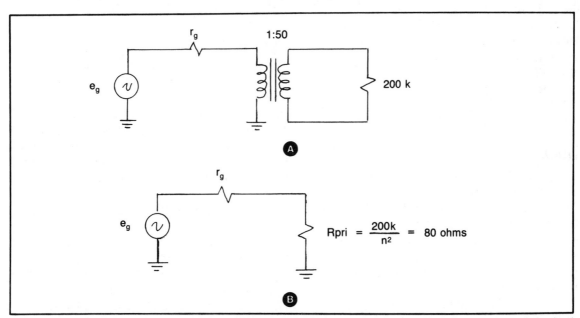

Fig. 12-2. Diagram (A) shows a step-up transformer and a resistive load. Diagram (B) indicates how the resistive load is reflected to the primary winding of the transformer.

$v2/v1 = n2/n1$
Where
   $v2$ = the voltage across the secondary winding.
   $v1$ = the voltage across the primary winding.
   $n2$ = the number of turns in the secondary winding.
   $n1$ = the number of turns in the primary winding.

In most instances, the actual number of turns in each winding is not known. The number of physical turns is not important. As indicated, the most meaningful term is the turns ratio. This ratio is equal to a number "n."

In the above example, the voltage required on the secondary of the transformer was 5000 volts. This value must occur when the primary voltage is 100 volts. The turns ratio "n" of the transformer is equal to:

$$n = n2/n1 = v2/v1$$
$$= 5000/100$$
$$= 50/1$$

This ratio indicates that, for every volt applied to the primary winding, 50 volts will appear across the terminals of the secondary winding.

Current Ratio

As the old saying goes, "Nothing in this world is free," and this same principle holds true for transformers. Although the value of the voltage has been increased, the current in the secondary winding has been reduced. Ohm's Law states that the current in an electrical circuit is equal to the voltage divided by the resistance. That is:

$$I = V/R$$
Where I = the current flow in amperes.
   V = the voltage in volts.
   R = the resistance in ohms.

In a transformer circuit, the current flowing through the load is equal to the secondary voltage divided by the load resistance. For the diagram shown in Fig. 12-2A, the load resistance is 200 kohms. This makes the secondary current equal to:

$I_{sec} = V_{sec}/R_{load}$
Where
   I_{sec} = the current flowing in the secondary winding.
   V_{sec} = the voltage across the secondary winding.
   R_{load} = the value of the load resistance.
      = 5000/200,000
      = 0.025 amps

To determine the current flowing in the primary winding, it is important to remember that the power output of a transformer cannot be greater than its input power. For a resistive circuit, this value is equal to the product of the voltage and current. Applying this rule to the circuit of Fig. 12-2A makes the power in the secondary circuit equal to:

$$P_{sec} = V_{sec} \times I_{sec}$$
$$= 5000 \times 0.025$$
$$= 125 \text{ watts}$$

To determine the primary current, it is only necessary to remember that the power being dissipated in the load must come from the input. Therefore, the source must be producing the 125 watts of power. The current in the primary winding can be determined by rearranging the power formula. The current in the primary circuit is:

$I_{pri} = P_{pri}/V_{pri}$
Where
   I_{pri} = the current flowing in the primary winding.
   P_{pri} = the power being supplied by the source.
   V_{pri} = the voltage across the primary terminals.

For the previous example, the current in the primary winding equals:

$$I_{pri} = 125/100$$
$$= 1.25 \text{ amps}$$

With this calculation, the relationship between the primary and secondary currents of a step-up transformer is established. The associated mathematics is shown below.

$$I_{sec}/I_{pri} = n1/n2 = n$$

In addition to the ratio, an important factor to note is that the number of turns is the inverse of the primary and secondary turns.

Impedance Ratio

Another factor of significant importance is the reflected primary load impedance. This value can be determined in one of two ways. First, if the primary voltage and current are known, the equivalent primary impedance can be obtained. This value is equal to the primary voltage divided by the primary current. That is:

$$Z_{pri} = V_{pri}/I_{pri}$$
$$= 100/1.25$$
$$= 80 \text{ ohms}$$

Where Z_{pri} = the reflected primary impedance.

The second method uses the turns ratio of the transformer to determine the reflected impedance. The impedance on the primary winding is a function of the square of the turns ratio. That is:

$$Z_{sec}/Z_{pri} = (n2/n1)^2 = n^2$$

Using the turns ratio from the above example together with the secondary impedance (200 kohms), the following result will be obtained.

$$Z_{pri} = Z_{sec}/(n)^2$$
$$= 200,000/(50)^2$$
$$= 80 \text{ ohms.}$$

The above material should provide a basic understanding on how a step-up transformer functions. In addition to the turns ratio, another transformer characteristic that is important is the frequency response.

TRANSFORMER FREQUENCY RESPONSE

A transformer has both a low and a high frequency limit. If the input frequency is beyond either of these limits, the transformer performance will not agree with the above calculations. To determine these limits, transformer frequency response is divided into three parts. An electrical model is then used to predict the transformer performance in each of the parts. The model usually reflects all the secondary elements to the primary winding. For the circuit of 12-2A, the model with the reflected values is shown in 12-2B.

The frequency analysis usually begins in an area called the mid-frequency range. Over the frequency spectrum covered by this area, the transformer is almost ideal and its performance can be predicted by the preceding set of equations. It should be noted that all transformers do not necessarily have the same mid-frequency range. For instance, a transformer used for a bass speaker will have a different mid-range than one that is used for a tweeter.

The diagram of Fig. 12-3A shows a transformer that is connected to a signal source (e_s). The resistance "r_g" is the internal resistance of that source. On the secondary winding, the load is a speaker and the capacity is identified as C_{spkr}. A model of the transformer is shown in Fig. 12-3B. In the mid-frequency range, the only elements that are important are the transformer winding resistances.

The resistor shown as r_p is the resistance of the primary winding. The value of r_s is the secondary winding resistance. In the model, the secondary resistance as well as the load capacity are referred to the primary circuit. To reflect the secondary resistance to the primary winding, its value must be divided by the square of the turns ratio. The speaker capacity, on the other hand, will be multiplied by the turns ratio.

In modern audio amplifiers, the value of r_g is usually less than one ohm, and the primary winding resistance does not usually exceed a few ohms. The secondary winding resistance can be in the range of 50 to 100 ohms. The value is determined by the number of turns and the size of the wire that is used in making this winding. If it is assumed that the resistance of the secondary is 100 ohms and the turns ratio is 50 to 1, the reflected value is 0.04 ohms.

Suppose that the speaker in the above example had a capacity of 500 picofarads. Multiplying this number by the square of the turns ratio makes

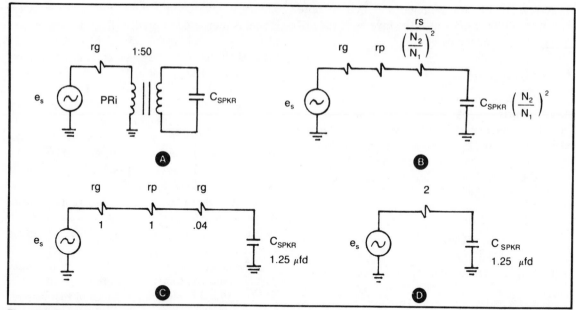

Fig. 12-3. Diagram (A) is a step-up transformer with a Capacitive Load. Diagrams (B), (C), and (D) are equivalent circuits that have been reflected to the primary winding.

the capacity, referred to the primary winding, equal to 1.25 microfarads. The circuit diagram shown in Fig. 12-3C reflects the above calculations. All of the resistance (r_g, r_p, and r_s) in this diagram can be added together. If the value of r_g and r_p were each one ohm, an equivalent circuit would be like the one shown in Fig. 12-3D. People who are familiar with electronic circuits should recognize this as a low pass filter.

The frequency response of this circuit will drop to -3 dB at a point where the impedance of the capacitor is equal to the value of the resistance. In this example, the upper frequency limit is 63.6 kHz. This limitation is due to the transformer winding resistance, and is not the main controlling factor. In this case, the performance is a circuit limitation. The following material will indicate how the transformer characteristics limit the total frequency response.

Low Frequency Transformer Limits

To determine the transformer low frequency limit, the inductance of the primary winding must be known. The low frequency limit can be determined from the circuit shown in Fig. 12-4A. When the value of the primary inductance (L_{pri}) equals the sum of the source resistance and the internal winding resistance, the voltage on the secondary winding will be equal to 0.707 (-3 dB) of the value that it had in the mid-frequency range. The frequency response of a transformer is shown in Fig. 12-4B. For the circuit of Fig. 12-4A, the secondary values are reflected to the primary winding by the turns ratio.

As an example of these calculations, suppose the transformer has a primary inductance of 1.5 milli-henries (0.0015 henries). If the impedance of C_{spkr} is significantly greater than the impedance of the primary inductance, the total value will not be affected by the speaker impedance. With the value of C_{spkr} removed, an equivalent circuit is shown in Fig. 12-5. The frequency where the inductive reactance is equal to the source resistance can be determined by rearranging the formula for the inductive reactance. This is shown below.

$$f = X_L/(6.28 \times L)$$

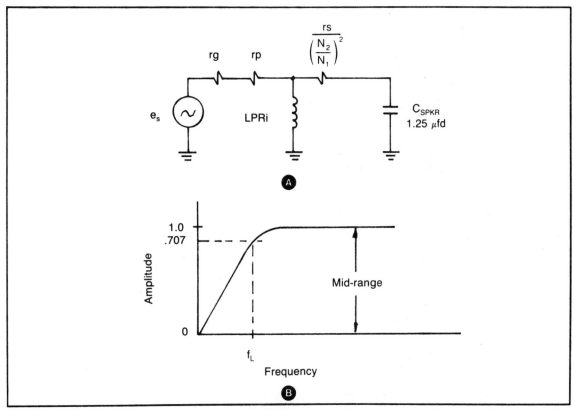

Fig. 12-4. Part (A) is the low frequency equivalent circuit for an electrostatic speaker and the step-up transformer. Part (B) indicates the low frequency response of the circuit shown in (A).

Where X_L = the impedance of the primary inductance.

L = the inductance of the primary winding.

For the circuit of Fig. 12-5, the value of X_L is equal to the sum of the source and the primary

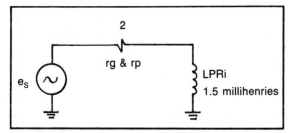

Fig. 12-5. The diagram of Fig. 12.4(A) has been simplified and the resultant low frequency circuit is shown in this diagram.

winding resistances. The low frequency limit is therefore equal to:

$$f = 2/(6.28 \times 1.5 \times 10^{-3})$$
$$= 212 \text{ Hz.}$$

This is the low frequency limit (f_L) of the transformer, and it will cause the voltage on the diagram of Fig. 12-4B to fall by 3 dB.

High Frequency Transformer Limits

The calculation of the high frequency limit is a little more involved than the one for the low frequency. This is because a number of additional factors must be known before the high frequency response can be determined. The circuit shown in Fig. 12-6A indicates some of the components that will affect the transformer high frequency perfor-

169

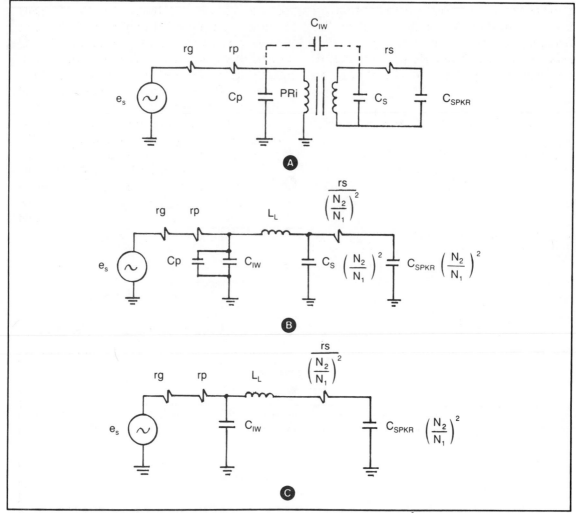

Fig. 12-6. Diagram (A) is the high frequency circuit for the transformer and the speaker capacitor. Diagram (B) is an equivalent circuit that has been reflected to the primary winding, and diagram (C) is a simplified high frequency circuit.

mance. The model shown in Fig. 12-6B is the equivalent circuit with all the values reflected to the primary winding. In this circuit, the unknown elements are the leakage inductance L_L, the interwinding capacity C_{iw}, the value of the secondary winding capacity C_s, and the primary winding capacity C_p.

Following the techniques used for the previous circuits, the diagram of Fig. 12-6B can be simplified. On the secondary, the winding capacitance C_s can be referred to the primary winding. The value of the interwinding capacity C_{iw} can also be moved

so that it also appears across the primary circuit. Because this capacity is between the two windings, it is not multiplied by the turns ratio. When it is placed in the primary circuit, it can be added to the value of C_p and the reflected value of C_s. When these changes are made, the equivalent circuit will be like the one in Fig. 12-6C.

One additional step is necessary to make the transformation complete. In the ideal analysis, it was indicated that all of the lines from the primary winding were linked to the secondary. In actual practice, this is not true. There is always some difference between the lines produced at the primary and those that arrive at the secondary. This difference gives rise to an additional term called the leakage inductance. The leakage inductance, referred to the primary winding, can be calculated by:

$$L_L = 2(1\text{-}k)L_p$$

Where L_p = the inductance of the primary winding.

k = the coefficient of coupling between the two windings.

L_L = the leakage inductance referred to the primary winding.

In the mid-frequency range, the value of "k" is equal to unity. When the frequency is increased, a greater number of lines do not link both windings and the value of "k" decreases. In the model, Fig. 12-6C, the leakage inductance appears in series with the reflected load impedance.

At this point, some additional simplification can be done. For instance, the value of C_{iw} is usually in the range of 100 to 500 nanofarads. If the source and the primary resistance are very low, C_{iw} will appear directly across the source and it will not limit the frequency response to the audible range. Also, the value of the secondary winding resistance will be divided by the turns ratio. This value will also be very low and it can be excluded from the final circuit. When these changes have been made, the equivalent circuit is shown in Fig. 12-7A.

The previous calculation for the speaker capacity provided a value of 1.25 microfarads referred to the primary winding. Suppose, in this circuit, the coefficient of coupling, "k," is 95%. This would make the leakage inductance equal to:

$$
\begin{aligned}
L_L &= 2(1 - 0.95) \times 1.5 \times 10^{-3} \\
&= 2(0.05) \times 1.5 \times 10^{-3} \\
&= 1.5 \times 10^{-4} \text{ henries}
\end{aligned}
$$

The voltage across the speaker will be down to

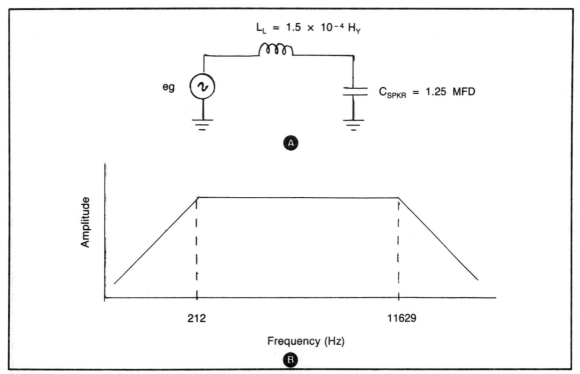

Fig. 12-7. The equivalent high frequency primary circuit with the reflected load impedance and leakage inductance. Diagram (B) is the overall frequency response of the transformer and the speaker.

0.707 when the reflected impedance of the capacitor is equal to the impedance of the leakage inductance. This can be calculated by the following equation.

$$f = 1/6.28(L_L \times C_{spkr})^{1/2}$$
$$= 1/6.28(1.5 \times 10^{-4} \times 1.25 \times 10^{-6})$$
$$= 11,629 \text{ Hz.}$$

This completes the calculations for both the low frequency and the high frequency limits of the transformer. The −3dB points for this example are located at 212 and 11629 Hertz. A graph of the transformers frequency response is shown in Fig. 12-7B.

TRANSFORMER MEASUREMENTS

There are a number of tests that can be made on a transformer to determine its performance characteristics. To perform these tests and evaluate the transformer, only some basic audio test equipment is required. Most of the characteristics mentioned previously can be evaluated by one of the following procedures.

Measuring the Turns Ratio

The first and easiest test to make on a transformer is the turns ratio. The diagram shown in Fig. 12-8 indicates the required test setup. As indicated, connect an audio oscillator to the input of an audio power amplifier. Begin by setting the oscillator frequency to the transformer mid-band frequency. If this point is not known, then use a convenient value like 1 kHz. Now connect the output of the amplifier to the transformer under test (TUT). Connect an ac voltmeter across the primary winding and adjust the oscillator voltage and the gain of the amplifier so that the voltage (v_1) is 1.0 volt. Next, move the voltmeter so that it is connected across the secondary winding.

Before making any actual measurements, adjust the oscillator frequency above and below the reference frequency that was just set. If the frequency can be changed by one octave from the reference value, and the output voltage does not appreciable change, this point is in the mid-frequency range of the transformer. If the reference value is not in the mid-frequency range, change its value until a frequency is located that will provide a stable reading for it and the other frequencies around the central value. Once the reference value has been set, the voltage reading can be recorded. The value of the turns ratio is equal to:

$$n = v_2/v_1$$

In the above setup there is nothing magical about using an input voltage of one volt. This value was chosen because it is large enough so the reading will not be influenced by any electrical noise. Also, if the transformer has a turns ratio that is 100 or 150 times the input, the secondary reading will still be within the range of most measuring instruments.

Primary and Secondary Inductance Measurements

The procedure for determining the primary and

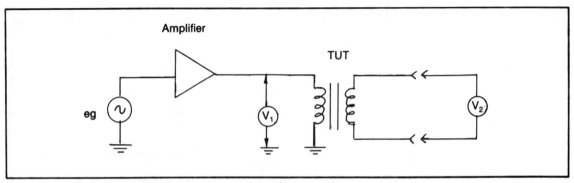

Fig. 12-8. A test method used to determine a transformer's turns ratio.

secondary inductance is the same. The only difference is which winding the instruments are connected to. The following procedure will describe how to determine the value of the primary inductance. To determine the secondary value, move the instruments to the secondary winding and repeat the procedure.

The diagram shown in Fig. 12-9 indicates how the instruments are connected. The starting procedure is the same as the one used to determine the value of the turns ratio. After connecting all of the equipment in the required fashion, set the oscillator to a reference frequency and then move the voltmeter to the secondary winding. Again change the oscillator frequency by plus and minus one octave. If the secondary voltage doesn't make any appreciable changes, the initial frequency is in the mid-frequency range of the transformer. This value can now be used as the reference point. If there is a significant change in the output voltage, change the frequency until a value is reached where the variation does not produce any significant change in the voltage. Once this frequency has been established, the voltmeter should be connected to the primary winding.

After making sure that the voltmeter is still reading one volt, disconnect the transformer and connect a variable resistor in its place. The value of the resistor should be about 100 ohms.

Adjust the resistor until the reading obtained on the voltmeter is the same as the one obtained with the transformer. After obtaining this reading, move the voltmeter to the output of the amplifier and measure the output voltage. With these two values, the unknown resistance can be determined by the following formula.

$$R_2 = (eo \times R_1)/(e_s - e_o)$$
Where R_2 = the value of the variable resistance
R_1 = the value indicated in the diagram
e_o = the voltmeter reading across R_2
e_s = the voltage at the source

The calculated value of R_2 in the above equation is equal to the reactance of the primary inductance. This value is related to the inductance by the following formula.

$$X_L = 6.28 \times f \times L$$

Because X_L is equal to R_2, the formula can be rearranged to determine the value of the inductance.

$$L = X_L/(6.28 \times f)$$

As an example of the above procedure, the value of e_o was 0.255 volts. The source voltage (e_s) was 1.0 volts, and the value of R_1 was 100 ohms. The oscillator frequency was set to 1000 Hz. Using the indicated numbers, the value of R_2 was 34.2 ohms. Substituting this into the equation for the inductance provides the following result.

$$L = 34.2/(6.28 \times 1000)$$
$$= 1.36 \text{ milli henries}$$

This is the primary winding inductance of the trans-

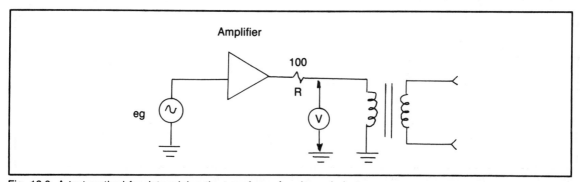

Fig. 12-9. A test method for determining the transformer's primary inductance.

former, and this value can be used to determine the low frequency limit of the transformer. If the secondary winding is connected in place of the primary winding, the same technique can be used to determine its inductance.

Measuring the Leakage Inductance

Previously, it was shown that the value of the leakage inductance can be determined by calculation. Using the test setup shown in Fig. 12-10, this value can also be measured. In this test, it is important that the oscillator frequency is low so that the reading is not affected by any capacity. A convenient value is 100 Hz.

The procedure for this test is the same as the one for determining the value of the inductance. In this case, however, the secondary terminals are shorted together. First, measure the voltage across the winding. Second, replace the transformer with a variable resistor. Adjust its value until the voltmeter equals the value that it read across the transformer. Third, measure the voltage at point "A." Fourth, substitute the measured values into the equation for R_2. Using the calculated value for R_2, substitute it into the equation for the inductance. The value obtained will be the leakage inductance reflected to the primary. If it is desired, the leakage inductance referred to the secondary winding can be performed by reversing the connections.

Measuring the Transformer Winding Capacity

For most electrostatic speaker transformers, the primary capacity is not a significant factor. The value is usually small and so is the source impedance. This combination will make the high end frequency limit outside of the audio range.

The diagram of 12-11 can be used to determine the capacity of a transformer winding. Figure 12-11A is used to measure the capacity of the secondary winding. This setup is similar to the one used to measure the secondary inductance. In this case, however, the oscillator frequency is increased in value until the voltmeter reading decreases to 0.707 of its mid-band value. At this point, the reactance of the winding capacity is equal to the series resistance. The capacity can be calculated by:

$$C_{sec} = (1.59 \times 10^{-1})/(f \times R)$$
Where C_{sec} = the secondary winding capacity
f = the frequency where the voltmeter reads 0.707 of its mid-band value.
R = the series resistance.

A similar technique is also used to determine the interwinding capacity C_{iw}. The electrical circuit is shown in Fig. 12-11B. Usually the primary capacity is much less than the value of C_{iw} and therefore it will not influence this measurement. Adjust the oscillator until the voltmeter reads 0.707 of its mid-band value. The capacity can be calculated according to the above formula.

BUILDING A HIGH VOLTAGE POWER SUPPLY

As already indicated, an electrostatic speaker needs a polarizing voltage. The exact value is a function of the type of speaker. A full-range speaker has a larger spacing between the plate and the diaphragm. It will require more voltage than a

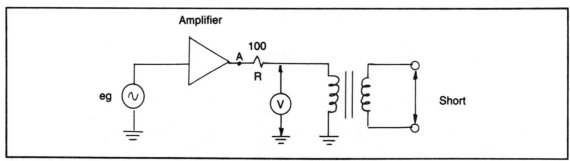

Fig. 12-10. A test method for determining the transformer's leakage inductance.

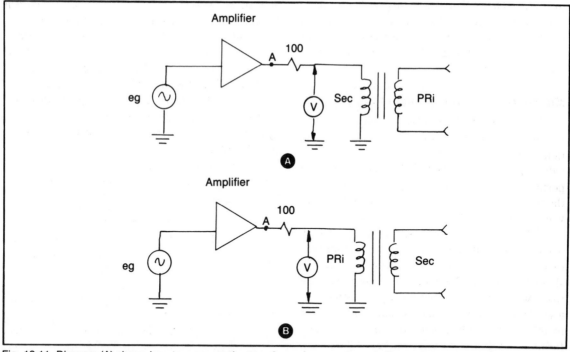

Fig. 12-11. Diagram (A) shows how to measure the transformer's secondary winding resistance, and (B) shows how to determine the transformer's interwinding capacity.

tweeter. The procedure described here is for the full-range speaker described in the preceding chapters. If a power supply for a tweeter is needed, the same procedure can be followed. The only difference will be the value of the transformer secondary voltage.

☐ Set the speakers aside and connect the components shown in Fig. 12-12. The diodes, capacitors, and resistors can be mounted on perforated board. Be sure to keep the ground connection away from the high voltage leads. The high voltage supply provides the bias voltage for two

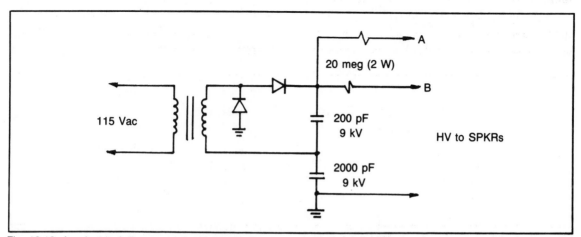

Fig. 12-12. An electrical diagram of the high voltage power supply for the speaker.

speaker panels. One high voltage power supply will be required for each stereo pair.

☐ Next, mount the audio transformer on each frame.

☐ Connect the common of the high voltage power supply to the center tap of the transformer.

☐ Connect a high voltage wire from each of the output resistors on the high voltage power supply to the diaphragm connecting screws on each panel. Use high voltage wire.

☐ Next, connect an insulated high voltage wire from the right side of the diaphragm across the top of the panel to the left side diaphragm connection. This wire should pass through the two 1/4 inch slots in the vertical ribs.

☐ From the upper panel, run a high voltage wire down the opposite side of the frame. At the same time, run a similar wire down from the lower panel. Connect the two wires together, and then solder them to one of the terminals on the audio transformer.

☐ On each of the speaker panels, connect the other end of these wires to the resistor that is connected to the four speaker panels.

☐ Repeat the last two steps for the speaker connections on the opposite side of the panel. Connect the wires to the opposite terminal on the transformer.

☐ On each of the panels, connect the ends of all of the resistors to the connection from the audio transformer.

☐ Repeat this last step for the resistors on the opposite side of the speaker.

☐ Connect the primary winding of the audio transformer to your audio amplifier. Connect the primary side of the high voltage transformer to its appropriate power source.

☐ Turn on your amplifier and slowly increase the audio volume.

The music level should increase with the volume setting. If it does not, turn everything off. Connect the high voltage meter to the center tap of the transformer. Turn the high voltage transformer back on and very carefully, with a high voltage probe, measure the voltage at the diaphragm connection. This voltage should be at least 4500 volts.

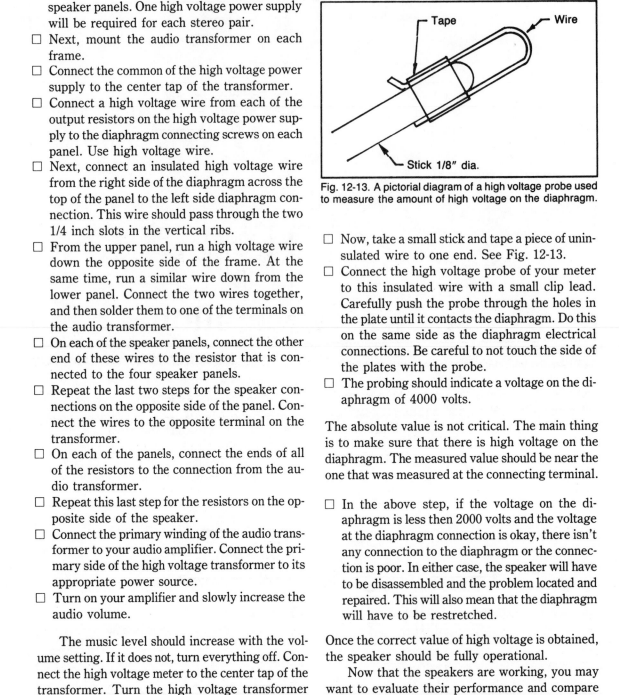

Fig. 12-13. A pictorial diagram of a high voltage probe used to measure the amount of high voltage on the diaphragm.

☐ Now, take a small stick and tape a piece of uninsulated wire to one end. See Fig. 12-13.

☐ Connect the high voltage probe of your meter to this insulated wire with a small clip lead. Carefully push the probe through the holes in the plate until it contacts the diaphragm. Do this on the same side as the diaphragm electrical connections. Be careful to not touch the side of the plates with the probe.

☐ The probing should indicate a voltage on the diaphragm of 4000 volts.

The absolute value is not critical. The main thing is to make sure that there is high voltage on the diaphragm. The measured value should be near the one that was measured at the connecting terminal.

☐ In the above step, if the voltage on the diaphragm is less then 2000 volts and the voltage at the diaphragm connection is okay, there isn't any connection to the diaphragm or the connection is poor. In either case, the speaker will have to be disassembled and the problem located and repaired. This will also mean that the diaphragm will have to be restretched.

Once the correct value of high voltage is obtained, the speaker should be fully operational.

Now that the speakers are working, you may want to evaluate their performance and compare your speaker to those of commercial electrostatic speaker manufacturers. This type of information is contained in the next two chapters.

Chapter 13

Speaker Evaluation

Speaker testing is performed by one of two distinct methods. The procedures can be classified as scientific and subjective. The scientific method uses different types of instruments to measure the speaker performance. The instruments are used to determine the electrical or the acoustical performance of the speaker.

SUBJECTIVE

The subjective evaluation is often performed by trained listeners. The critical factor is how the speaker sounds. The test is conducted by placing the speakers in a listening area. Using a tape recorder or a record player, a variety of musical selections are played. The listeners try to evaluate the speaker performance against some arbitrary "golden standard." Quite frequently, selections or small parts are played many times. The listeners then rate the speaker performance by what they hear or sometimes by what they didn't hear.

In actual practice, this subjective type of evalu-

ation is the easiest to perform. It does not require any special equipment. It does require a variety of musical selections and a good ear for music. The program material can be divided into three parts. For instance, a good organ recording, like Widor's Organ Symphony No.5, can be used to indicate the speaker bass performance. An alternative selection is "Pink Floyd and the Dark Side of the Moon." The first part of this recording has a very low frequency beat tone. The frequency and the beat demonstrate the speakers bass response and its transient capability.

There are a number of recordings that can be used for high frequency evaluation. The "Pines of Rome" is one example. In addition to this, records that contain clapping are excellent for indicating high frequency transient capabilities of the speaker. If the clapping is clear and distinct, there is good high frequency definition.

The middle range is best evaluated by using an orchestra and a singer. There are many fine recordings that fit into this category and the listener

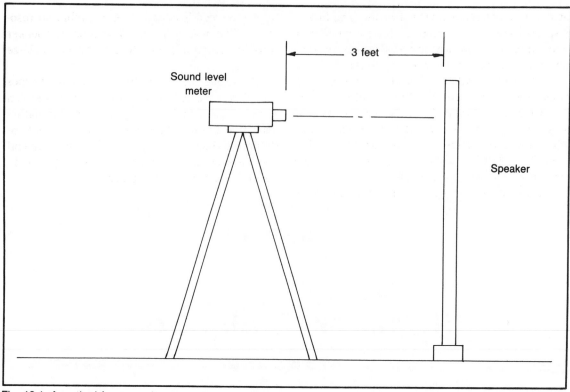

Fig. 13-1. A method for measuring a speakers acoustic output.

should choose one that is familiar.

SCIENTIFIC

The scientific evaluation of a speakers' performance uses instruments to measure its acoustic output. The diagram shown in Fig. 13-1 uses a sound level meter and an audio oscillator to measure the speaker frequency response. If the microphone is placed close to the speaker, there will be a reasonable amount correlation of between the measured results and the speakers actual performance.

If the microphone is far away and the measurement is performed indoors, the pickup will also include room reflections. The results can change as a function of the frequency, the measuring location, and the speaker position. This will make the readings very difficult to interpret. To overcome this problem, a pink noise generator can be used in place of the audio generator. This creates an addi-

tional problem. If the output has some irregularities, how can the associated frequency be identified? The solution is to use either an octave band

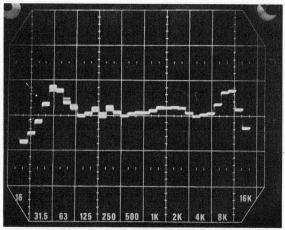

Fig. 13-2. The acoustical response of the electrostatic speaker described in this book.

analyzer or a selective level voltmeter. The first is a special type of instrument that has a number of internal filters. In the least expensive type, the output of a microphone is connected to the analyzer and the operator switches in the different frequency bands and records the result on a meter.

An expensive type of analyzer uses an oscilloscope as a display. Crown Manufacturing Co. of Elkhart, Indiana, makes a real time analyzer called the RTA-1. The frequency response of this speaker system was measured with this instrument. The results are shown in Fig. 13-2. The resonant peak on the low end is caused by the diaphragm resonance. The peak at 16 kHz is due to the speaker capacity resonating with the transformer leakage inductance.

Other manufacturers have more exotic types of analyzers. Some have computers so that they can store the data and do some special types of mathematical analysis. While both methods provide information about how a speaker performs, the end result must satisfy the requirements and the pocketbook of the principal listener.

Chapter 14

Commercial Electrostatic Speakers

In the preceding chapters, a description was given on how an electrostatic speaker works and how one can be built. The purpose of this chapter is to show some of the concepts used by manufacturers of commercial electrostatic speakers.

As of this writing, there are two major manufacturers of electrostatic speakers. The oldest firm is the "Acoustical Manufacturing Co." of England. It produces products under the trade name of Quad. The president of this company, Peter J. Walker, is a well known proponent and authority on this type of speaker. See the article in Chapter 15.

QUAD

Mr. Walker started Quad, which stands for "Quality Unit Amplifier Domestic" in 1936. Although the official company name is the "Acoustical Manufacturing Co.," the name Quad is easier to remember and is often used in its place.

The first electrostatic speaker produced by Quad was 31 inches high, 34-1/2 inches wide, and

10-1/2 inches deep. In addition to the audio transformer and high voltage power supply shown in Fig. 14-1, there are three electrostatic panels. Two of them are bass speakers and they are connected to a high voltage power supply of 6 kilovolts. The third panel is a 1-1/2 inch wide tweeter. It is connected to a 1.5 kilovolt tap on the high voltage power supply. A schematic diagram of the speaker is shown in Fig. 14-2, and the schematic for the power supply is shown in Fig. 14-3.

ESL 63

During the 25 years that followed the introduction of the Quad, it came to be regarded as a standard or reference speaker. It would probably have this same designation today except that it has been replaced by the model ESL 63. This unit, shown in Fig. 14-4, is affectionately called "Fred." This is an abbreviation for "Full Range Electrostatic Doublet."

The model 63 is 36.4 inches high, 26 inches wide, and is 10.6 inches deep. With an input volt-

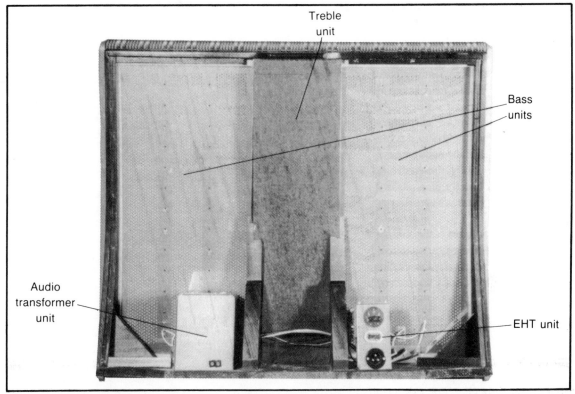

Fig. 14-1. The rear view of the Quad electrostatic loudspeaker showing the bass units, treble unit, the audio step-up transformer and the high voltage power supply.

age of 2.83 volts rms, the speaker sensitivity is 86 dB at one meter. The maximum peak program voltage for an undistorted output is 40 volts and the permitted peak is 55 volts. The maximum acoustic output at two meters is two newtons/m^2 and this is measured on the speaker axis.

The electronics for the ESL 63 are shown in Fig. 14-5. This rather elaborate circuit includes two additional circuits to protect the speaker from damage. Figure 14-6 is a diagram of the protection circuits and the high voltage bias supply. In this diagram, one protection circuit limits the maximum input voltage and the other is used to detect fault conditions. If a fault occurs, the protection circuit will short the input signal and thereby prevent the speaker from being damaged. Over the frequency range of 20 Hz to 20 kHz, the frequency response is very flat and has a variation of less that 0.5 dB. The distortion is also extremely small. It does not

exceed a value of 1% at an output of 45 watts. There is a large difference between this value and that of a conventional electromagnetic speaker.

Ideal Speaker

In basic sound theory, most textbooks refer to an ideal radiator as being a pulsating sphere. If the sphere expands and contracts as a function of the acoustic signal, then the sound would radiate outwards in a circular or spherical pattern.

Although the ESL 63 uses a flat diaphram, the speaker is segmented so that it produces a pattern that is similar to the ideal radiator. The technique used to accomplish this feature is a tapped delay line.

To give some insight into how this feature works, consider the diagram of Fig. 14-7A. This diagram shows three separate segments of the

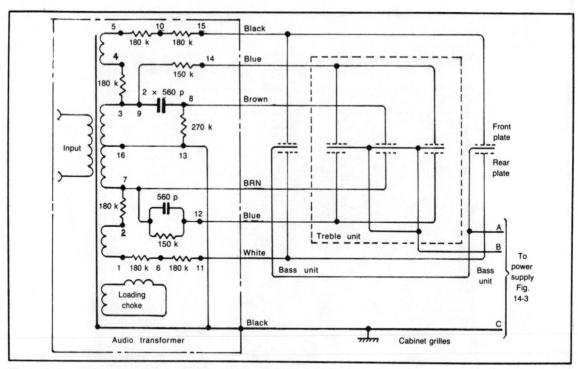

Fig. 14-2. Circuit diagram for the Quad electrostatic speaker, showing the equalizing resistors and the audio step-up transformer.

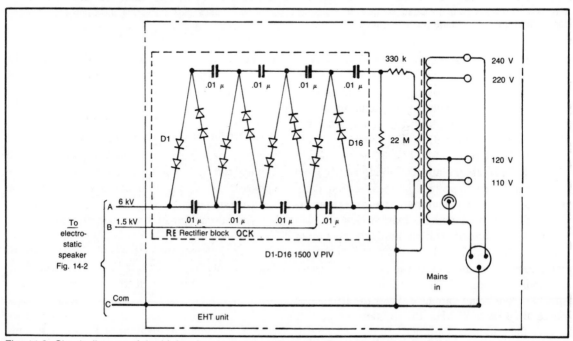

Fig. 14-3. Circuit diagram of the high voltage power supply for the Quad electrostatic speaker.

Fig. 14-4. Photo of the Model 63 electrostatic loudspeaker.

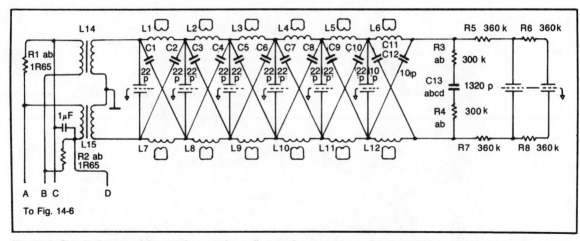

Fig. 14-5. Circuit diagram of the speaker panels, audio transformer and equalizing network for the Model 63 electrostatic speaker.

speaker. The segment marked S_1 is connected directly to the signal source. Segment S_2 is connected to S_1 through the delay circuit D_1. Segment S_3 is connected to the delay circuit D_2 and this in turn is connected to segment S_2.

Now, suppose that the input receives a signal that looks like a pulse. This type of waveform could be due to the plucking of a string. Because segment S_1 is connected directly to the input, the sound

from this section of the speaker will immediately appear at the output of this segment. The sound wave will propagate outwards from this segment as shown in Fig. 14-7B. This same pulse will not appear at the output of segment S_2 or S_3 because of the delay created by the delay circuits.

The time delay introduced by the delay circuit D1 is 20 microseconds. Therefore, twenty microseconds after the pulse has appeared at the output

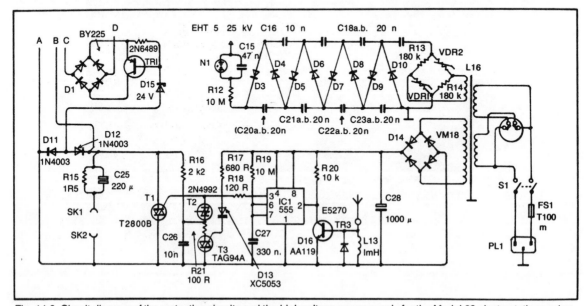

Fig. 14-6. Circuit diagram of the protection circuits and the high voltage power supply for the Model 63 electrostatic speaker.

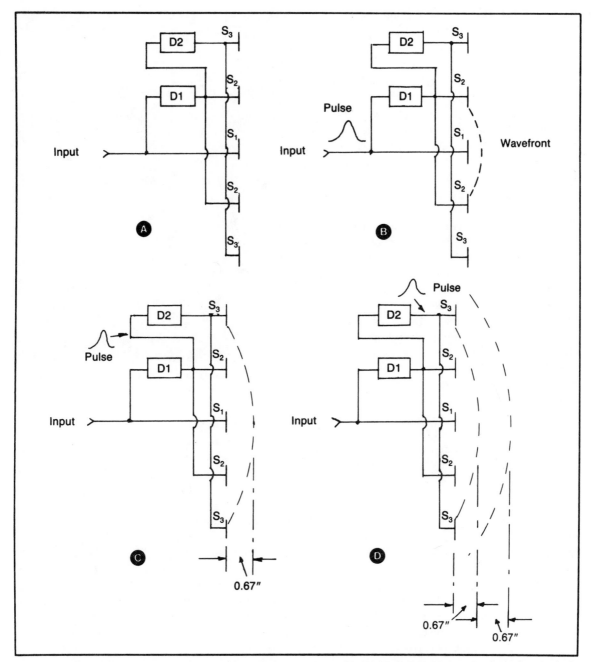

Fig. 14-7. A pictorial diagram for explaining how the wavefront from a Model 63 electrostatic speaker is made spherical.

of segment S_1, it will also appear at the output of S_2. During this time, the sound wave from the first segment will travel outwards at 13,440 inches per second. At the end of the 20 microsecond delay, the pulse produced by segment S_1 will have moved 0.672 inches away from the speaker. This is shown in Fig. 14-7C. This same process will be repeated for segment S_3. The delay circuit D_2 will postpone the output of segment S_3 for an additional 20 microseconds. During this time, the wavefront from both S_1 and S_2 will move another 0.672 inches. This is shown in Fig. 14-7D. If a line is drawn so that it links each of the wavefronts together, it will have a spherical shape.

There are a total of six segments in the ESL 63 and each segment produces a delay of 20 microseconds. By the time that the last segment produces a pulse, the wavefront from the first segment will have traveled about 1.6 inches.

In testing these speakers, Mr. Walker has also done something that is unique. While the traditional tests are performed with sound measuring equipment, a new type of test has also been devised. Two speakers are placed opposite each other. They receive the same signal, but one, the device under test, has the waveform inverted. The two speakers are placed near each other and a microphone is placed in the center between the two speakers. Because the speakers are perfectly matched, the sound from one speaker will be canceled by the sound from the opposite speaker. The result is that the microphone will produce no output. An example of the test setup is shown in Fig. 14-8.

Mr. Walker's unique design, his attention to details, and the perfection of the corresponding test system are the result of many years devotion to the development of the electrostatic speaker.

Fig. 14-8. A novel test method used to determine the matching between two Model 63 electrostatic speakers.

ACOUSTAT

The other company, Acoustat, has a much shorter history than Quad and is presently owned by David Hafler, a well known audio designer and entrepreneur. Their first product consisted of an electrostatic speaker with an internal hybrid high voltage amplifier (patent 4,324,950). This product appeared on the market in the early 70's.

There are some very distinct advantages in using a hybrid amplifier to drive an electrostatic speaker. One of the first is the elimination of the transformer that is required to match the speaker to the amplifier. Transformers, because they contain iron, usually cost a lot of money. This is especially true if they have a wide frequency response and a large step-up ratio. These two conflicting requirements add additional cost to that already provided by the use of iron.

By using vacuum tubes in the output circuit, both the transformer cost and its associated manufacturing problems are eliminated. An additional benefit of a tube type circuit is a better match between the source and the load impedance. The tube, by its very nature, is a high impedance device. The speaker, which is a capacitor, is a high impedance load. Therefore, a high impedance source is driving a high impedance load and this is an optimum situation. Tube circuits, on the other hand, have some problems of their own. Both the advantages, as well as the disadvantages, must be weighed.

One of the problems associated with having an amplifier that is built into the speaker is that it tends to limit the number of customers that will buy such a unit. The reason for this is that most customers already own an amplifier. The built-in unit would tend to make the existing one obsolete. Another fac-

Fig. 14-9. A pair of acoustic electrostatic loudspeakers.

tor is that audio enthusiasts are dedicated to a specific type of amplifier and may not want the one that is built into a speaker system.

Because it is very difficult to build a transformer that has a very high step-up ratio and a wide frequency response, the new design used two transformers. The design, which is patented, uses a frequency selective transformer circuit. In this way, each device can be optimized for its particular application.

In this new design, the audio spectrum was divided into two sections. One section used a transformer with a 200 to 1 step-up ratio. This provides an audio signal to the lower frequency section of the speaker. The other transformer has a 60 to 1 step-up ratio. It is used to cover both the mid- and high-frequency range of the speaker. As indicated, the circuit also contains a number of resistors and capacitors. A current example of the Acoustat product line is shown in Fig. 14-9.

Chapter 15

Noteworthy Articles

Since the end of World War II, there have been a number of articles published in audio magazines on electrostatic speakers. These articles are often referred to in subsequent articles. Unfortunately most of them are out of print and copies are difficult to locate. I have selected several of the most notable ones and have reprinted them in the following pages. The articles are reprinted with the kind permission of both the publishers and authors of the respective materials.

15.1 Telestar-Shaped Electrostatic Speaker

by R. J. Matthys

PART 1

Would you like to have the very best loudspeaker known today? I firmly believe that the electrostatic speaker is the finest loudspeaker that anyone knows how to make today. Furthermore, you can make one yourself easily and inexpensively in your own basement workshop, with a few ordinary tools. Individual electrostatic tweeter units can be made for 15 to 40 cents each. Individual electrostatic woofers can be made for about $3 to $10 each. This article is written for a specific purpose: To describe the design and construction of electrostatic speakers so that others can build and enjoy them.

The first part of this article describes the general characteristics of full-range electrostatic speakers. The second part shows how to design one. The third part tells how to build your own electrostatic speaker and sufficient data is given to build a tweeter or to start you on the way to building a full-range unit.

GENERAL CHARACTERISTICS

The modern electrostatic speaker consists of a thin plastic diaphragm located in the center of a small air gap between two parallel metal grids or plates. A crosssectional view of one is shown in Fig. 15-1. The diaphragm in this unit is coated on both sides with graphite to make it electrically conductive, and it is biased with a high dc voltage with respect to the two metal grids. The electrical connections to the speaker are shown in Fig. 15-2. Push-pull audio signal voltages are applied to the two metal grids, and this drives the diaphragm back and forth by means of the electric field forces developed between the diaphragm and the metal grids. The sound must pass through the metal grids, and to permit this the metal grids usually con-

sist of an array of parallel round rods or wires, spaced at intervals to allow air to pass through them. The high voltage dc bias supply provides very little current, as the only load is the leakage current through the air gap spacers. The speaker is usually designed to be connected to the 8 or 16 ohm output on a power amplifier, and the step-up transformer shown in Fig. 15-2 steps up the low voltage on the 8 or 16 ohm tap to the high level required at the speaker plates. This step-up transformer can be an ordinary audio output transformer connected backwards so that its low impedance secondary winding is actually used as the primary.

Electrostatic speakers have been made that will cover the entire audio frequency range from 20 cps to 20,000 cps with a single diaphragm. But, a single diaphragm speaker is very inefficient. For reasons to be given later, it is much more efficient to use a two, three, or even a four way speaker system. A large diaphragm is used as a woofer and proportionately smaller diaphragms as mid-range and tweeter units. The size of the air gaps (d in Fig. 15-2) between the diaphragm and the push-pull metal grids or plates is important, and varies inversely with frequency. The air gaps in a woofer might be 0.1 inches while a tweeter might have air gaps of 0.001 inches. Crossover networks are used to feed the proper frequency range to each speaker.

The outstanding sound quality of the electrostatic speaker is due almost entirely to two factors: 1. the very low mass of the moving diaphragm, and 2. the electric driving force being applied uniformly over the entire diaphragm area. The diaphragm has low mass because it is very thin, on the order of 0.00025 to 0.0005 inches thick. The mass of such a thin diaphragm is approximately

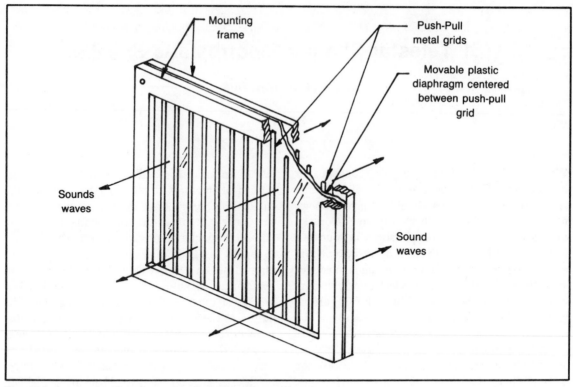

Fig. 15-1. A cut-away view of a push-pull electrostatic speaker element.

equal to a 1/4 inch thick layer of air! The low mass gives the speaker excellent transient response because the diaphragm can be moved quickly and the resistance of the air load damps out any "overshoot" of the diaphragm. The low mass of the di-aphragm also gives a flat frequency response up to 20000 or 30000 cps where it starts to drop off at 6 dB per octave.

The second factor, applying the driving force uniformly over the whole diaphragm area, almost

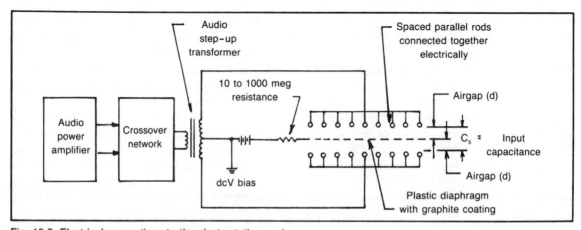

Fig. 15-2. Electrical connections to the electrostatic speaker.

completely eliminates "cone breakup." Cone breakup is the major cause of tone color in moving coil speakers. Thus, the second factor gives the electrostatic speaker a degree of naturalness and transparency that must be heard to be appreciated.

A third factor is low distortion. Janzen and Hunt both report distortion levels of 0.5 percent, which is much lower than for moving coil speakers.

The low frequency cutoff for an electrostatic speaker is the same as it is for a moving coil speaker—the fundamental resonant frequency of the diaphragm in free air. The frequency response is flat down to approximately this frequency. The fundamental resonant frequency of an electrostatic speaker diaphragm is inversely proportional to its diameter. Thus the fundamental resonance, and consequently the low frequency response, can be lowered by increasing the speaker diameter. An 8 inch diaphragm will have a fundamental resonance of about 40 cps. Diaphragm material is available up to 36 inches wide, and consequently the frequency response and the fundamental resonance can be extended down to about 10 cps if desired.

The low mass of the diaphragm, being approximately equal to a 1/4 inch layer of air, has a very good impedance match directly to the air load on the speaker. This means that no baffles, horns, or cabinets of any kind are needed. The author's test, and also tests reported by Walker show that the use of a baffle, horn, or cabinet of any kind actually degrade the sound quality of the electrostatic speaker because of the internal resonances inherent in these devices. What a contrast to moving coil speakers, where these devices are needed to beef up speaker performance! The best way to mount an electrostatic speaker is as a free-standing unit without a cabinet of any kind, letting the diaphragm radiate freely from both sides. Using one as part of a room divider or a wall would give excellent results.

The efficiency of the electrostatic falls in between that of the normal high efficiency cone speaker and the so called low efficiency bookshelf types. Briggs reports the electrostatic speaker as being 3 to 6 dB less efficient than a good high efficiency cone speaker. This agrees with the authors experiments.

The acoustical directivity of the electrostatic is almost the same as that of a moving coil speaker of equal size, which means it is highly directive at high frequencies and corrective measures are needed. The corrective measures can take various forms. Walker describes several of them, one being to make the tweeter diaphragm in the form of a long narrow strip. Malme describes an interesting method of electrically accomplishing the same thing—the horizontal width of the diaphragm decreases uniformly as the frequency increases. The author prefers to use an array of tweeters mounted on a spherical surface to solve the directivity problem.

The electrostatic speaker is inherently a high impedance device. And the lower the speaker's frequency range is, the higher is its input impedance. This means high voltages are required to operate the speaker, especially at low frequencies. To indicate some approximate values, the bias voltage for a tweeter might be 200 volts dc. The bias for a mid-range unit might be 2000 volts dc, while a woofer might have a bias voltage as high as 20000 volts dc. These voltages are not as dangerous as one might think, because the very high resistance (10 to 1000 megohms) in series with the bias supply naturally limits the current. However, to prevent any accidents the speaker is enclosed by a grounded metal screen.

The electrostatic speaker has one undesirable characteristic—the input impedance of the speaker is almost a pure capacitance over its entire frequency range. The capacitive input impedance is probably the most important single factor in the design of an electrostatic speaker because of the drastic effect it has on efficiency and amplifier loading. This is discussed later in more detail.

There is a definite limit to the acoustic power that can be obtained per unit area of the diaphragm. This limit is voltage breakdown across the gaps between the push-pull metal grids and the diaphragm. The speaker response is linear right up to the point of voltage breakdown. To increase the power output beyond this point, the radiating area of the speaker must be increased.

An electrostatic speaker cannot generate as

much power per unit area as a moving coil speaker, and consequently the electrostatic must have more radiating surface for the same acoustic power rating. When the power rating of an electrostatic speaker is increased, it is more efficient to add more speakers of the same size in parallel than to increase the size of the speaker diaphragm. The reasons for this are given later.

The preceding characteristics basically determine what an efficient full-range electrostatic speaker will look like: It will be quite thin, 2 to 3 inches at most; it will have a relatively large surface area and will be a two, three, or four-way system containing woofers, mid-ranges and tweeters; the speaker will be free-standing in the room and will not use a cabinet or baffle of any kind; the woofer, mid-range, and tweeter sections of the complete speaker will each consist of an array of identical speakers whose diaphragm size has been scaled to that frequency range; the individual speaker diaphragms can be round, square or rectangular in shape.

A three-way system might consist of the following: The woofers would all be alike with a diameter of 20 inches and air gaps of 0.2 inches for a fundamental resonance of 20 cps; each mid-range unit would have a diaphragm diameter of about 2 inches and air gaps of 0.02 inches for a fundamental resonance of 200 cps; each tweeter unit would have a diaphragm diameter of 0.2 inches and air gaps of 0.002 inches for a fundamental resonance of about 2000 cps. The number of woofers, mid-range, and tweeter units is chosen so that the total diaphragm area in each frequency range is sufficient to produce the acoustic power required in that frequency range. The size and resonant frequencies given are approximate, and are based on using Saran, 0.0004 inch thick, as the diaphragm material. If a different material or thickness is used, the sizes and frequencies will change.

DESIGN

The design of an electrostatic speaker is primarily based on four factors: input capacitance, efficiency, diameter of the diaphragm, and the size of the air gaps between the diaphragm and each push-pull plate. A flat frequency response is obtained by maintaining a constant amplitude audio signal between the push-pull plates at all frequencies.

The speaker input capacitance or load impedance as seen by an amplifier consists almost entirely of the electrical capacitance between the metal surfaces of the two push-pull plates. Over the audio frequency range of 20 cps to 20000 cps, the impedance of this capacity will vary by 1000 to 1. Connecting a load whose impedance varies by a 1000 to 1 to a constant impedance source, such as a power amplifier, means that a tremendous mismatch in impedance occurs over most of the frequency range. This makes it impossible to get a good impedance match, and consequently if the entire frequency range is covered by only one diaphragm the efficiency will be low.

If the speaker is a two-way system, the frequency range each speaker must cover is only half the total, and the impedance variation of each speaker as seen by the amplifier is then only about 30 to 1. The efficiency of the two-way system is thirty-two times greater than a one-way system or single- diaphragm speaker because of the reduced impedance mismatch. If the speaker is a three-way system, each speaker covers only one third of the frequency range, and the total impedance variation of each speaker as seen by the amplifier is only 10 to 1. The efficiency of the three-way system is about three times greater than the two-way system. If the speaker is a four-way system, the impedance variation is reduced to about 6 to 1, and its efficiency is about twice as good as the three-way system. Thus, for maximum efficiency and to reduce the variation in load impedance seen by the power amplifier, a full-range electrostatic should be designed as a multi-way speaker system.

Amplifiers do not like to drive the capacitive load presented to them by an electrostatic speaker. There are three reasons for this. First, the input impedance of the speaker varies with frequency, and amplifiers like to work into a constant load impedance and not into a load that changes with frequency. Also, the low load impedance that occurs at higher frequencies drastically limits an amplifier's power output at high frequencies. When the speaker is a multi-way system, the woofer, mid-range, and tweeter sections are each connected to the amplifier with a different transformer turns ratio, so as to give a more constant load impedance over the whole audio frequency range. The step-up turns ratio for each section is proportional to the size of the air gaps in that section.

The second reason amplifiers don't like capacitive loads is that the load line for the power output tubes become a circle instead of a straight line, and the performance of the amplifier's power output stage changes. In practice, the crossover coupling networks used between the amplifier and the speaker drastically change the speakers capacitive input impedance to a much more resistive impedance, and this helps the amplifier loading problem considerably. Janzen has used the coupling network to improve the input impedance of the KLH Model Nine full-range electrostatic speaker so that it is resistive over half the audio frequency range and does not vary more than about 35 percent from its nominal impedance value over the 20 cps to 20000 cps frequency range.

The third reason amplifiers do not like capacity loads is that most hi-fi amplifiers use feedback and work best with resistive loads. The large capacity load presented by an electrostatic speaker can ruin an amplifier's transient response and also make the amplifier become unstable. This problem is discussed later in more detail in the section on the crossover network and amplifier loading effects.

The second major factor in electrostatic speaker design is efficiency. Without giving the derivation, the efficiency of an electrostatic speaker can be shown to be

Efficiency = $(Vb/d)^2 \times (k/f_d)$

Where
- k = a constant.
- f = frequency.
- d = the air gap distance between the diaphragm and each plate.
- Vb = bias voltage on the diaphragm.

The term in parenthesis, $(Vb/d)^2$, is the bias voltage gradient in volts-per-inch in the air gap between the diaphragm and each plate. This term says that for maximum efficiency the bias voltage gradient should be as high as possible, which means just short of corona and voltage breakdown. Note that it is the bias voltage gradient in volts-per-inch that is important, and not just the bias voltage. A woofer has a larger air gap than a mid-range or a tweeter, and consequently will need more bias voltage to get the same voltage gradient. The author uses a bias voltage gradient of 100 volts-per-0.001 inches.

The terms f and d (frequency and air gap size) in the denominator of the efficiency equation show that the efficiency decreases as both the frequency and the air gap size increase. The efficiency decreases as the frequency increases because of the greater reactive amplifier power that must be "dumped" into the speaker's input capacitance at high frequencies to maintain a constant voltage between the push-pull plates.

The air gap size affects the efficiency because the energy stored in the input capacitance is proportional to the air volume enclosed between the push-pull plates. The mechanical force that drives the diaphragm is proportional to the square of the voltage gradient in the air gap. The same voltage gradient can be obtained with a small gap as with a large gap, and since less energy has to be stored if the volume is smaller, the efficiency increases as the air gap size becomes smaller. Thus, for maximum efficiency, the air gap is made as small as possible for maximum diaphragm travel.

A woofer has the same efficiency per unit area as a tweeter because the tweeter has a smaller air gap than a woofer, as the diaphragm amplitude is much less at high frequencies. To put it another way, the frequency and air gap terms (f and d) in the efficiency equation complement each other, and consequently woofers, mid-ranges, and tweeters all have the same efficiency per unit area.

The diameter of a single electrostatic diaphragm (round or square) is about 1/24 of the wavelength of sound at the diaphragm's resonant frequency. Since the air load on a diaphragm is reactive and not resistive when the diameter is less than one-third of the wavelength, a single electrostatic diaphragm will see a reactive air load in the frequency range between the fundamental diaphragm resonance and about eight times this resonant frequency.

Walker has shown that an electrostatic speaker reacts quite differently to a reactive load than does a moving-coil loudspeaker. With a reactive air load, the amplitude of an electrostatic diaphragm increases at 12 dB per octave as the frequency decreases, instead of the 6 dB per octave of a resistive air load. If the air gap is increased to handle the larger diaphragm amplitude that occurs with a reactive load, the efficiency will be lowered. The best solution is to add speakers of the same size in parallel until the diameter of the speaker array is

one-third the wavelength of sound at the fundamental resonant frequency of the diaphragms. This solution solves the reactive air load problem by making the air load resistive at all frequencies above the fundamental diaphragm resonance. Another way of accomplishing the same thing is to make the diaphragm rectangular, with the length of each diaphragm equal to eight times the width.

To make the air gap as small as possible for maximum efficiency, it is important to know what the maximum diaphragm travel is. Maximum travel occurs at the lowest frequency each speaker radiates. The maximum diaphragm amplitude at different frequencies is shown in Fig. 15-3. This is a calculated curve, based on a bias voltage gradient

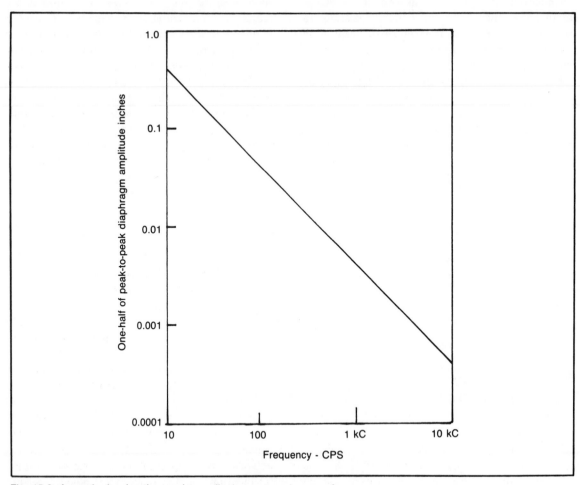

Fig. 15-3. A graph showing the maximum diaphragm travel versus frequency.

194

of 100 volts-per-0.001 inches, with the peak value of the audio input voltage between one plate and the diaphragm set equal to the bias voltage. The air load on the diaphragm is assumed to be resistive. The author's experience indicates that the actual diaphragm amplitude is somewhat less than that shown in Fig. 15-3.

Another factor affecting efficiency is the shunt capacitance in the speaker frame. It is very easy for the shunt capacitance in the frame between the push-pull grids to be two to three times greater than the "useful" capacitance through the moveable part of the diaphragm. This means that two-thirds to three-fourths of the total audio power into the speaker would be wasted in the capacitance of the speaker frame without doing any useful work in moving the diaphragm. The shunt capacitance can be minimized by reducing the surface area of the frame between the grids, and by using an air gap spacer material that has a low dielectric constant. The shunt capacitance in the frame of the electrostatic tweeter made by the author amounted to 50 percent of the "useful" capacitance between the grids. Thus, one-third of the audio input power is wasted in the frame capacitance of this tweeter.

The third major factor in electrostatic speaker design is the diameter of the diaphragm. The diaphragm diameter determines the lowest frequency the diaphragm will radiate. The low frequency cutoff is the frequency of the fundamental diaphragm resonance, which is inversely proportional to the diameter of the diaphragm. The larger the diaphragm, the lower the cutoff frequency.

For reasons of efficiency and stability, it is desirable to use the smallest diaphragm diameter, which means the fundamental resonance should be as high as possible. The smallest diameter is obtained by setting the fundamental resonance a little below the lowest frequency to be radiated by the diaphragm. For example, a mid-range speaker designed to cover a frequency range of 200 cps to 2000 cps might have its fundamental resonance placed about an octave lower than 200 cps, or at 100 cps. A diaphragm diameter of 4 inches will give a fundamental resonance of about 100 cps. Application of the minimum-diameter rule to woofers,

mid-ranges, and tweeters results in tweeters of small diameter, mid-range units of medium diameter, and woofers of large diameter; with the fundamental diaphragm resonance of each being set about an octave below the low end of each speaker's frequency range.

Stability Problems

There are two stability problems in the electrostatic speaker. These are the static and dynamic stabilities of the diaphragm. The static stability problem will be discussed first. When the bias voltage is applied to the diaphragm, the resulting electric field between the diaphragm and the two push-pull plates acts as a spring which pulls the diaphragm away from its center position toward one of the two plates. Because the diaphragm is stretched taut in its mounting frame, this mechanical tension also acts as a spring which pulls the diaphragm back toward its center position. Thus, we have two spring forces pulling the diaphragm in opposite directions. For the diaphragm to be stable, the mechanical tension in the diaphragm must be greater than the electric field forces generated by the bias voltage. If the tension is too low, the electric field forces will pull the diaphragm away from the center, and the diaphragm will oscillate back and forth from one plate to the other, making a noise like a stack of paper being shuffled. See the section "Diaphragm Tension" in Chapter 4.

There are two solutions to the static stability problem. The first is to reduce the diameter of the diaphragm. This will increase the spring constant of the diaphragm tension. The second is to increase the air gap which will decrease the spring constant of the electric field bias forces. These two solutions lead to a certain ratio of diaphragm diameter to air gap size that must not be exceeded if the diaphragm is to be stable. Limited experiments by the author indicated that diaphragms of any size, made of 0.0004 inch thick Saran Wrap, will be statistically stable if the ratio of diaphragm diameter to air gap size (L/d) is about 100 to 1 or less. This ratio is based on a bias voltage gradient (Vb/d) of 100 volts-per-0.001 inch, and assumes that the diaphragm has been stretched taut in the speaker frame so as to obtain a suitable diaphragm tension.

The static stability problem does not appear to be much of a practical limitation in designing an electrostatic speaker. In the tweeter built by the author, the ratio of diaphragm diameter to air gap size needed for static stability gave an air gap size very close to what was needed for maximum diaphragm travel. If an audio oscillator is available, it is easy to experiment with this instability effect. The ratio of the two spring constants can be measured by noting how much the fundamental resonant frequency of the diaphragm changes when the bias voltage is applied. The fundamental resonance of the author's tweeters drops about 20 percent when operating bias of 1500 volts dc is applied.

The second stability problem is the dynamic stability of the diaphragm. When an audio signal is applied to the push-pull plates, the diaphragm moves away from center, moving in turn toward each of the push-pull plates. To prevent the diaphragm from being "pulled into" one of the plates when it gets very close to one, a large resistance is put in series between the bias supply and the diaphragm. This resistance provides a condition of constant charge operation on the diaphragm, and reduces the bias voltage on the diaphragm in proportion to the position of the diaphragm toward either plate. In this fashion, the voltage difference between the diaphragm and the nearest plate goes to zero as the diaphragm approaches it. There is no arcing if they happen to touch, because there is no voltage difference between them at the instant of touching. Hunt has shown that if the RC time constant of this resistance and the capacitance between the diaphragm and one of the push-pull plates is at least four times greater than the time interval of one-half cycle of the lowest frequency to be radiated, the diaphragm will be dynamically stable at any location between the plates.

Because the diaphragm is clamped at the edges, it does not move as a rigid plate but forms a curved surface when displaced from its center position. The only way to obtain true constant charge operation for each part of the diaphragm under this condition is to put a high series resistance on the

diaphragm itself in the form of a high resistance coating. The high resistance in series with the diaphragm and the high resistance coating on it have several other advantages in addition to making the diaphragm dynamically stable, such as: 1. Reducing the even and odd harmonic distortion to 0.5 percent or less, and 2. limiting the short circuit current if the speaker happens to arc over.

Design Summary

The design of a full-range electrostatic speaker is summarized as follows. To obtain high efficiency, the speaker is designed as a two, three or four-way system. The woofer, mid-range and tweeter sections will each consist of several speakers connected in parallel, preferably so that the diameter of the array in each section will be at least one-third of the wavelength of the lowest frequency that each is required to radiate. The diaphragm diameter, air gap size, and bias voltage of each speaker increase directly as the frequency range and the fundamental resonance of that speaker are lowered.

To get the best efficiency the diaphragm diameter is made as small as possible, and is selected to place the fundamental diaphragm resonance about an octave below the lowest frequency the diaphragm is required to radiate. With mid-range and tweeter speakers the crossover frequency is considered to be the lowest radiated frequency. For best efficiency, the air gap is made the smallest size that will still allow for maximum diaphragm travel. Fig. 15-3 shows the maximum diaphragm travel as a function of frequency. Figure 15-3 can also be used to determine the approximate diaphragm diameter needed to obtain a particular fundamental diaphragm resonance. To do this, the frequency scale is interpreted as the fundamental resonant frequency desired, and the air gap scale is multiplied by 100 and interpreted as the diaphragm diameter that will give this resonant frequency.

To make the diaphragm stable under static conditions (bias voltage only, no audio signal) the ratio of the diaphragm diameter to air gap size (L/d) should not exceed 100 to 1. To make the diaphragm stable under dynamic conditions (bias voltage and audio signal) and also to obtain the very low distortion that the speaker is capable of, the resistance in series with the bias supply and the resistance of the graphite coating on the diaphragm must be increased as the fundamental diaphragm resonance is decreased. The RC time constant of the sum of these two resistances times the capacitance of the diaphragm to one plate should be equal to at least four times the time interval of one half cycle of the lowest frequency that each diaphragm will radiate. For maximum efficiency, the bias voltage gradient is set at the highest possible value, just short of corona and voltage breakdown. The maximum bias voltage gradient, (Vb/d), is about 80 to 120 volts dc per 0.001 inches.

The power rating of the speaker is proportional to the total diaphragm area in each frequency range. For a constant power rating at all frequencies, the total diaphragm area should be the same in each frequency range. If more power is wanted, more speakers must be added in parallel, as the acoustic power per unit of diaphragm area is limited by voltage breakdown. If desired, the total diaphragm area in each frequency range can be pro-rated to match the power vs. frequency requirements of music.

The high frequency response is limited by the mass-per-unit-area of the diaphragm to about 20,000 to 30,000 cps with present diaphragm materials, with a 6 dB per-octave roll off above this point. The low frequency response is limited only by the diameter of the diaphragm. The larger the diaphragm, the lower the cutoff frequency. Saran Wrap is available up to 36 inches wide, which would give a low frequency cutoff of about 10 cps.

For maximum efficiency, the shunt capacitance in the frame around each diaphragm should be minimized, as it can absorb 25 to 75 percent of the audio power into the speaker. This power is wasted.

The Coupling Network

The coupling, or crossover network, used between the amplifier and the electrostatic speaker is very important, much more so than for a moving-coil speaker. The crossover network for a tweeter will be discussed first. Figure 15-4A shows an L-C crossover network for coupling to an electrostatic tweeter. This network was used by Janzen in his Model 130 electrostatic tweeter. Figure 15-4B shows the amplifier output impedance, the L-C crossover elements, the step-up transformer to the high impedance tweeter and the capacitive input impedance (Cs) of the tweeter itself. Figure 15-4B also shows two resistors, R1 and R2, which play an important role in the network.

Both the frequency response and the input impedance of the coupling network provide useful information. For a tweeter, the audio voltage between the push-pull speaker plates should be constant above the crossover frequency and should drop off at 12 dB per-octave below the crossover frequency. The input impedance of the crossover network should be as constant as possible over the frequency range to make it easier for the amplifier to drive the speaker.

The frequency response of a 500 cps crossover network for a tweeter is shown in Fig. 15-5. The data in Fig. 15-5 was taken from measurements on the author's tweeter. It shows that what was supposed to be a high pass network is actually a bandpass network. With R1 and R2 equal to zero, an undesirable peak occurs in the response curve at each end of the bandpass. The two other curves in Fig. 15-5 show the correct value of R1 (about 11 kohms) will eliminate the peak at f_{co} near the crossover frequency, and that the correct value of R2 (about 500 ohms) will eliminate the high frequency peak at f_h. A flat frequency response in the bandpass is thus obtained.

The behavior of the network can be explained by redrawing Fig. 15-4B using the equivalent circuit for the step-up transformer as in Fig. 15-4C. What happens is that the resonant peak at or near the crossover frequency f_{co} is caused by C1 and L1 going into series resonance at this frequency, and R1 is used to limit the current at this resonance. The resonant peak f_h at the high end of the pass band is caused by the transformer leakage inductance (L_{leak}) and the speaker input capacitance (a^2Cs) going into series resonance at this frequency, and R2 is used to limit the current at this resonance.

197

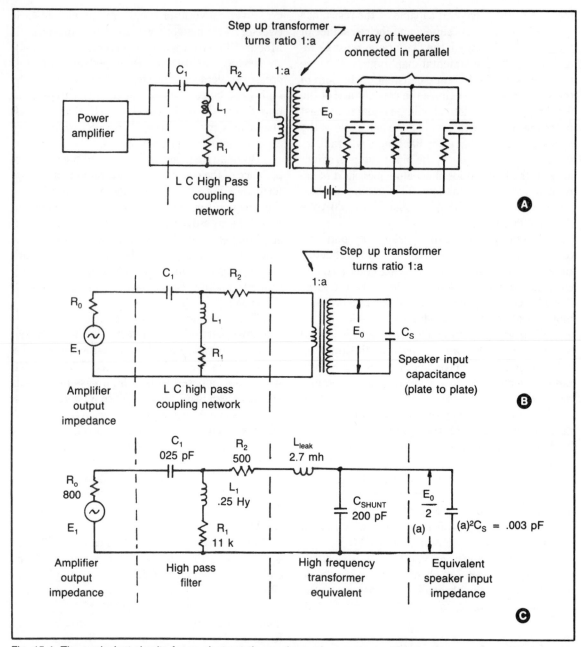

Fig. 15-4. The equivalent circuits for an electrostatic speaker and a crossover network.

The load impedance that the amplifier sees is the input impedance of the crossover network. The input impedance of the author's 500 cps crossover network with an electrostatic tweeter as a load is shown in Fig. 15-6. The input impedance curve in Fig. 15-6 shows series resonances at 800 cps and 110,000 cps (f_{co} and f_h), and a parallel resonance at 3000 cps (f_p). The resonance at f_p is caused by the parallel resonance of L1 with the speaker input capacitance (a^2Cs). The resistors R1 and R2 affect

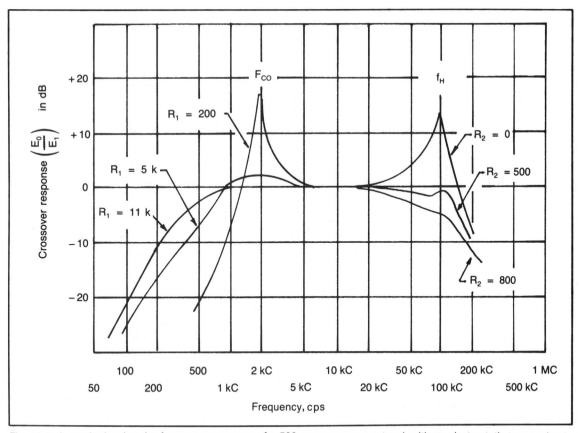

Fig. 15-5. A graph showing the frequency response of a 500 cps crossover network with an electrostatic tweeter load.

the resonant frequencies to a certain extent and hence the frequencies are slightly different from what would be calculated from just the inductive and capacitive elements.

Normally, the step-up transformer and high pass filter would be connected to the 8 or 16 ohm output tap of the power amplifier. The author chose to bypass the amplifier output transformer, however, and connected the high pass filter directly to the plates of the power output tubes as shown in Fig. 15-7. The amplifier used to drive the tweeter is a 60 watt Dynakit Mark III amplifier. The step-up transformer used in the high pass network is a UTC LS 33, which for many reasons is almost ideal for the purpose. For experimental work, it provides a large variety of turns ratios for matching almost any tweeter capacitance to the amplifier.

The output tubes in the Dynakit Mark III am-

plifier have a rated load impedance of 4300 ohms plate to plate. If you wish to connect the electrostatic tweeter described in this article to the 16 ohm output tap on your amplifier, the impedance of the high pass filter elements should be reduced by the ratio of the square of the impedances, $(16/4300)^2$, and the transformer step-up ratio should be increased by the square root of the impedance ratio, $(16/4300)^{1/2}$. Any other amplifier output impedance such as 4 or 8 ohms can be accommodated in a similar manner.

Network Design

The design of the coupling network between the amplifier and the tweeter is basically a trade-off between efficiency and the highest frequency to which the tweeter should provide full power output. This is because the tweeter's capacitive input

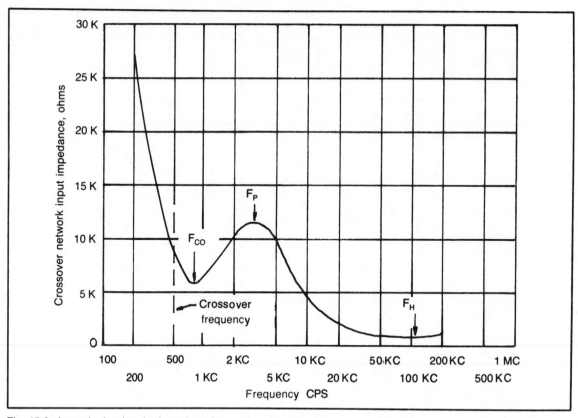

Fig. 15-6. A graph showing the input impedance of a 500 cps crossover network with an electrostatic tweeter load.

impedance at high frequencies decreases as the frequency increases, and when the impedance drops below the amplifier's rated load impedance, the amplifier's maximum available power output also drops off. For instance, if one wanted maximum power at all frequencies up to 20,000 cps, and if the amplifier's rated plate to plate load impedance was 4300 ohms, then the capacitive input im-

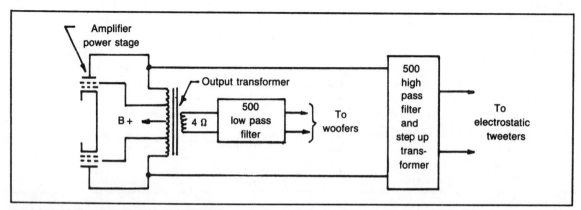

Fig. 15-7. A diagram that shows how to connect the electrostatic tweeter and a moving coil woofer to their respective crossover networks and then to the amplifier.

pedance of the tweeter as seen by the amplifier at the primary of the step-up transformer should be 4300 ohms at 20000 cps. This is the impedance of a 0.0018 microfarad capacitor. The turns ratio of the step-up transformer is then adjusted so that the actual input capacitance of the tweeter, which is the capacitance between the two push-pull speaker plates, is reflected to the transformer primary as 0.0018 microfarads.

If you are not a hi-fi purist, you can "fudge" a little and improve the efficiency somewhat by saying that full power to 20000 cps is not needed for music reproduction, and that full power to 11000 cps or so with gradually decreasing power to 20000 cps would be adequate. The author fudged, and 4300 ohms at 11000 cps represents a capacitance of 0.003 microfarads. The transformer step-up ratio was adjusted to reflect 0.003 microfarads on the primary instead of 0.0018 microfarads. The fudging increased the efficiency by 65 percent.

Referring back to Fig. 15-4C, the capacitive load impedance seen by the amplifier (a^2Cs), has been selected as 0.003 microfarads. Once this capacitance value is selected, the values of the other components in the tweeter coupling network are fixed with the exception of L1. The other components are determined as follows: the capacitor C1 should be about ten times larger than (a^2Cs) as it is in series with the speaker input load capacitance, and any voltage drop across C1 is wasted in terms of speaker efficiency. C1 in Fig. 15-4C was chosen as 0.025 microfarads, and represents an 11 percent voltage loss in terms of the 0.003 microfarad speaker load capacitance. The leakage inductance and shunt capacitance of the step-up transformer, which should be as small as possible, are determined by the transformer selected. R2 is set equal to the impedance of the speaker, (a^2Cs), at the upper resonant frequency, f_h, which is the resonant frequency of the transformer leakage inductance (L_{leak}) with the speaker capacitance (a^2Cs).

The resonant frequency, f_h, can be determined by measuring the values of (L_{leak}) and (a^2Cs) individually or by sweeping the frequency range with an audio oscillator and watching for the resonant peak at f_h in the frequency response of the net-

work with a VTVM. R1 is set equal to the impedance of C1 at the crossover frequency, which in this case was 500 cps. The value of L1 apparently has to be determined experimentally with an audio oscillator and VTVM, and is selected to eliminate any peaking or drooping in the response curve at the crossover frequency. L1 has a second useful purpose in "unloading" R1 from the amplifier at the high end of the frequency range where the amplifier is heavily loaded by the 0.003 microfarad speaker load capacitance.

Woofer and Mid-Range Crossover Networks

The author has not yet built a crossover network for an electrostatic woofer or mid-range speaker, so only a few guidelines will be offered. The basic crossover network shown in Fig. 15-4A can be used for a mid-range speaker by adding an appropriate inductance in series with R2. For a woofer, the components C1, R1 and L1 in Fig. 15-4A would be eliminated and an appropriate inductance would be added in series with R2. The values of the various components in the crossover networks would be selected to give the desired crossover frequencies.

There may be other kinds of crossover networks that would work well with electrostatic woofers and mid-range speakers. For example, if the crossovers were designed as RC networks instead of RLC, it may be possible to use the input capacitance of the speakers themselves as the capacitance elements in the network.

Amplifier Loading Effect

The author was curious as to what effect a capacitive load would have on the amplifier's power output at high frequencies, since the load line for the power output tubes becomes a circle instead of a straight line. Figure 15-8 shows the maximum undistorted plate-to-plate output voltage versus frequency of the author's 60 watt Dynakit amplifier for various resistive and capacitive loads. The amplifier response is flat up to the frequency where the reactance of the load capacitance plus the 0.0015 microfarad winding capacitance in the out-

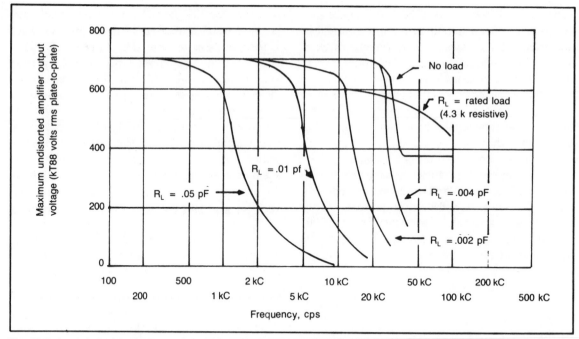

Fig. 15-8. A graph that shows the maximum amplifier output voltage versus plate-to-plate load impedance for the author's 60 watt dynakit amplifier.

put transformer equals the rated load impedance of 4300 ohms. The maximum output voltage then drops off at 9 or 12 dB per octave about that point. The amplifier's maximum voltage output with the actual crossover network and electrostatic speaker load is slightly better than that indicated by Fig. 15-8. The maximum output voltage (measured at the push-pull speaker plates) corresponds approximately to the curve for the 0.002 microfarad load in Fig. 15-8.

When tested with square waves, the amplifier exhibited excellent transient response at high frequencies with the electrostatic tweeter and 500 cps crossover network as a load. To make the test realistic, two moving coil woofers were connected to the amplifier at the same time through a 500 cps low-pass network. No ringing or overshoot was observable, and while a little rounding of the corners of the square wave was present, it was much less than expected.

The outstanding transient response of this amplifier with a capacitive load is due to the design

of the feedback network used in it which I think makes the Dynakit one of the best amplifiers commercially available for driving an electrostatic speaker. The amplifier's one small drawback in its otherwise excellent design appears to be a slight tendency toward low-frequency instability. The author's Dynakit exhibited a 6 dB peak in its frequency response at 8 cps (with no load on the amplifier). Both the peak at 8 cps and the tendency toward low-frequency instability were eliminated by changing the KT88 grid coupling condensers in the amplifier from 0.25 microfarads to 2.0 microfarads.

PART 2

Electrostatic speakers are best built in 3 or 4 way systems for best impedance matching and efficiency.

SPEAKER CONSTRUCTION

Electrostatic speaker units are very easy to make. The construction of the author's tweeter is shown in Fig. 15-9 through 15-12. For convenience, the tweeter units are made in groups of six. The dimensions of one group of six tweeters are shown in Fig. 15-9. Each diaphragm is rectangular, with a size of approximately 1.6 × 1.8 inches and a fundamental resonance of about 350 cps. The mechanical assembly of one group of six tweeters is shown in the crosssection views in Fig. 15-10A and B. Figure 15-10C and D shows the mechanical details of the grid spacers.

Each tweeter group consists of a stretched Saran Wrap diaphragm spaced midway between two grids of 1/16 inch diameter brass rods, using two pieces of 0.015 inch thick Cadco high-impact polystyrene as air gap spacers to maintain the two air gaps at precisely 0.015 inches each. The diaphragm, the air gap spacers, and the brass grids

are held together between two stiff mounting frames of 1/8 inch thick epoxy-glass laminate. The assembly is held together with 4-40 screws. The input capacitance between the two push-pull plates is 122 picofarads for each group of six tweeters.

To put a graphite coating on the diaphragm, the diaphragm is stretched out on a sheet of masonite, and pulled semitaut with Scotch tape around the edges. A very thin layer of Dixon's Microfyne graphite is applied to the diaphragm and rubbed in vigorously using Kleenex. Graphite is added until the diaphragm resistance measures about 10 to 100 megohms with the ohmmeter probes about one-half to one inch apart on the diaphragm surface. The coating should be uniform, and this is checked by moving the two ohmmeter probes in parallel across the diaphragm surface in

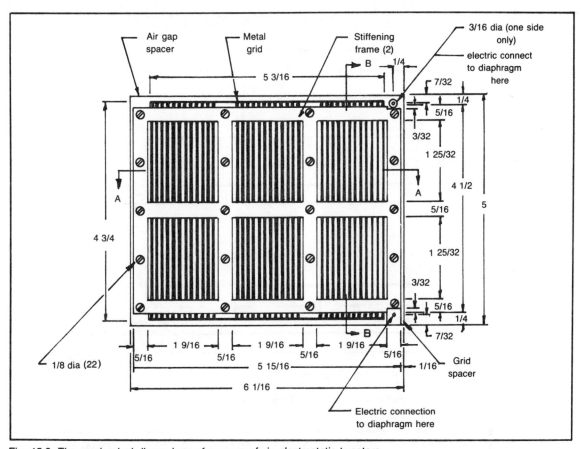

Fig. 15-9. The mechanical dimensions of a group of six electrostatic tweeters.

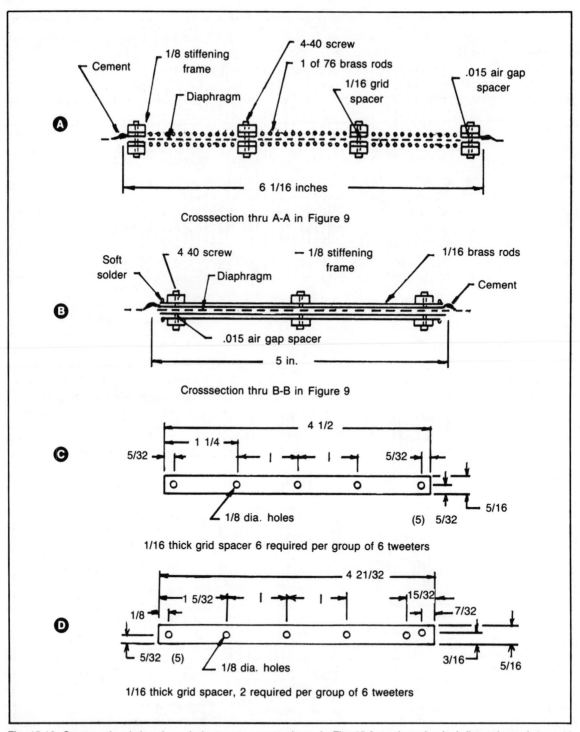

Fig. 15-10. Crosssectional view through the tweeter group shown in Fig. 15-9, and mechanical dimensions of the grid spacers needed.

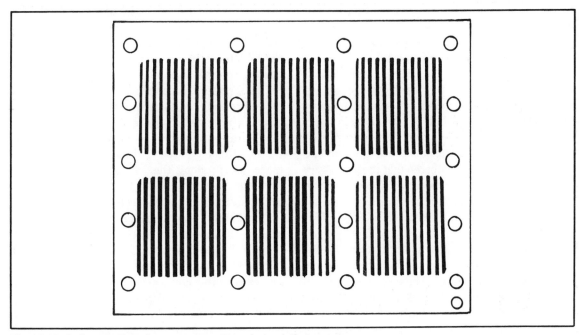

Fig. 15-11. A diagram that shows a group of six electrostatic tweeters.

several directions. If too much graphite is used, the diaphragm resistance will be too low. Any excess graphite is removed by rubbing the diaphragm vigorously with Kleenex. In practice, the resistance of the diaphragm coating does not seem to be critical. When the resistance of the coating is satisfac-

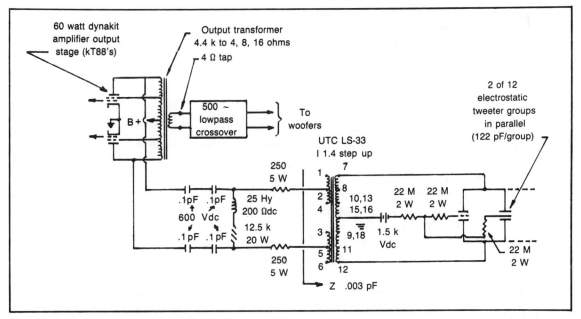

Fig. 15-12. A crossover network for the 500 cps electrostatic tweeter.

tory, the diaphragm is turned over and graphite is applied to the other side in the same manner.

To avoid shorting out the air gap spacers, the graphite operations should be performed in a separate area and your hands washed immediately afterwards, especially before handling the air gap spacers. One sweaty fingerprint loaded with graphite placed across the edge of one of the air gap spacers will provide a high resistance leakage path across the spacer and short out the diaphragm bias supply. It must be remembered that there is a very high resistance in series with the dc bias supply, and a high leakage resistance across one of the air gap spacers will act as a partial short on the bias supply.

To keep the diaphragm tightly stretched in the speaker assembly, the diaphragm is cemented to one of the air gap spacers. The diaphragm, which is still stretched out on the masonite hardboard, is first pulled taut by applying more Scotch tape around the edges of the Saran. One of the air gap spacers is then laid on the stretched diaphragm and cement is applied around the outside edge of the air gap spacer. The location of the cement on the air gap spacer is important, and is shown in Fig. 15-10A and B. The cement must be kept off the spacer surfaces that determine the 0.015 inch air gap spacing, otherwise the air gap will not be uniform.

Each of the push-pull metal grids consists of a parallel array of 1/16 inch diameter brass rods spaced by 1/8 inch intervals. They are soldered together into a grid by means of two brass rods soldered across the two ends of the grid. All of the rods in the array must be very straight and in the same plane to obtain a uniform air gap. If one of the rods should be closer than the others to the diaphragm, voltage breakdown will occur at that point. This will limit the bias voltage that can be applied to the speaker, and as a result the speaker's efficiency will be reduced.

Because straight brass rod is hard to find, it is necessary to test each rod for straightness. An easy test is to roll them one by one across a flat surface, such as a piece of plate glass, and watch for "cracks of light" under the rods. Only 70 percent of the rod

material obtained by the author was useable. To insure that all of the grid rods lie in the same plane, they are clamped between two flat plates during the solder operations. Although not necessary, the spacing between rods can be made uniform by placing short extra rods as spacers in the gaps between the rods during the soldering operation. The extra rods are removed after the soldering operation.

The air gap spacers are cut from a sheet of plastic 0.015 inches thick with scissors and a razor blade. Burrs along the edges of the diaphragm openings are scraped off with a razor blade. The grid spacers are cut from sheets of epoxy glass laminate 1/16 inch thick. They must be the same thickness as the brass rods. Because sheets of plastic vary in thickness, especially near the edges, the thickness of the air gap and grid spacers must be measured with a micrometer to make sure they are the correct size and uniform thickness.

Electrical connections to the graphite coating on the diaphragm are made by means of two screws in the upper right and lower right corners of the tweeter frame as shown in Fig. 15-9. An oversized hole is cut through the air gap spacer and the stiffening frame on one side in the corner of the frame, as shown in Fig. 15-9, so that the screw head contacts the graphite coating on the plastic diaphragm. In similar fashion, a second screw makes contact to the graphite coating on the other side. The electrical diaphragm connections may be seen a little clearer in Fig. 15-11 where the two diaphragm connecting screws are shown with soldering lugs attached to them.

Crossover Network and Bias Supply

The tweeter crossover network is shown in Fig. 15-12. The 0.25 henry air core inductor was wound by hand and its dimensions are given in Fig. 15-13. The high voltage bias supply is shown in Fig. 15-14. The crossover network and the bias supply were placed in a 6 × 11 × 13 inch wood box instead of a metal box so as not to affect the air core inductor. Connection to the amplifier was made by means of a socket on the rear of the amplifier chassis. The plates of the amplifier output tubes were connected

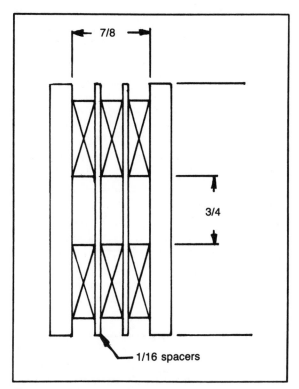

Fig. 15-13. A mechanical diagram of the coil form for making the inductor for the 500 cps crossover network. Also included are construction details.

to this socket. Disconnecting the crossover network at this socket makes the amplifier available for other purposes when desired.

Mounting the Tweeter

The electrostatic tweeter described here was designed for a two-way corner speaker system using two 15 inch moving coil woofers which the author had on hand. The complete tweeter array contains a total of 72 individual tweeters. To eliminate directional effects, each group of six tweeters is mounted facing in a slightly different direction so as to form an approximately spherical surface covering a solid angle of 90 by 60 degrees. To do this, the tweeters are first attached to a flexible sheet of 3/64 phenolic-cloth laminate. Six V-shaped slits are made between the tweeters along the top and bottom edges of the sheet which is then bent backward and fastened to five vertical 3/4 inch

dowels. The dowels fasten the tweeter array into a recess in the front wall of a 50 cubic foot bass reflex cabinet. The dimensions of the flexible mounting sheet are shown in Fig. 15-15. The tweeter recess is covered with a plastic grill cloth to make it more decorative.

Tools Needed

The 500 cps tweeter can be made by almost any hi-fi hobbyist in his basement workshop. The few tools needed are:

1. Coping saw or jig saw to cut the stiffening frames.
2. Inexpensive 0-1 inch micrometer to measure thickness of the air gap and grid spacers.
3. 100 watt soldering iron for soldering the brass rods and grids.
4. Dc VTVM-ohmmeter to measure the resistance of the diaphragm coatings and the diaphragm bias supply.
5. Dc high voltage accessory probe for the above.
6. A homemade clamping jig (two flat plates) to hold the brass rods in a flat plane while being soldered into grids.
7. 1 foot by 1 foot piece of plate glass for testing the straightness of brass rods.
8. 2 foot by 2 foot piece of Masonite hardboard to hold each diaphragm stretched out flat while applying the graphite coating.

If you want to build a full-range electrostatic or redesign the tweeter described here, an audio oscillator and an ac VTVM will also be needed to measure the frequency response and input impedance of the crossover networks, the input capacitance of the speaker elements, the leakage inductance of the step-up transformers, and the fundamental resonant frequencies of the diaphragm.

Cost

The electrostatic speaker units, by themselves, cost very little to make. One 5 × 6 inch group of six tweeters cost the author $2.50 each. Almost all of the cost is for the stiffening frames. Using

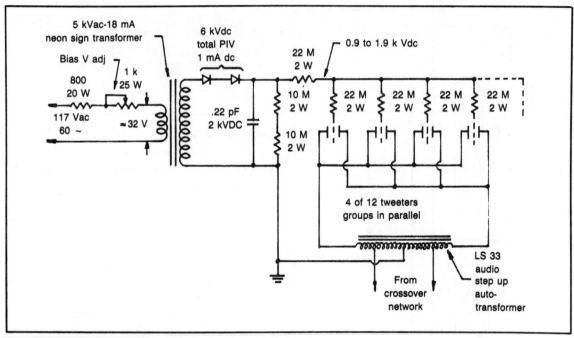

Fig. 15-14. High voltage power supply for the electrostatic tweeters.

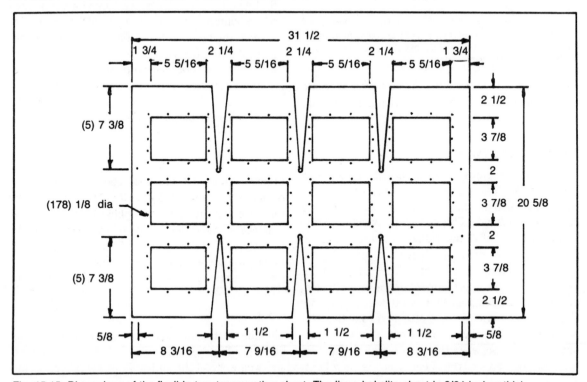

Fig. 15-15. Dimensions of the flexible tweeter mounting sheet. The linen bakelite sheet is 3/64 inches thick.

208

phenolic-cotton laminate, instead of epoxy-glass laminate, for the stiffening frames would reduce cost to about $1.50 per group of six tweeters, and if tempered masonite were used, the cost would drop to about 75 cents per group of six tweeters.

Parts for the high voltage power supply cost $6.00 at the local surplus store. Parts for the cross-over network came from the junk box except for the air core inductor. The wire for each cost $1.00. The only expensive item in the tweeter is the step-up transformer costing $24.00.

This gives a total of $40.00 for a 72 unit tweeter array, using tempered masonite for the stiffening frames. The cost of making a full-range three-way system is estimated at $120 to $150. In comparing this cost to a moving coil speaker system, remember that the full-range electrostatic does not need a speaker cabinet.

Speaker Materials

The selection of the right plastic for the various parts of the speaker is important. Many plastics were tested to determine which was best for the various parts of the speaker.

The diaphragm must be tough, tear resistant, and have a low mass-per-unit-area. Mylar and Saran Wrap are suitable diaphragm materials. The 1/4 mil (0.00025 inch) thick Mylar has less mass-per-unit-area, and consequently it has a slightly higher cutoff frequency than the Saran Wrap, but the author was unable to get a uniform resistance coating on Mylar. Mylar also gave trouble with wrinkles and creases when graphite was applied to it. Saran Wrap, 0.4 mil (0.0004 inches) thick, is very cheap and is available from any grocery store. Saran shrinks when heat is applied, and this turns out to be useful in tightening the diaphragm to attain a specific resonant frequency. The writer has used both an electric hot plate and hot air from an electric hair dryer to shrink diaphragms. The key to successful shrinking seems to be many "warm" passes over the heat source rather than one "hot" pass.

The air gap spacers should be a low-creep material with a low dielectric constant, and it should not "track." Tracking means that the material will form a carbon track along the path of an arc over. If the speaker should happen to arc over and a carbon track occurred, the track would make a high resistance leakage path across the air gap and short out the diaphragm bias supply.

The dielectric constant of the air gap spacers directly affects the amount of shunt capacitance in the speaker mounting frame, and hence affects the speaker's efficiency. Doubling the dielectric constant doubles the amplifier power wasted in the frame capacity. Polystyrene, high impact polystyrene, Lexan, Delrin, and epoxy-glass laminate are suitable materials for air gap spacers. Delrin is the best material if cost is no object because of its mechanical stiffness, stability, and (apparently) the lowest creep of any of the thermo plastics. It has the disadvantage that its dielectric constant is a little high (3.7). Epoxy laminated with glass cloth also has the disadvantage of a high dielectric constant (5.8). Lexan is stiff and mechanically stable, but its edges "burr over" when cut and this warps the diaphragm out of flat. Polystyrene is a very good material because of its low dielectric constant (2.6) and very high insulation resistance, but it is not available any thinner than 1/32 of an inch. The author used Cadco high impact polystyrene, which is rather soft mechanically but has the advantage of a low dielectric constant (about 3.0) and low cost.

The grid spacers should have very high mechanical stiffness and be dimensionally stable. Either epoxy-glass laminate or phenolic-cloth laminate are good materials for grid spacers.

The stiffening frames should be the stiffest possible material at lowest cost. The stiffening frames should not be too thick or they will act as "tunnels" to the sound coming from the diaphragm. Although epoxy-glass laminate is the most rigid of any suitable material, it also is the most expensive and dulls cutting tools very rapidly. The best material for stiffening frames appears to be phenolic-cloth laminate. For a big speaker with several woofers, tempered masonite hardboard would be a good choice because of lower cost.

The adhesive used to fasten diaphragms to the air gap spacers was General Cement No 32-2A Plastic Cement, available at most radio parts stores. General Cement No 346 Epoxy Cement also was used. These two adhesives were only marginally satisfactory, but were the best of many adhesives tried. The graphite used was Dixon's Jet-4 microfyne Graphite, available at most hardware stores.

Miscellaneous

Although the directivity of a single electrostatic diaphragm is just as bad as that of a moving coil speaker of the same size, the effect is greater with an electrostatic because it has a flat power response curve whereas a moving coil speaker does not. Because of this, an on-axis frequency response cure on a single electrostatic unit will show a rising response characteristic with frequency. Since an electrostatic speaker system usually contains many tweeters connected in parallel, one cure for directivity is to fan them out on a spherical surface so that each one faces outward in a slightly different direction. Another interesting approach suggested by Walker is to cover one whole wall of the room with electrostatic speakers.

The electrostatic speaker is not a perfect speaker. The diaphragm exhibits standing wave resonances at various frequencies, and these can be seen by observing the reflection of a light bulb on the diaphragm while the frequency is varied. As might be expected, the biggest resonance is the fundamental resonant frequency of the diaphragm. The metal grids also exhibit resonance effects, and several electrostatic designs have applied damping materials to the grids to reduce these resonances.

The depth positioning of the woofer, midranges, and tweeters with respect to each other is important if good transient response is wanted. All of the speakers should be in approximately the same plane, whether or not that plane is flat or spherical, and should be connected in phase as well. Musical transients lose their sharpness if the higher harmonics from a tweeter arrive at the listener's ear either sooner or later than the fundamental frequencies from the woofer. On several speaker systems, the author could tell by listening if the tweeter was more than 1/4 inch away from the plane of the woofer. For moving coil speakers, this plane seems to be almost halfway between the voice coil and front edge of the cone. The time delays in the crossover networks should affect this depth positioning, but they don't seem to, and the author doesn't understand why not. If the tweeter is out of phase with the woofer, the sound jumps back and forth from one to the other instead of becoming fused into a common "wall of sound." These two effects can make the difference between just an ordinary sounding speaker system and a good one.

A full-range electrostatic is the finest loudspeaker the author has ever listened to. For the same reasons, the electrostatic tweeter is the finest tweeter the author has ever heard. The technical reasons behind this good performance are given in the first part of this article. The performance of an electrostatic is so good that the very best auxiliary equipment is required to demonstrate its performance.

This article was written to help others build their own electrostatic speaker. I'm sold on them as being the best loudspeaker that anyone knows how to make today. Why don't you build one and see for yourself?

(1) Publication is by permission of Audio magazine.

Wide-Range Electrostatic Loudspeaker

P.J. Walker

PRINCIPLES OF DESIGN FOR OPERATION AS WELL AS HIGH FREQUENCIES AND NEGLIGIBLE DISTORTION

A closer examination of underlying principles leads to the conclusion that the electrostatic loudspeaker may well supersede the moving coil for high quality sound reproduction. Designs recently developed have proved to be capable of reproducing the full audio-frequency range, with harmonic distortions no higher than those of the associated amplifier.

Every loudspeaker designer must at some time or other have looked longingly at the electrostatic principle of drive as a solution to his problems of improving quality of reproduction. The movement of a diaphragm driven all over its surface is entirely predictable. The diaphragm can be as light as required. The impedances influencing performance can be predominantly acoustic and, since there are no shape restrictions, entirely under the control of the designer.

What has held it back? First, the fact that in its generally known form it is intrinsically non-linear and even in a push- pull construction linearity can only be approached for small amplitudes. Second, in order to obtain adequate sensitivity, the available gap is small, the diaphragm movement limited and largely stiffness controlled, both factors restricting its use to high frequencies. Third, as it is essentially a capacitive electrical load, it is difficult to match to an amplifier.

The first of these objections, that of nonlinearity, can be removed completely by an expedient which is spectacular in its effectiveness and simplicity. The second and third difficulties will resolve themselves, as we shall see later, when the designer makes his choice of the interdependent mechanical, acoustical, and electrical variables.

Figure 15-16A shows diagrammatically the connection of conventional electrostatic loudspeaker in which the polarizing voltage is applied to the center diaphragm and the signal in push-pull to the outer perforated fixed plates. Under conditions of no signal (Fig 15-16B), and assuming the diaphragm to be central, there will be equal and opposite attractive forces on the diaphragm. If one fixed plate is now made positive and the other negative so that the diaphragm will be deflected to the right, the effective capacitance will increase, and to satisfy the relationship $Q = CE$ the charge Q will also increase and will be supplied by a current i during the movement. The force acting on the diaphragm per unit area will, however, be proportional to:

$$((E + e/2)/d_2)^2 - ((E - e/2)/d_1)^2$$

The relationship will be non-linear. Note that the charge Q, although varying, does not enter directly into the relation.

Suppose that after having charged the diaphragm electrode, the source of polarizing potential is disconnected (Fig. 15-16D). The diaphragm now carries a constant charge Q which experiences a force proportional to the product of the field intensity and the charge. The force will be independent of the position of the diaphragm between the plates since both Q and the distance between plates are constants; the only variable is the applied voltage. Note that the difference between d_1 and d_2, although varying, does not enter into the relationship.

The above is perhaps an over-simplification,

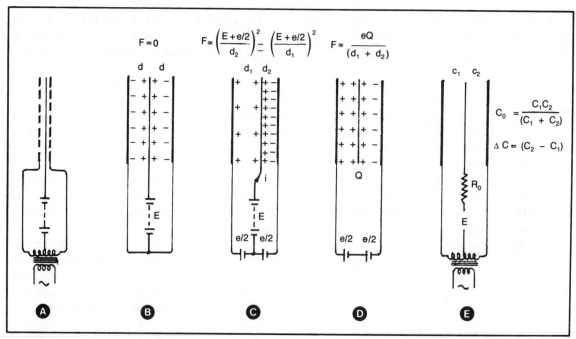

Fig. 15-16. The essential differences in the operation of electrostatic loudspeakers with "constant charge" and "constant voltage" on the center diaphragm.

but it shows that distortion is not necessarily inherent in the electrostatic principle.

The "constant Q" method of operation has another very important advantage in that it reduces the risk of collapse, which occurs at large amplitudes with the conventional method of connection, when the negative stiffness resulting from electrical attraction exceeds the positive mechanical stiffness of the diaphragm. As the diaphragm approaches one of the fixed plates, the capacity is increased but as the charge Q has been assumed constant, E must fall since $E = Q/C$.

Professor F. V. Hunt of Harvard University has shown that the criterion for dynamic stability under large excursions is that the time constant R_oC_o of the charging circuit (Fig. 15-16E) should be large compared with $1/2f$, the half period of the applied frequency. This also supplies the condition for low distortion and Professor Hunt gives the results of measurements (Fig. 6-14) showing the dependence of second harmonic distortion on both the degree of unbalance due to displacement of the central electrode (in terms of C/C) and of the ration of time

constant to half period $2fR_oC_o$. Even when this latter parameter was reduced to unity and the diaphragm displaced by a distance equivalent to a capacity unbalance of 25 per cent, the second harmonic did not exceed 0.5 percent, when driven at 150 c/s by 780 V rms (plate to plate) with a polarizing voltage of 500. Third and higher harmonics were always less then the second.

So much for the driving mechanism; it now remains to see how it fares when coupled to the air and to an amplifier.

It will help in understanding the broad principles involved if we start by considering a loudspeaker whose diaphragm is large compared with the longest wavelength of sound to be reproduced. Under these conditions, the mass reactance of the air load on both sides of the diaphragm can be neglected and the impedance per unit area 2pc offered to the motion of the diaphragm is predominantly resistive (pc = 42 mechanical ohms per cm^2). With constant voltage driving the diaphragm, the force will be proportional to the applied signal voltage and independent of frequency.

212

If the load is resistive, the velocity, and also the acoustic power output, will be independent of frequency.

At very high frequencies, the mass reactance of the diaphragm can exceed the radiation resistance and will cause a falling off in velocity when the force remains constant; the acoustic output will then decline by 6 dB/octave, but with suitable choice of diaphragm material, not until a frequency of 20 to 25 kc/s is reached. (How different from the average moving coil in which the cut-off starts at about 1000 c/s and must be sustained by focusing of high frequencies along the axis or by juggling with cone "break-up.")

Similarly, at low frequencies, a 6 dB/octave falling off with reducing frequency will result when the reactance due to the stiffness (reciprocal of compliance) of the diaphragm exceeds the resistance air load. This state of affairs is shown graphically in Fig. 15-17. Unfortunately, it is not so easy to put the frequency at which the stiffness begins to exercise control outside the audible range. The choice of stiffness will be dictated by the necessity of constraining the diaphragm against the forces associated with the polarizing voltage. Under "static" conditions ($2fR_oC_o$ less the unity) these forces can increase as the diaphragm approaches the fixed plates and must be limited by a suitable choice of stiffness, polarizing voltage and plate spacing. The plate spacing also determined the electrical capacitance of the loudspeaker, and the impedance offered to the amplifier at the frequency chosen for "matching".

Thus, the bandwidth, available for constant output under the acoustic conditions postulated, is limited at low frequencies by the diaphragm stiffness required for stability and at high frequencies by the conditions of matching to the amplifier. (The

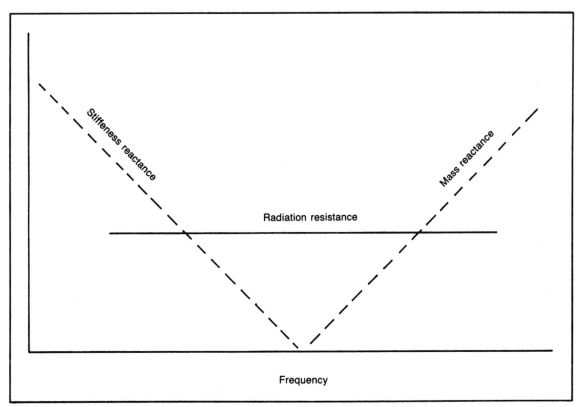

Fig. 15-17. A graph showing the variation in the acoustical and mechanical impedances with frequency in a diaphragm that is large compared with the wavelength.

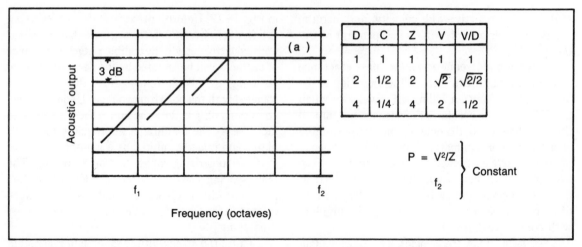

D	C	Z	V	V/D
1	1	1	1	1
2	1/2	2	$\sqrt{2}$	$\sqrt{2}/2$
4	1/4	4	2	1/2

$$P = V^2/Z$$
$$\left.\begin{array}{c}\\ \\ f_2 \end{array}\right\} \text{Constant}$$

Fig. 15-18. Low frequency response can be extended at the expense of "apparent efficiency," by increasing the plate spacing and re-matching to the amplifier at f2, the upper frequency limit.

inertia cut-off will always be well above the matching frequency and can be ignored.)

The true efficiency of an electrostatic loudspeaker is very high indeed, but it is difficult to realize because of the large wattless current which has to be provided due to the electrical capacity of the loudspeaker unit. Thus, it is necessary to waste watts in the amplifier or in resistances associated with crossover networks of which the loudspeaker may be part. For purposes of simplification, therefore, it is convenient to use the term "apparent efficiency" the meaning of which is the ratio of the acoustic power output of the loudspeaker to the amplifier volt-ampere output necessary to provide the required voltage across the loudspeaker capacity.

The way in which the designer can trade bandwidth for "apparent efficiency" is illustrated by Figs. 15-18 and 15-19. In both cases, we assume the maximum output will be available at the high frequency matching limit, and that constant voltage will be available at this and lower frequencies.

In Fig. 15-18, let curve (a) represent the response with a given electrode spacing $D = 1$. If we double the spacing, the diaphragm stiffness re-

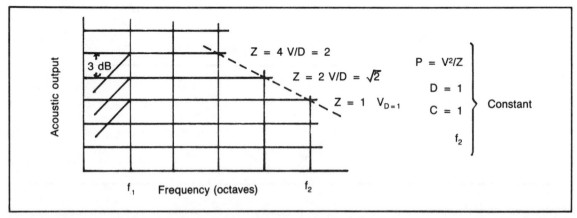

$$Z = 4 \ V/D = 2$$
$$Z = 2 \ V/D = \sqrt{2}$$
$$Z = 1 \ V_{D=1}$$

$$P = V^2/Z$$
$$\left.\begin{array}{c} D = 1 \\ C = 1 \\ \\ f_2 \end{array}\right\} \text{Constant}$$

Fig. 15-19. Alternatively, with constant spacing and a fixed low frequency limit the high frequency response can be extended, again at the expense of "apparent efficiency," by varying the frequency f2 at which the capacitive impedance is matched to the amplifier.

quired for stability can be halved and the low frequency cut-off goes down an octave. At $D = 2$, the capacitance is halved and the impedance doubled, but because the power is limited the volts rise by only 2 when the amplifier is re-matched. Thus, the field strength V/D available to drive the diaphragm is reduced and the response falls by 3 dB. We have thus gained an octave for a drop of 3 dB in output, and, of course, the necessity of finding twice the polarizing voltage.

We can, if required, regain the lost efficiency by re-matching an octave lower at the top end, as shown in Fig. 15-19. If we re-match an octave lower, Z will be doubled and V will increase to 2, so there will be a 3 dB rise in acoustic power for the loss of an octave at the high frequency end.

Since very high efficiencies are not a prerequisite of high quality reproduction, it is convenient to arrange the apparent efficiency to be similar to the efficiency obtained from present day commercial moving coil speakers. Setting the efficiency at this level and applying polarizing voltages permissible in the given air gap, we find that the available bandwidth for level response is about four to five octaves.

Below the low frequency cut-off, we have the stiffness of the diaphragm controlling response, a large proportion of it under conditions where the "apparent efficiency" is high and wasted. (At low frequencies, the impedance is high, and less power is required to maintain constant voltage.) The effect of this mechanical stiffness is best considered when we deal with possible forms of loading, since it can be lumped in with the acoustical circuit loading the loudspeaker.

A high polarizing voltage is desirable in order to place a high value of charge Q on the diaphragm. Each small unit area of the diaphragm can be fed with a high voltage at very high impedances, thus charging up that part of the diaphragm in relation to the fixed plates. In this arrangement of the loudspeaker, where the signal is applied to the fixed plates only, there are no signal currents due to the wanted signal in the diaphragm itself, so that this arrangement of high impedance charging of each unit area of the diaphragm is permissible, and is

essential for linearity in any practical construction. Any tendency for the air to conduct between the diaphragm and the fixed plate at any point in the loudspeaker merely causes a slight drop in the voltage at that area on the diaphragm, so that in this way high voltages can be applied without any danger of sparking.

Since the charge on the diaphragm is unvarying, it follows that the force on the diaphragm is completely independent of the position of the diaphragm in the space between these electrodes and the system in linear. With this arrangement, it is no longer necessary to restrict the allowable motion of the diaphragm to a small percentage of the available gap. Again, there is no restriction to the ration of signal voltage to polarizing voltage. The only non-linear element entering the system at all is that due to the compliance of the diaphragm, and, since in most designs, this is not a controlling factor in the motion of the diaphragm, its importance is small. There is no difficulty in producing units on this principle, the distortion content of which is even lower than that of present day amplifiers, and many times better than a moving coil loudspeaker of normal efficiency.

We have seen that it is now possible to design loudspeakers on the electrostatic principle for a given bandwidth, over which the forces are acting directly on to the air. We have seen that this bandwidth can be placed anywhere in the audio range and that linearity represents considerable improvement on anything hitherto produced. The design of a loudspeaker unit on such principles is therefore purely one of applying it to its acoustical load to give any required performance.

We have so far assumed the simple case of 2pc loading on the diaphragm. Ignoring horn loading for the moment, this can only be achieved in practice at very high frequencies, or for cases where the diaphragm is very large indeed.

A simple single unit construction for high frequencies is shown in Fig. 15-20. This loudspeaker covers the range from 1000 cps to the upper limits of audibility. Such a unit could, of course, be used with conventional moving coil speakers for low frequencies, but the assumption that moving coil units

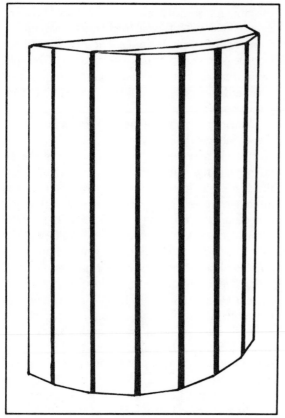

Fig. 15-20. A pictorial diagram of a high frequency unit with dimensions large compared with wavelength designed to cover from 1000 c/s to the upper limit of audibility.

reliable figures below 1%. Inspection of the residual waveform indicates that the distortion due to the units is considerable lower than this figure.

Similar remarks apply to frequency response, due to the fact that is virtually impossible to achieve perfect loading conditions. Measurements produce responses which are within 2 dB of the predicted curves, but the major part of these small discrepancies may be attributed to the approximations assumed in the structures used for loading.

Since 1953, electrostatic loudspeakers have been the subject of joint development between Ferranti, Ltd., of Edinburgh, and The Acoustic

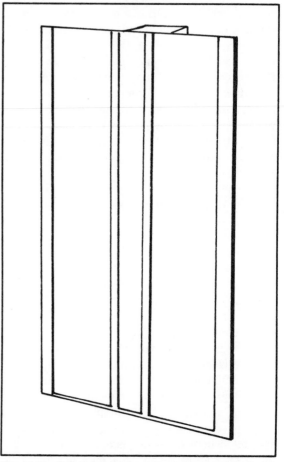

Fig. 15-21. A pictorial diagram of a more complex design which, with proper acoustic loading, covers the range from 40 c/s to the upper limit of audibility. Measurements on this and the unit of Fig. 15-20. Indicate a total harmonic distortion of less than 1 percent.

operate like distortionless pistons at low frequencies is very far from the truth. It is obviously desirable to introduce the benefits of the electrostatic principle throughout the whole frequency range.

By way of showing what can be done, Fig. 15-21 shows a more complex design of electrostatic loudspeaker which, when properly loaded, covers the whole frequency range from 40 cps up to the limits of audibility. In a future article, it is proposed to discuss the operation of such loudspeakers, i.e., when size is no longer large compared to wavelength, and to show the basis of design approach for the whole frequency range.

Distortion measurements on these units gave figures well below 1%. Measurements were made out of doors, and noise, wind, and other restrictions due to imperfect conditions made it difficult to get

Manufacturing Co., Ltd., of Huntingdon. Some of the techniques involved in the design of these loudspeakers are the subject of joint patent applications by P.J. Walker and D.T.N. Williamson.

PROBLEMS OF AIR LOADING

In the first part of this article we showed that it was possible to design and construct electrostatic drive units which were capable of applying a force which virtually acted directly on to the air, and we showed that this force was linear. This state of affairs applied over a bandwidth of several octaves for any single unit, depending upon the efficiency required from that unit, and it was further shown that bandwidth could be placed anywhere in the audio range.

Different Requirements of Moving Coil and Electrostatic Drive Units

The only mechanical impedance likely to affect performance is the suspension compliance of the diaphragm, necessary to offset the negative compliance due to electrical attraction. We can therefore begin to draw an electrical analogue circuit of the mechanical elements of the loudspeaker as in Fig. 15-22, showing the force fed in series with a capacitance. In practice, the compliance will considerable exceed the electrical negative compliance, so that this capacitance C_2 is almost solely due to the diaphragm compliance.

For simplicity, we will restrict consideration to units driven from constant-voltage sources, so that no elements need be included to indicate amplifier source impedance.

Since the loudspeaker will be coupled to the air, we can now add the front air load radiation resistance R_f and the front air load mass M_f, and we can include the impedance (Z) which represents the impedance presented to the back of the diaphragm.

The impedance (Z) may include dissipative terms in the form of absorption and/or acoustic radiation resistance. With most acoustic devices, the analogy elements change with frequency and the problem as with all loudspeaker design, is to arrange matters so that the power developed in the radiation resistance(s) is independent of frequency.

The electrostatic unit differs from the moving coil in that there is no large mass component (cone and speech coil) which normally appears as a large inductance in series with C_d. The absence of this inductance profoundly alters the requirements for

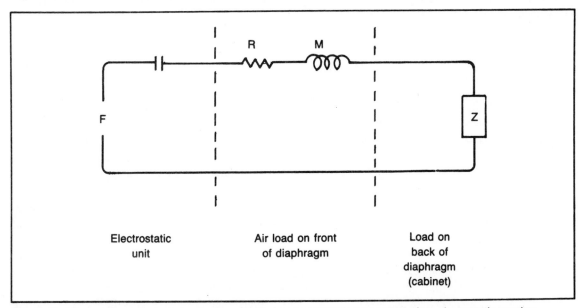

Fig. 15-22. Elementary equivalent circuit of mechanical and acoustical parameters of an electrostatic speaker.

Z and, since Z is the cabinet or back enclosure, it is to be expected that the form of cabinets, for electrostatic units will follow trends entirely different from those that have been evolved for moving coil units. A further difference is that the shape of the diaphragm area is more versatile, so that R_f and M_f may be independently varied over reasonable limits.

Due to the absence of large mass, we can, if we wish, arrange the constants so that R_f is large compared with the other elements, and therefore becomes the controlling factor for the equivalent current in the circuit, ie., the velocity of motion of the diaphragm. This means that the impedance looking back into the loudspeaker can be very low. When this is so, any increase in the acoustic resistance on the front of the diaphragm will result in reduced power output. If, on the other hand, the impedance of the loudspeaker is made to appear high by arranging that the total impedance is large compared with R_f then an increase in acoustic resistance on the front of the diaphragm will result in increased power output. This ability to control the impedance looking back into the diaphragm is a useful feature in designs where R_f is subject to fluctuations due to surroundings, horn reflections, etc., and, in particular, where one loudspeaker unit is influenced by another unit at cross-over frequencies.

In order to show the action of an electrostatic unit, which is small compared to the wavelength of the radiated sound, it is convenient to commence with a circular shape, because impedance information is readily available for such a shape. Load impedance for other shapes is best obtained by considering the diaphragm as a number of unit areas of equal size and calculating the impedance of each unit area, taking into account the mutual radiation due to the presence of all other unit areas.

Figure 15-23 shows the load on a piston operated in an unlimited atmosphere without a baffle. The diaphragm compliance reactance $X_c(E)$ is also drawn. Between f1 and f2, the controlling factor is the air mass, and the velocity of motion will vary directly with frequency until resonance between $X_c(E)$ and X_{ma} is approached. R, however, falls

rapidly with frequency, and the power output will fall at approximately 6 dB per octave with declining frequency. Exactly the same would occur with a moving coil unit, the control this time is the mass of the cone and speech coil designated $X_m(MC)$. $X_c(MC)$ is the moving coil suspension compliance.

Multiple diaphragms without baffles form the basis of design for loudspeakers to provide the directivity of a doublet. Such a system has useful attributes in relation to the listening rooms, a subject to be dealt with in a later article.

Above f2, the velocity of the moving coil unit would still be controlled by $X_m(MC)$ (except for cone "break-up") and, since the resistance becomes constant, the response will fall with increasing frequency. Above f2, the velocity will be controlled by the air load resistance, and the response will be independent of frequency.

Extending this comparison to units in very large baffles, we have the curves of Fig. 15-24. Here, the radiation resistance varies with the square of the frequency below f2. With a moving coil, the response will be level below f2 and will fall with frequency above f2. With the electrostatic, the response will be level below f2 and also level above f2, but there will be a step in response so that the output level above f2 will be 3 dB higher than that below f2.

A simple arithmetical example will make clear the reason for this step. With a constant force (F) applied to the diaphragm, the velocity of movement will be $F/(R_2 + X_2)^{1/2}$ and the power expended usefully in the radiation resistance will be P = $(F/(R_2 + X_2)1/2)^2 \times R$. At f_B in Fig. 15-24, neglecting Z due to the declining air mass reactance, we have for a constant for F = 1, P = R/R_2 = 2/4 = 1/2. At f_A, on the other hand, the air mass predominates and, if R can be neglected in calculating the velocity of motion, P = R/X_2 = 0.01/(0.2)² = 0.01/0.04 = 1/4, or half the power at f_B. A similar relationship will be found for any other pair of values of R and X at points below f2.

This change in level can be overcome by deviating from the circular piston shape. For wavelengths which are large, compared to the diaphragm size, the resistance per unit area is dependent upon the

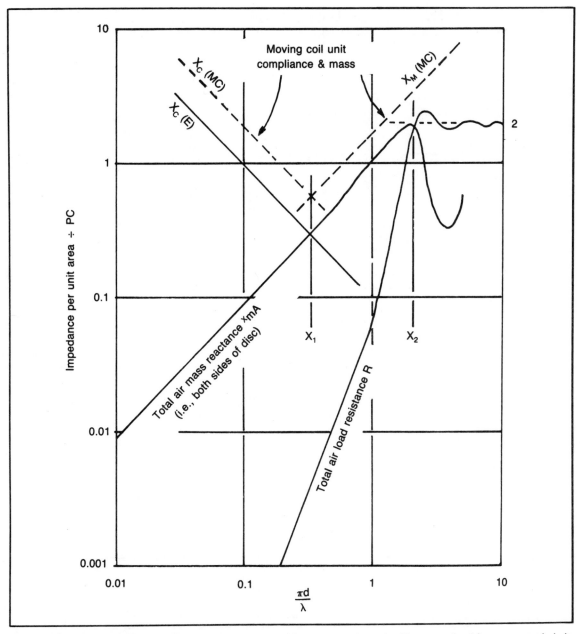

Fig. 15-23. Mass and radiation resistance loads on circular diaphragm in free air. The normalized frequency scale is in terms of the relationship of diaphragm size to wavelength.

new area and not upon the shape, whereas the mass is mainly dependent upon the smaller dimension. By elongating the diaphragm shape, the output level below f2 can be made equal to that above f2.

We have, so far, been considering a comparatively small diaphragm in a flat baffle, the latter being very much larger than the piston, and the size of the complete system is obviously that of the baf-

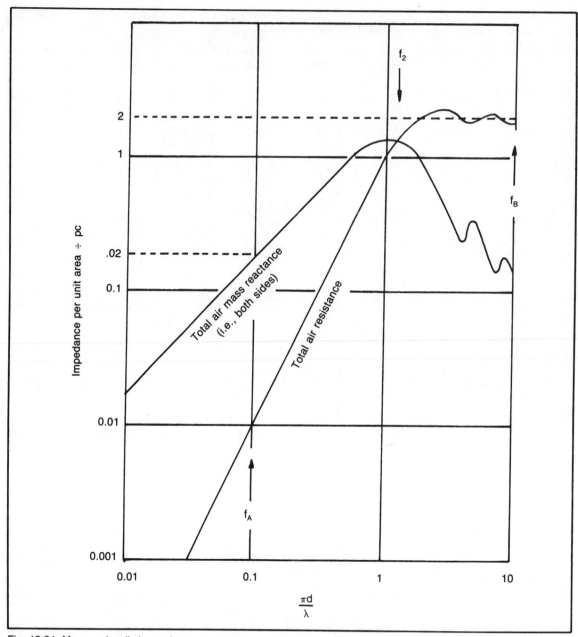

Fig. 15-24. Mass and radiation resistance curves for a circular diaphragm in a large baffle. The power radiated at any frequency fa well below f2 is half that radiated at frequencies fb well above f2 (see text).

fle. The reason that the piston has been kept small is purely for convenience of the moving coil unit, because its diaphragm is driven at only one point. In the electrostatic case, we no longer have this re-striction, and it will always be preferable to increase the size of the piston (without increasing the total size of the complete system). This will usually be necessary because there is a limit to the available amplitude of movement, and thus, for a given power output per unit area, we have a minimum limit to the radiation resistance in order that the diaphragm excursions may be attainable. Increasing the size of the piston for a given power output has the double advantage of reducing power requirements per unit area, and where the loading is below 2pc, of increasing the radiation resistance per unit area, and therefore reducing the amplitude required to provide that power output. For reasons of efficiency, we shall, in any case, limit the high frequency response of the unit so that optimum design is obtained by increasing the area of the diaphragm to the point where the piston just begins to become directional at the frequency which we have chosen for crossover (set by the efficiency laid down in the design requirement).

Continuing the consideration of the air load on diaphragms, reference should be made to horn loading. Here, we have large resistive and mass components due to the horn. Figure 15-24 shows the load of an idealized horn to which has been added $X_m(MC)$, the cone mass of a typical moving coil loudspeaker which might be used with such a horn. It will be seen that, at low frequencies, the cone mass is largely swamped by the horn impedance, so that the design of horns for electrostatic units differs very little from the design for moving coil units. Although we can now have the advantages of a virtually distortionless driving unit, we are still left with the disadvantages of practical horns, which are present independent of the drive units. Horns are normally used to match the high impedance of moving coil diaphragms to the low impedance of the air. Since we have no such fundamental mismatch with the electrostatic loudspeaker, and since diaphragm shape and size are not fundamentally restricted, we shall not normally have to resort to the use of horns to the same degree. It should be remembered, however, that nay back enclosed volume is a direct function of throat area, so that in some applications it is possible to use space for providing a length of horn in exchange for saving in size of capacitive enclosure. Again, we may wish to restrict the front wave expansion in order to maintain a reasonable resistance per unit area at

low frequencies (utilizing the corner of a room, for example).

One of the most desirable diaphragm shapes for electrostatic designs is that of a strip having a length (together with floor or wall image) large compared to $\lambda/3$ at the lowest frequency of interest, and a width small compared to wavelength at the highest frequency of interest. The strip may be curved along its length if desired, provided the radius of curvature is not less than $\lambda/3$ at the lowest frequency.

To consider the load on such a strip, it is convenient to assume the strip as being infinite in length (legitimate provided it is at least $\lambda/3$ in length). With such a diaphragm, there will be no expansion of sound in the direction of the length since all pressures along the length of the strip will be equal. Expansion from any given element of the diaphragm takes place in one plane only and will therefore take the form $S = S_0x$. This is the expansion of a parabolic horn. At low frequencies, the front air load resistance is falling directly with frequency (instead of f2 as with the circular piston shape). The advantages of the strip shape may now be enumerated:-

(a) The air resistance even at low frequencies (since R α f) is sufficient to develop adequate power with reasonable diaphragm amplitude.
(b) The narrow diaphragm gives good dispersion for several octaves (up to the frequency at which width $\lambda/3$).
(c) The narrow diaphragm enables other units to be placed close to it, thus being less than 1/4 wavelength apart at the crossover frequency.
(d) The frequency limitations, amplitude at the low end, and directional problems at the high end, fit in nicely with the 4 - 5 octave range which we established in Part I of this article for satisfactory efficiency. Thus a strip shape can form one basis of design for our ideal—the perfect loudspeaker.

It will be obvious that a curved front source similar to that illustrated in of Fig. 15-20 in Part I of this article will give similar distribution to a strip, and, due to the large surface, smaller spacing may be used and high efficiency may thus be achieved. In such a case however, the diaphragm must be large compared to wavelength in both dimensions, because it is the nature of curved surfaces to become directional when the radius of curvature is comparable with the wavelength. When the diaphragm is large compared to the wavelength, it is impossible to design an intimate acoustic crossover. This small inherent imperfection would appear to preclude its use in a "perfect" loudspeaker design, although its "efficiency" advantages will have obvious applications in some practical compromise designs. Although designs free to the air on both sides have useful attributes, it is obviously desirable also to produce loudspeakers in cabinet form, enclosing the rear. This rear enclosure, if it is to be of reasonable size, will be the controlling factor for the diaphragm velocity, at least at low frequencies.

With any unit, the high frequency limit will be set by efficiency requirements, and the low frequency limit by amplitude limitations or by the compliance of the enclosure in series with the diaphragm compliance. This compliance will resonate with the air mass on the front and back of the diaphragm (unless the diaphragm is large that the loading is pc - for example, as in the curved diaphragms previously mentioned). Since the total mass is small, the resonance will usually occur above the lowest frequency of interest. It may be dealt with in two ways, (1) by adding acoustic mass within the cabinet to reduce the resonant frequency to the lowest required frequency, or (2) critically damping the resonant frequency and maintaining response below this frequency either by re-matching or by a secondary acoustic resonant circuit, or both.

There are innumerable ways in which either of these alternatives may be achieved. Consider the first alternative. Suppose that the enclosure is made deep and narrow (or fitted with partitions so that it appears deep and narrow to the loudspeaker): then, at wavelengths just under four times the depth, the reaction on the diaphragm will be positive. This will effectively force the resonance to the

1/4 wavelength resonance of the depth of the enclosure. Absorbent wedges may now be fitted to control the resonance and to present a purely resistive load at all high frequencies. Sound compression within the wedges becomes isothermal, decreasing the speed of sound, so that the depth of the enclosure can be reduced accordingly.

Figure 15-25 shows the impedance of a strip unit loaded on this principle together with a curve showing the power output radiated as sound for constant applied voltage. The output is extended by more than an octave over that which would be obtained if the same volume of enclosure were allowed to act as a lumped capacitance.

Turning now to the second method of extending the low frequency range, Fig. 15-26 shows a diaphragm loaded by a capacitance leading through resistance and inductance into a larger capacitance. Both volumes have dimensions many times less than the wavelength in the ranges where they are operative.

If the constants are adjusted to give a step in response as the frequency is lowered, then the total volume of the enclosure is reduced accordingly and the response restored to level by re-matching at the step frequency.

Figure 15-27 shows a strip diaphragm loaded by a capacitance with series resistance, all elements continuing along the whole length of the structure. With this assumption, there will be no waves in the enclosure along its length so that the constants can be calculated on a sectional element of thickness. If the crosssection of C_2 has dimensions which are many times smaller than the wavelength, then C_2 will behave as a capacitance (independent of length). If this proviso is not met, then R_2 must be distributed to avoid C_2 appearing as a multiresonant circuit.

Where the unit crosses over to another unit for low frequencies, then R_2 must be adjusted to give a Q of 0.7 so that the crossover components are already present in the acoustic circuit.

When the lower-frequency unit is arranged so that the two diaphragms are close and intimately coupled, then R_1 will be increased in value by the mutual radiation of the low frequency unit. R_2 is

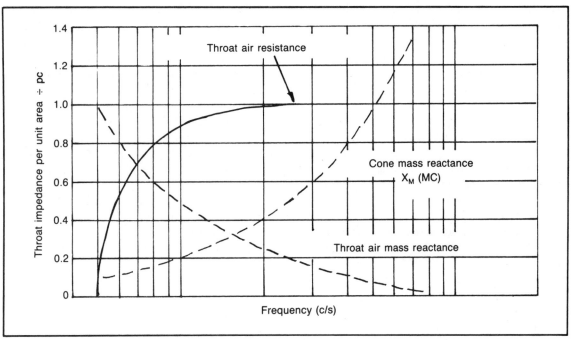

Fig. 15-25. A graph that relates the throat air resistance curves of idealized horn with moving coil mass reactance superimposed.

then reduced to restore Q and we find that if R_1 is larger than R_2 a useful self-compensating effect takes place.

If the voltage applied to the low frequency unit is reduced at crossover due to tolerance in its crossover components, then R_1 is automatically reduced and the output of the high frequency unit increases at crossover. At crossover, $P_{out} \propto R_1/(R1 + R_2)^2$.

Where the enclosure of Fig. 15-27 is used for the unit covering the lowest part of the audio range, bass response may be extended by re-matching or by introducing a secondary resonant circuit and utilizing back radiation from the diaphragm. If an aperture is provided at one end of the enclosure, when the enclosure length is 1/4 wavelength, resonance will occur along its length, and there will be radiation from the aperture. 3/4, 5/4 resonances, etc., will not arise, because the enclosure is excited by a force distributed along its length. At frequencies above the 1/4 wavelength, the enclosure will behave approximately as a capacitance, as if the aperture were not present.

The next part of this article will deal with electrostatic units as part of delay lines and the application of various complete designs, "built in," "boxed in" and "doublet" in relation to the listening room. Complete electrostatic loudspeakers can take several different forms, each of which, in terms of frequency response, distortion, and sound dispersion, can meet a specification virtually to perfection. When the listening room and subjective factors are considered it becomes impossible to lay down a rigid specification. To adopt a quotation "Each design is perfect, but some designs are more perfect than others"!

COMPLETE SYSTEMS

In the first part of this article, we showed that for a given size, the apparent efficiency of an electrostatic unit my be increased by reducing the bandwidth which that unit is required to cover. An obvious method of increasing the overall efficiency of a complete electrostatic system, therefore, is to

Fig. 15-26. Strip loudspeaker, long compared with wavelength, and of width d, mounted in a wall, with the back of the diaphragm loaded by a tube with cross-sectional area equal to that of the diaphragm and of length 5d, blocked at the far end. Resistance (fiber-glass wedge) included in tube to control impedance.

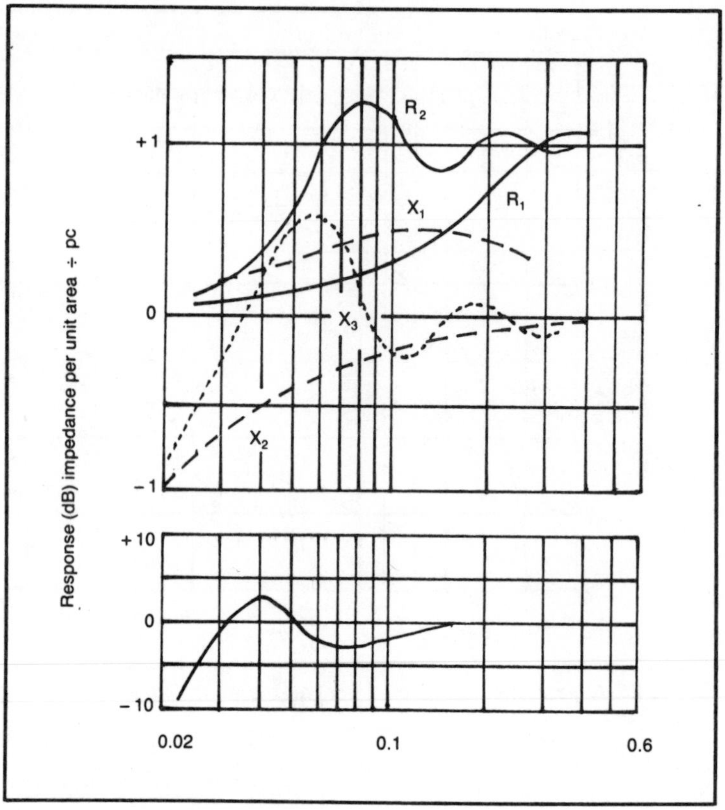

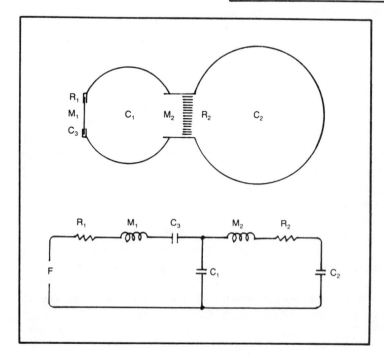

Fig. 15-27. Diaphragm loaded by an equivalent capacitance C1 leading through an acoustic mass and resistance M2 and R2 into a larger capacitance C2.

224

divide the system into a convenient number of frequency bands and to feed them via crossover networks. Optimum design is obtained by increasing gaps and areas with decreasing frequency.

An alternate method of increasing apparent efficiency is to subdivide the loudspeaker area into a number of smaller units each covering the whole frequency range, the units being coupled by inductors so that the whole loudspeaker becomes a transmission line. (Fig. 15-28.) The acoustic radiation resistance appears as conductance in parallel with each capacitive element. For a fixed total area, and neglecting losses, the efficiency varied directly with the number of subdivisions.

Consideration of these two systems shows that frequency division has considerable advantages over transmission line divisions for most complete systems of domestic size and power requirements. First, if a single nine-octave unit is subdivided into a two-unit system, the apparent efficiency is increased 16 times. To obtain the same increase by transmission lines division would require a minimum of 12 divisions. Unless the total area of the loudspeaker is large, and the plate separation small, the capacitance of each section of the transmission line becomes very small indeed and requires a correspondingly large inductance which must be relatively high Q.

This apparent efficiency advantage of frequency subdividing over transmission line dividing holds until the bandwidth of each unit is reduced to two octaves.

Apart from transmission line subdivision applied to individual units of a frequency-divided system, practical considerations normally limits transmission line techniques to large area diaphragms. When such is the case, however, additional facilities are available to the designer both in the accurate control of directional characteristics and in providing a constant phase contour, independent of frequency.

Loudspeaker/Room Relationships

In discussing various possible forms of complete electrostatic systems, a novel situation arises. The quality criterion of a loudspeaker usually con-

centrates on three performance parameters, as measured in an unlimited atmosphere. (a) Ability to produce a required sound intensity over the audio spectrum with negligible non-linearity distortion. (b) The sound pressure over the designated listening area should be independent of frequency throughout the audio range. (c) Operation should be aperiodic.

Complete loudspeakers designed on the principles which we have been discussing are capable of meeting these three requirements to a new and exciting degree. We shall see that different designs and approaches differ not so much in terms of (a), (b) and (c) above, but in other factors of importance to quality reproduction; factors which have previ-

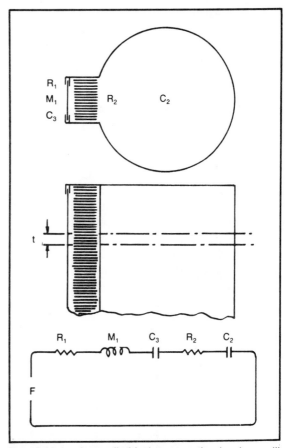

Fig. 15-28. In a long cylindrical structure the air column will be driven equally at all points along its length and no appreciable longitudinal standing waves can be established at frequencies other than that corresponding to f4.

ously had to take second place or have been masked in the struggle for (a), (b) and (c).

Corner Mounting

There has been a strong tendency in loudspeaker design to make use of the corner of a room. This is because, at low frequencies, the air load resistance for a given size of diaphragm is increased 8 times over that of an unlimited atmosphere.

Since the ratio of cabinet "stiffness" to air load resistance is independent of diaphragm size, any increase of resistance due to boundary walls and floors fundamentally reduces the size of cabinet required for a given performance.

As an example, the form of corner electrostatic loudspeaker illustrated in Fig. 15-29 and designed for full performance down to 40 cps utilized an internal resonance with a Q of 3 and a built-in enclosure of 10 cubic feet. Fundamentally the enclosure size could be reduced either by (1) increasing Q, (2) reducing the power and apparent efficiency requirements, or (3) restricting frequency range. Any one factor may be traded for any or all of the others.

It should be noted that with the diaphragm area of Fig. 15-29 the resistance could be substantially increased by reshaping the whole of the low frequency area near the floor so that, with the boundary reflections, its dimensions laterally and vertically are similar. Such a form, with suitable shaped treble unit above it, can be designed to give level response in direct radiation to the listening area so that the (a), (b), (c) requirements are not affected. Homogeneity, on the other hand, due to the

physical spacing of units, is destroyed. This may be more important than is generally realized, particularly in rooms of normal domestic size.

The high frequency section (center strip in Fig. 15-29) is sealed at the rear by an enclosure of width equal to that of the strip and incorporating a fibreglass wedge to offer almost pure resistance throughout the range of the unit. This sealing is necessary in order to maintain front air load resistance by preventing coupling between front and back.

Figure 15-30 shows an entirely different form of corner design. The diaphragm area covers the whole surface and extends around the back to form an enclosed cylinder. Every part of the diaphragm carries the whole frequency range. The surface area is divided into units to form a transmission line. The total volume is 15 cubic feet. The step in diameter is introduced because the transmission rotates around the top portion and thence around the bottom portion. The time delay in the sound expanding from the top portion to the diameter of the bottom portion is equal to the time delay of the electrical voltages in the transmission line.

The complete assembly is placed a small distance from the corner of a room so that the boundary reflectors are aiding at the lowest frequency of interest. The large diaphragm area together with the boundary reflections provide a loading approximately equal to pc at 30-40 cps. Internally there is acoustic resistance treatment so that there will be resistive loading at high frequencies, changing to a capacitive load due to the lumped enclosure at low frequencies. Simplified equivalent circuits for high and low frequencies are shown in Fig.

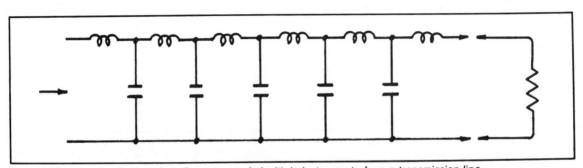

Fig. 15-29. Capacitive loudspeaker elements coupled with inductances to form a transmission line.

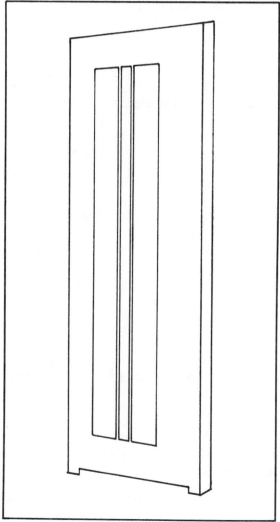

Fig. 15-30. A wide-range electrostatic loudspeaker in a resonant corner enclosure.

15-31. The turnover occurs at about 400 cps and it is obvious that, with constant voltage, the response will be level above 400 cps and drop at 6 dB/octave below this frequency. This is corrected by progressively re-matching to the amplifier below 400 cps. The section shape may be elliptical to give a degree of direction at high frequencies.

It is obvious that the corner boundaries will introduce peaks and troughs throughout the frequency range. These are, however, exactly the same as occur naturally with speech or music

originating near boundaries in a room. To what degree these effects are important must at the present time be a matter of conjecture. It can safely be said that the subjective effect is by no means as alarming as the appearance of the response curve.

The advantage of a corner position has already been noted. This advantage is not gained without considerable detriment in other directions. If we wished to excite every room resonance to its fullest extent with a sound source of high internal impedance, we put this source in a corner because this is the position of high impedance for every mode. In placing our loudspeaker in a corner therefore we are placing it in the worst possible position if our aim is smooth aperiodic sound.

Although the present trend appears to be to

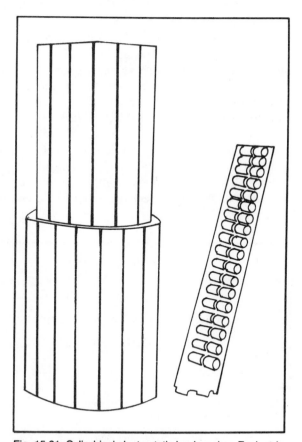

Fig. 15-31. Cylindrical electrostatic loudspeaker. Each strip carries the full frequency range and the sections are coupled to form an electrical transmission line. The inductor assembly is at the right.

tolerate this state of affairs in the interest of the organs's 32 foot rank (or reduction of cabinet size), the inherent smoothness of electrostatic loudspeaker one experienced is not lightly thrown away, and there is added impetus in attempts to improve the loudspeaker/room relationship.

Double Wall Enclosure

The strip "twin" unit design of Fig. 15-29 may be built into a wall in such a way that most room modes are not excited or are excited only feebly. If it is an outside wall, the rear enclosure may be added externally. If it is an inside wall it may spread over the wall so that from the appearance point of view it has virtually disappeared. Figure 15-32 shows the general form of installation. The strip unit extends from floor to ceiling and the low-frequency sections are backed by 5 inch wide enclosures 4 1/2 feet in length, with fibre-glass wedges incorporated. The impedances and response are shown in Fig. 15-25. With the dimensions of the example, $d = 10$ inches since both 5 inch units are coupled and the response will be within 3 dB of 1 kc response down to 35 cps. These figures include floor, one wall and ceiling, but do not, of course, include the effects of other room boundaries. Assuming a 2 inch thick wall for rigidity, the volume of a room of 300 square feet floor area would be reduced 2%.

There can be no initial excitation of floor to ceiling modes because vertical excitation is evenly distributed. Modes excited in a direction parallel to the wall on which the speaker is mounted will be reduced in number. Assuming a rectangular room, the number of modes excited will be some four times less than the number excited by a corner floor position.

As can be seen by the following summary, this form of loudspeaker leaves little more to be desired.

1. The enclosure being "built-in" can be completely rigid.
2. The only fold in the enclosure is narrow compared to wavelength and being close to the diaphragm can cause no reflections in the range of that unit.
3. The loudspeaker and its enclosure are completely predictable.
4. The (a), (b) and (c) requirements previously mentioned can be met virtually to perfection.
5. Radiation throughout the whole frequency range is homogeneous; there is no source displacement and no phase problems at crossover.
6. Total radiated energy (as well as axial pressure) is independent of frequency.
7. The loudspeaker/room relationship is good.

Item 6 deserves further mention. The normal frequency response specification of a loudspeaker

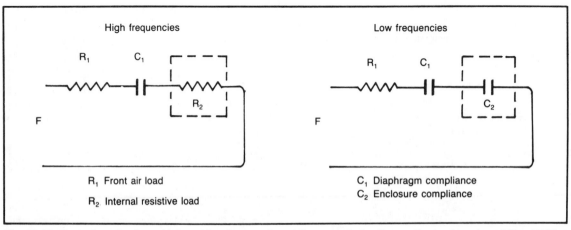

Fig. 15-32. Equivalent circuits at high and low frequencies of the acoustic loading on the loudspeaker of Fig. 15-31.

is in terms of sound pressure produced on the axis or over a limited listening arc. The mean spherical radiation (total power output) is not usually specified, although it will have a profound effect in a room because the intensity of indirect sound is dependent upon it. If high-frequency radiation is limited to a segment of 90×30 degrees (a typical figure), and bass radiation is hemispherical, and if the axis response is level, then there will be a step of 12 dB in the mean radiated response. This produces an artificial step in the acoustic ratio (ratio of direct to indirect sound) producing unnatural hardening of the reproduced sound.

Doublet Sources

We now come to consideration of the doublet as a sound source and we shall see that it possesses properties of considerable significance in improving loudspeaker/room relationships. By a doublet, we mean a diaphragm radiating on both sides.

If we assume a 12 inch—15 inch unit (moving coil or electrostatic) mounted in a 4 foot—5 foot baffle, we find that the acoustic system has three main faults. (1) the acoustic air load falls to very low values at wavelengths larger than the baffle size. (2) The acoustic load is very irregular at low frequencies and (3) reflections from the baffle edge occur at higher frequencies. The second and third faults can be mitigated by adopting peculiar shapes.

If, instead of a baffle, we construct a composite electrostatic unit of the same area, the position is completely altered. The resistance per unit area and the total working area are both increased so that the air load is many times that of the baffle case. The load and consequently the performance, is regular and predictable.

The construction is that of strip units progressively increasing in plate spacing and area from the center line. Due to the air load resistance involved for each strip, the permissible bandwidth is reduced over that which could be obtained if the back radiation were sealed off and it is necessary to split the frequency range into three to obtain efficiency comparable to a two-way "sealed" system.

Any unloaded strip considered alone will have a resonant frequency when the diaphragm stiffness reactance equals the air load mass reactance. This is, however, placed below the frequency range of the strip, so that the mutual radiation of the adjacent strip carrying a lower frequency range increases the radiating area and prevents the application of any effective mass. The complete system is therefore entirely free of resonance except at one low frequency (usually at 30 to 35 cps). The Q of this resonance is adjusted to maintain a response to this frequency.

The complete loudspeaker has a cosine characteristic and this is substantially maintained through the range. It cannot radiate sound in the direction of its surface, horizontally or vertically, so that it cannot excite room modes in two of the three room dimensions. It will only excite modes in the remaining dimension when placed at a region of maximum velocity for that mode. (The impedance looking into the loudspeaker is low.)

Having a "cosine" polar characteristic, the mean spherical radiation is reduced by a factor of 3 at all frequencies, so that quite apart from freedom of mode excitations, any colour due to the room is reduced by a factor of three. This is exactly analogous to a "velocity" microphone. In the same way, a "velocity" microphone is used in place of a "pressure" microphone to reduce studio colour due to the listening room.

Listening tests comparing "pressure" and "velocity" speakers of otherwise similar characteristics indicate that a velocity characteristic may well have important features for high quality reproduction. An electrostatic loudspeaker of this type correctly positioned in the room meets all requirements as did the "wall" form previously described, with the addition of an even better loudspeaker/room relationship. The fact that it needs to be free standing well within the room may or may not be advantageous.

The more the acoustic ratio is reduced (provided always that it is reduced equally at all frequencies), the more one approaches the state of affairs that the pressure at the ears is a replica of the pressure at the position of the microphone in the concert hall or studio (ideal headphone conditions).

It must be emphasized that many arguments for and against this condition have been proposed. It is outside the scope of these articles to enter these arguments other than to say that, with a monaural channel, the choice must be an aesthetic one. A complete listening room can be designed to produce pressures throughout the room which are more or less equal to the pressure at the studio microphone.

A tube of small diameter compared to wavelength fitted with a piston at one end, and terminated at the other by a resistance of pc will give pressures anywhere in the tube which are directly proportional to piston velocity and independent of frequency. Provided that the area of the piston equals the tube crosssectional area, and then the requirement of small diameter disappears.

A rectangular room with a diaphragm covering one wall and correct termination on the opposite wall meets the requirements. The space behind the diaphragm must be at least 10 inches deep and treated like the speaker in Fig. 15-30. the equivalent circuit is the same as Fig. 15-31. The sound absorption treatment of the opposite wall must ideally be several feet in depth.

Sound intensity throughout the room is independent of position (including the distance from the diaphragm). The apparent sound source is always in a direction perpendicular to the diaphragm and, of course, moves as the listener moves.

The same loudspeaker may be used for stereophony. With transmission line matching and feeding the signal at one end the wavefront will be tilted, due to the time delay. Separate signals may be fed from either end to produce two tilted waveforms, one for each signal. Since each apparent origin is perpendicular to its wavefront, the aspect angle from the listener is a constant and entirely independent of the listener's position over a large triangular area (Fig. 15-33). The relative intensity of the two signals is also constant.

A fixed angle, two channel system of this type may be obtained with a less elaborate listening room. The strip arrangement of Fig. 15-32 may be installed horizontally instead of vertically. If each unit is a transmission line along its length, then two cylindrical wavefronts will be produced with exactly the same feature of constant aspect angle already described. See Fig. 15-34.

To summarize, the electrostatic principle is capable of surmounting the present limitations of other methods of speaker drive. It is capable of overcoming the present tweeter/woofer concept to produce a closely coupled, integrated assembly. The problem of loudspeaker/room relationships (common to all loudspeakers) still remains, although the design versatility of the electrostatic makes it possible to design for optimum relationship if these can ever be defined for a monaural channel.

A closer understanding of the relative importance of the many factors involved are needed. (a) Source movement with frequency, (b) Homogeneity, (c) Acoustic ratio, (d) Mode excitation, (e)

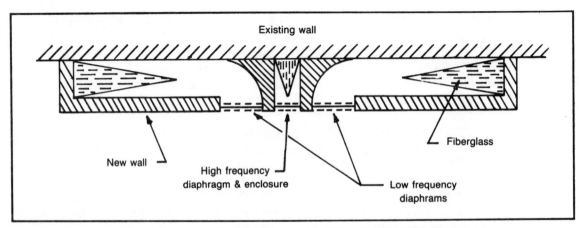

Fig. 15-33. Sectional plan showing one method of rear enclosure for a strip electrostatic unit.

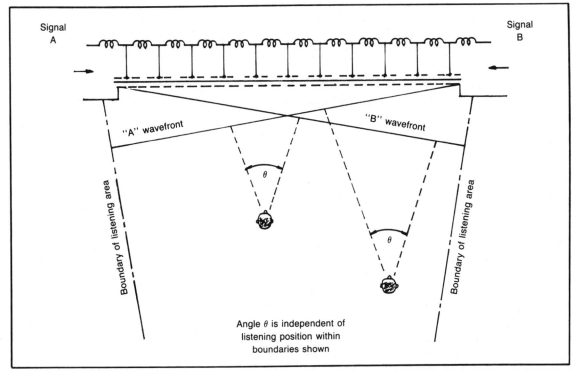

Fig. 15-34. Stereophony from a single transmission line loudspeaker, with separate channels feeding each end of the line.

Phase contour, etc. All are factors which can only be tentatively assessed after long usage.

The author wishes to thank Ferranti Ltd. for permission to publish the result of work jointly carried out, and to acknowledge the invaluable work of D.T.N. Williamson, W.D. Olliphant, and their colleagues at Edinburgh. Thanks are due to J. Watson, J. Collinson, and others at the Acoustical Manufacturing Company, and to the several specialists, who have been able to assist with problems in their own field.

Published by permission of Mr. Peter J. Walker

A Wide-Range Electrostatic Speaker

by Charles I. Malme, Massachusetts Institute of Technology, Cambridge Massachusetts

A newly designed wide-range electrostatic loudspeaker incorporates: (a) push-pull operation with a light, 20 inch diameter, peripherally-supported diaphragm; (b) a high-resistivity coating on the diaphragm surfaces to give constant-charge operation without the use of an external series resistor; (c) a bias voltage of 16 kv applied through a corona-ring around the edge of the diaphragm; (d) a high output-voltage audio amplifier to provide a driving signal of 4.5 kilovolts rms; (e) large diaphragm excursion to allow adequate low-frequency reproduction; and (f) electrical segmentation of the diaphragm to give broad directivity patterns at all frequencies.

The experimental electrostatic loudspeaker is capable of a frequency response essentially flat within +/– 8 dB from 16 cps to 16000 cps. Total harmonic distortion at 16 cps is 6 percent. The figures quoted are for a sound pressure level of 80 dB (re 2×10^{-6} micro-bars) measured at a distance of 6 feet on the loudspeaker axis in an anechoic chamber.

INTRODUCTION

Most people think of the electrostatic loudspeaker as an invention of the "high-fidelity era." The idea of using a condenser to produce sound is almost a century old, however, and can be traced back to Lord Kelvin. In the 1880's, Amos Dolbear, a professor at Tufts University, patented and produced a telephone system using condensers for both the transmitter and the receiver. Around 1930, during the radio boom, several workable electrostatic loudspeakers were invented and manufac- tured. These speakers never achieved commercial success because they were unable to compete with the more rugged electromagnetic "hornless loud- speaker" invented by Rice and Kellog.

The builders of electrostatic loudspeakers in the 1930's were handicapped by a lack of suitable materials. The light plastic films and insulating materials such as Mylar and Lucite, which we have today, were not available. Instead such materials as cast iron, bakelite, aluminum foil, and sheet rub- ber had to be used.

The simultaneous occurrence of rapid advances in plastic technology and mounting public interest in high-quality sound reproduction during the late 1940's provided a logical incentive for renewed re- search in electrostatic loudspeaker units (or ESLU). Recent research has resulted in several practical designs which are now commercially available. Most of the currently successful electrostatic loud- speakers are designed to operate only at the high- frequency end of the audio spectrum, however. Very few wide range designs have been tested, and at present only a very limited number are sold com- mercially.

The advantages of a wide-range ESLU become immediately evident when the principles of its oper- ation are considered. The diaphragm in such a speaker is a plastic film weighing only a few grams. The force applied to this film is distributed over its entire surface. Thus the force developed by the transducer operates essentially on the air itself in- stead of on a paper cone. Another advantage is the control obtainable over the directivity pattern by using either curved electrodes or an electrically seg- mented diaphragm. Because of its relative freedom from resonance effects, the ESLU has a much smoother pressure response than most electromagnetic loudspeakers.

In spite of the advantages listed above, a number of problems have stood in the way of the development of an ESLU to cover the entire audio spectrum. The primary problem in the design of a wide range ESLU is that of adequate low-frequency reproduction. This problem involves a compromise between diaphragm area and stationary electrode spacing. The few existing low-frequency electrostatic loudspeakers have attempted to solve the problem by using a large radiating area composed of small diaphragm segments. This type of loudspeaker usually has the segments arranged in an arc, giving an excellent dispersion of sound at high frequencies. At low-frequencies, however, it is necessary to insure that the diaphragms of all segments operate in phase to prevent mutual cancellation. This requirement means that (a) the resonance frequencies of the diaphragms must all be identical, or (b) the diaphragms must be operated with sufficient loading to maintain "in-phase" operation. Both conditions are hard to achieve in practice.

Another method of producing low-frequencies involves the use of a moderate size diaphragm capable of large excursions. Achievement of large excursions necessitates a wide stationary electrode separation and, consequently, a large signal voltage.

Current electrostatic loudspeaker designs obtain a high voltage audio signal by using a standard audio output transformer connected in reverse. This arrangement limits the achievable audio signal because of transformer leakage inductance, core losses, and insulation problems.

A more satisfactory method of obtaining the high-voltage audio signal is through the use of an amplifier capable of delivering a large output voltage in the order of kilovolts. Achievement of large signal voltage capability then removes the restriction on allowable fixed electrode separation and paves the way for a wide-range ESLU design using a diaphragm of moderate size.

A test of the validity of this idea was made by the construction of an experimental ESLU using a high-output voltage audio amplifier as the signal source. The following discussion outlines the details of the design and testing of this amplifier-loudspeaker combination.

PERTINENT THEORY

The electrostatic loudspeaker that was studied was basically a push-pull design using constant charge operation. The theory of this type of electrostatic transducer has been worked out very elegantly in the literature. Consequently the following discussion will cover only the theoretical considerations involved in the design of the experimental wide-range ESLU.

It has been shown that if an electrostatic loudspeaker is to be truly free from distortion, it is necessary that the charge on the diaphragm not only remain constant but also remain in a fixed position on the diaphragm as it moves between the stationary electrodes. If this condition is strictly adhered to, the relationships for the force on the diaphragm can be derived very simply as

$$f_e = Q_1 E(t) \text{ newtons} \qquad (1)$$
$$\text{where} \quad Q(t) = 2e_o A E_b/d \text{ coulombs} \qquad (2)$$
$$\text{and } E(t) = e(t)/2d \text{ volts/meter} \qquad (3)$$
$$\text{Defining } C_o = e_o A/d \text{ farads} \qquad (4)$$
$$\text{then } f_e = [C_o E_b/d]e(t) \text{ newtons} \qquad (5)$$

where E_b = bias voltage (volts)
  $e(t)$ = time varying signal voltage
  d = diaphragm to electrode spacing (meters)
  A = diaphragm area (meters^2)
  e_o = 8.85×10^{-12} (farads/meter)

In equation (5), the coefficient multiplying $e(t)$ can be thought of as the turns ratio of an ideal electro-mechanical transformer.

Equation (5) is a relationship derived frequently in the literature, usually after the authors have made several assumptions to satisfy stability and linearity criteria. This underscores an important point: a push-pull electrostatic loudspeaker operating with a constant stationary charge on its diaphragm is an inherently linear device that becomes non-linear only under special circumstances; on the other hand, a push-pull electrostatic loudspeaker with an electrically conducting diaphragm is an inherently non-linear device that becomes linear only if certain conditions are not exceeded.

The linearity of the electrical transduction relationship must be preserved in the mechanical system if the loudspeaker is to be free from distortion. This can be done by using sufficient tension in the diaphragm to insure a linear compliance. If the tension of the diaphragm is too low, the force-displacement relationship will be that for a supported membrane. This would be definitely undesirable because it involves the third power of the diaphragm displacement and is therefore nonlinear.

When sufficient tension is put in the diaphragm, it behaves as a stretched membrane. The displacement is then given by:

$$x = Z/4T(a^2 - r^2) \qquad (6)$$

when a circular membrane of radius a is assumed and x is the displacement at distance r from the center. Z is the normal force per unit area, and T is the tension of the membrane. This linear displacement relationship is accompanied by a smaller cubic term for most realizable values of diaphragm tension. For small displacements, however, the cubic term can be neglected.

HIGH OUTPUT-VOLTAGE AUDIO AMPLIFIER

The following requirements were considered in the design of an amplifier to operate an electrostatic loudspeaker:

a. The output voltage should be at least several kilovolts rms.
b. The output voltage should be delivered to the speaker differentially, i.e., in push-pull.
c. No output transformer should be used.
d. The amplifier should have a gain sufficient to give full output for 1 volt rms input.
e. The response should be flat within +/- 2 dB from 20 to 20000 cps.
f. Sufficient negative feedback should be incorporated so that the output impedance of the amplifier is well below the speaker impedance at all frequencies.

The high output voltage required from this amplifier motivated a search for suitable output tubes. Fortunately, the National Union 2C53 high voltage triode was found to possess suitable characteristics. This tube is designed for use as a shunt regulator in high voltage power supplies.

The performance of the output tubes was investigated in a test circuit, and a general push-pull design was evolved as shown in Fig. 15-35. The amplifier incorporates 45 dB of negative feedback to reduce the differential mode output impedance to about 6 kilohms at 1 kc/s. A push-pull arrangement of the amplifier inside the feedback loops allows the elimination of cathode bypass condensers without sacrificing gain. Because direct coupling has been used wherever possible, the phase in the low frequency region is controlled by only two time constants.

The maximum output of this amplifier is 4.5 kilovolts rms. It can be delivered into a load requiring up to four watts of audio power. The response curve is flat within +/- 4 dB from 20 to 20000 cps at maximum power output. A gain of 80 dB provides full output for an input of 0.45 volts rms. A maximum total harmonic distortion of 0.7 percent was observed at 1 kc/s at an output voltage of 4.3 kv rms.

The unbypassed cathode resistors reduce the common mode gain of the amplifier to a value much lower than that of the differential mode. This must be done to prevent the hum voltage in the 8 kv power supply from traveling around the loop and overdriving the output stage. The hum signal does not appear in the push-pull output, but an excessive amount of common mode hum voltage on the grids of the 2C53's would cause non-linear distortion products to appear in the signal delivered to the ESLU. The primary limitation in the design of this amplifier is a result of the high impedance level of the feedback loop. A voltage rating of at least 6 kv was needed, so the use of a resistor of considerable physical size was unavoidable along with its attendant stray capacity and coupling problems. The middle of the feedback loop is at an impedance level of around 13 megohms. Thus a stray capacity of only 1.2 picofarads could cause high-

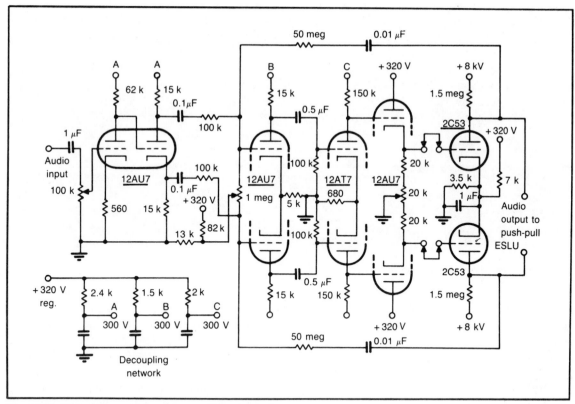

Fig. 15-35. High output-voltage audio amplifier circuit diagram.

frequency attenuation beginning at 10 kc/s.

The feedback loop limitation made it difficult to stabilize the amplifier at the high frequency end by the usual means of extending the frequency response of the feedback loop far beyond the frequency response of the amplifier. An alternate method was used. This method consisted of designing the bias circuit of the final stage so that a large increase in signal level on the grids would cause the tube bias to shift in the proper direction to reduce the stage gain. The effective time constant of the bias circuit, i.e., the time required for the bias to shift appreciably, was made about 0.2 sec., so that the amplifier could pass normal loud transients in program material.

An unfortunate by-product of this method of stabilization is a reduction in signal handling capacity above 10 kc/s. The power handling requirements of an audio amplifier are quite modest above 5 kc/s,

however, so it was decided that the present design would be adequate. The amplifier chassis is shown in Fig. 15-36.

EXPERIMENTAL ELECTROSTATIC LOUDSPEAKER

As mentioned previously, the primary problems involved in the design of a wide-range ESLU are in the low frequency range. A logical design procedure would first resolve the necessary compromise between diaphragm size and allowable excursion. For the experimental unit discussed in this article, a circular diaphragm 20 inches in diameter was used.

The initial diaphragm-to-electrode distance was chosen to be 1/4 inch. The spacing was selected after preliminary experiments with a small ESLU proved that a displacement of this order of magni-

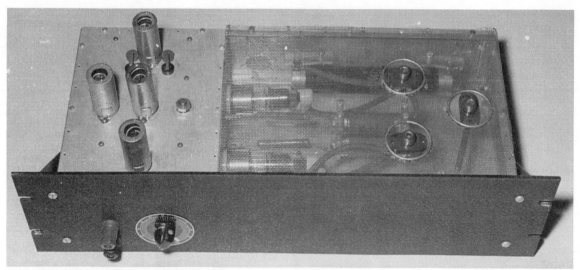

Fig. 15-36. High output-voltage audio amplifier.

tude was possible. Further modifications are anticipated as the design is advanced by experimentation.

The Diaphragm Assembly

The diaphragm material selected was Mylar plastic film 1/4 mil thick. The weight of a sheet of this material is approximately equal to that of a sheet of air 7 mm thick. Consequently, if the fundamental resonance of the diaphragm is set at a sufficiently high frequency, the higher order resonances will be completely damped by the resistive component of the air load. This dampening is necessary if the ESLU is to have a smooth response.

The frequency of the fundamental resonance as determined by diaphragm tension was set at the lowest frequency of interest in the audio range. When the resonance of the "gravest" mode is placed at 20 cps, it has the very beneficial effect of increasing the efficiency of the ESLU at the end of the audio spectrum where it is usually wanting.

The method of mounting the diaphragm is shown in Fig. 15-37. It is stretched between two acrylate plastic annuli with an outside diameter of 27 1/2 and 28 inches. The tension is controlled by wedges inserted between quadrants of the larger annulus. Rubber cement was used to hold the Mylar diaphragm to the quadrants. The assembly was prevented from buckling when tension was applied by first cementing the smaller annulus with the corona ring to the diaphragm as shown in Fig. 15-38. The smaller annulus (a) was attached with a small quantity of rubber cement to allow the cement to flow under pressure. Thus when the quadrants of the tensioning annulus (b) were forced apart by the wedges (c), the stretching action was not blocked by the smaller annulus. The friction fit of the corona ring (d) around the periphery of the smaller annulus provided the electrical connection to the diaphragm (e).

After the assembly was complete, the diaphragm tension was adjusted until the design value was reached, as determined by deflection measurements. The entire assembly was then placed between the fixed electrodes and clamped into the baffle to prevent further changes in tension.

Before being mounted, the diaphragm was coated with a material of high resistivity to give the constant charge operation discussed earlier. A commercially available compound used for removing the electrostatic charge on plastic records was found to have a resistivity of the right order of magnitude when sprayed on the diaphragm in a thin layer.

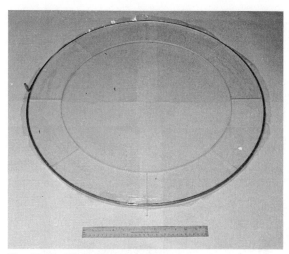

Fig. 15-37. ESLU diaphragm mounting.

Constant charge operations of push-pull ESLU's is usually achieved by inserting a large series resistor between the bias voltage supply and the diaphragm. The value of this series resistance is determined by a stability criterion requiring the time constant of the series resistance and the electrode-diaphragm capacitance to be longer than the half period of the lowest frequency.

The active electrode-diaphragm capacitance of the experimental ESLU is approximately that of a parallel-plate condenser of the same dimensions. It was calculated to be 270 picofarads. If 20 cps is chosen as the lowest frequency of interest, the required value of series resistance would have to be greater than 100 megohms. One is then faced with the fact that, if an external series resistor of this magnitude were used, any current leakage from the diaphragm would cause a considerable drop across this external resistor and would reduce the effective bias voltage.

Even when the required high value of series resistance takes the form of a high resistive coating on the diaphragm, the stability criterion cannot be ignored. In this case, however, the resistance and capacitance are distributed so that a simple time

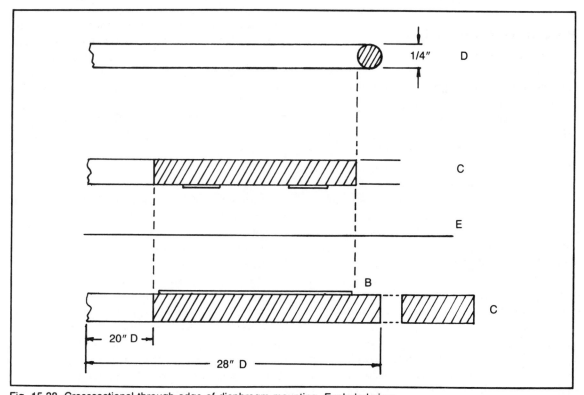

Fig. 15-38. Crosssectional through edge of diaphragm mounting. Exploded view.

constant calculation cannot be made. Calculation of the required surface resistivity was based on the presumption that the diaphragm shape at maximum excursion is paraboloidal. If the surface were too conductive, charges could flow cyclically toward and away from the center region. The item of interest, therefore, is the resistance of the surface as measured from a central region of the diaphragm to a region near the supporting rings. A relation giving this resistance as a function of surface resistivity can be developed from the equation for the capacitance of a coaxial cable. Thus,

$$R = (ps/6.28) \times \log(r_2/r_1)$$

where R is the resistance in ohms measured from a conducting ring of radius r_1 to a second conducting ring of radius r_2 across a surface of resistivity ps. If R is required to be larger than 100 megohms and a value of 2 is assumed for the radii ratio, ps is required to be greater than 9×10^8 ohms. An average conductivity of 2.5×10^{-10} mhos (ps = 4×10^9 ohms) was used in the experimental ESLU. The conductivity of the inactive area between the supporting rings was made considerably greater than that of the active diaphragm to minimize any voltage drop due to current leakage.

The Fixed Electrodes

Figure 15-39 is an illustration of the type of electrode construction used in the ESLU. It is not considered to be the optimum design but was used because of experimental flexibility and ease of construction. The electrodes are seen to consist of two plastic half-rings supporting a wire grid work. The wires are 1/8 inch iron weldrods and are uninsulated. They are embedded in grooves cut in the plastic rings. Additional support and vibration dampening are provided by the styro-foam strips cemented to the wires, dividing the unsupported wire lengths into three unequal parts.

The spacing of the wires was determined by the electrode-to-diaphragm distance. It was necessary that the electrodes be electrically equivalent to a solid plate and acoustically equivalent to an open window, so a compromise was indicated. For-

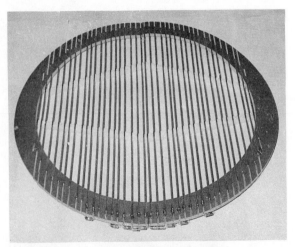

Fig. 15-39. ESLU fixed electrode construction.

tunately, the capacitance of a parallel array of conductors spaced a distance d above a conducting plate is approximately equal to that between two parallel plates until the distance between the conductors becomes appreciably larger than d. Since the electrode-to-electrode spacing is 1/2 inch, a mean center-to-center wire spacing of 1/2 inch was selected as a good compromise. The acoustic resistance of the resulting grid is negligible at all frequencies of interest.

The Speaker Baffle and Final Assembly

The baffle used for the experimental ESLU is a 4-foot square piece of 3/4 inch plywood. This type of baffle was chosen because of its simplicity and the experimental nature of the project.

Figure 15-40 shows the completed ESLU with its associated high voltage audio amplifier and power supplies. The baffle is supported on a wooden base by two cross braces. The high voltage bias supply is mounted behind the baffle on the wooden base close to the corona ring charging terminal.

Because the optimization of baffle design was not considered to be part of the ESLU design problem, the arrangement described above was used throughout all subsequent test procedures. The limitation imposed by this type of baffle should be borne in mind when considering the results

Fig. 15-40. A wide-range electrostatic loud-speaker and associated electronics.

reported in the following section. The baffle dimensions of four feet on a side allows front to back cancellation to take place below 140 cps. Consequently, the sound-pressure response of the loudspeaker could normally be expected to begin falling off at a rate of 12 dB per octave below 140 cps (assuming a constant volume velocity).

The design of a suitable enclosure would be relatively straightforward should this type of loudspeaker prove to be desirable as a commercial product. Such an enclosure could logically contain also the amplifier and the necessary power supplies to give an integrated unit with only two input requirements: a 1-V audio signal from a preamplifier and 110 volts ac from the power line.

PERFORMANCE CHARACTERISTICS OF THE EXPERIMENTAL LOUDSPEAKER

The results of the design considerations in the previous section were checked by calculating the theoretical response of the ESLU. This can be done by several methods, including the one based on a solution of the complete differential equation governing the motion of the diaphragm. It was found more convenient, however, to use an electrical analogue circuit, the parameters of which were determined by the design values for the electrical and mechanical components. The analogue circuit and the radiation impedance were obtained from a text on acoustics.

The sound pressure response measured on the axis of the first experimental ESLU compared quite well with that predicted by the analogue circuit. The fundamental resonance of the diaphragm occurred at 16 cps (20 cps calculated) with a secondary resonance at 70 cps. The secondary resonance was found to be the "0.2" natural mode of a circular membrane. All higher resonances were effectively damped by the air load. A small Fiberglass pad placed in the center of one of the fixed electrodes introduced enough dampening to eliminate the secondary resonance peak without reducing low-frequency response. This pad was left in place as a permanent part of the ESLU.

Since the diaphragm was operating as a large piston at high frequencies, it exhibited the sharp beamed response expected from a piston 20 inches in diameter. On axis, the pressure response rose at 6 dB per octave above 150 cps until the reactive load on the amplifier caused a high frequency roll off at 8 kc/s. When the microphone was located 15 degrees off axis, the response shown in Fig 15-41 was observed. The peak and valley pattern apparent at frequencies above 2 kc/s is a result of the small secondary lobes in the radiation pattern of a large piston.

A de-emphasis of high-frequency response was accomplished by electrical segmentation and was done in such a manner to cause only a small, narrow area of the diaphragm to be driven by high frequency signals while still allowing a low frequency signal to drive the entire surface. Since the physical construction of the fixed electrodes utilized parallel- connected vertical wires, the insertion of appropriate resistances between the separate wires converted the fixed electrodes into an R-C trans-

mission line for a centrally applied signal voltage.

The resistance values selected effectively reduced the radiating area by a factor of 2 for each doubling of frequency. The diaphragm was thus electrically divided into separate radiating areas that became decoupled at the correct frequency to give the necessary reduction in the total area. As a matter of convenience, the radiating surface was divided into six separate electrical areas. This manner of diaphragm segmentation was easily accomplished and seemed to provide as much control of frequency response as a larger number of segments. The segmenting resistors can be seen in Fig. 15-39.

The response of the ESLU after segmentation is shown in Fig. 15-42. The results show that two benefits were obtained: first, the response was much more uniform and the broad directivity pattern eliminated the peaks of Fig. 15-40; and second, reproduction of high frequencies was improved by the reduction of the capacitive load on the amplifier at high frequencies. The upper curve in Fig. 15-41 illustrates the effect of an electrical network used in the amplifier input to correct for some of the low frequency roll-off caused by the 4-foot-square flat baffle.

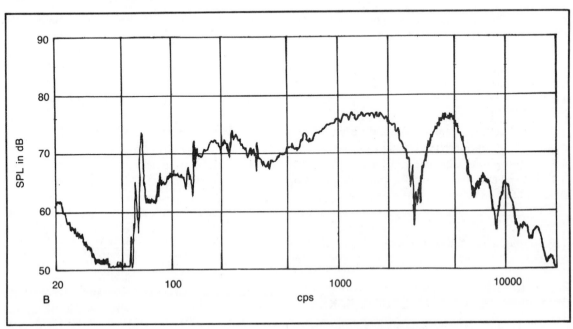

Fig. 15-41. Response of first experimental model, 15 degrees off axis, 6 feet from ESLU.

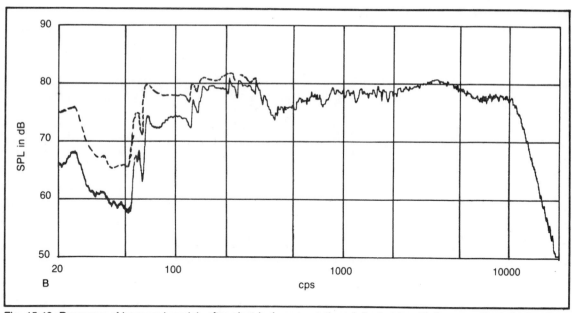

Fig. 15-42. Response of improved model, after electrical seqmentation of diaphragm, 15 degrees off axis, 6 feet from ESLU. Note upper curve with electrical compensation, lower curve without compensation.

The transient response of the ESLU was investigated by using tone bursts at various frequencies. The loudspeaker was observed to follow the input signal accurately without "ringing."

The waveforms produced by the ESLU at various low frequencies are shown in Fig. 15-43. These

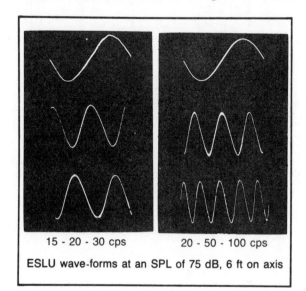

| 15 - 20 - 30 cps | 20 - 50 - 100 cps |

ESLU wave-forms at an SPL of 75 dB, 6 ft on axis

Fig. 15-43. Waveforms produced at low frequencies.

waveforms were produced at an SPL of 75 dB (re 0.0002 microbars) as measured in an anechoic chamber at a distance of 6 feet on the axis of the loudspeaker.

All previously discussed tests of the loudspeaker were conducted in an anechoic chamber which provided a reasonably good simulation of free space. However, a loudspeaker is, in general, not used in free space but in a room with resonant characteristics.

To measure the performance of the ESLU in a more representative listening room, it was set up in a studio with a volume of 1350 cubic feet. This room had a reverberation time of 0.8 seconds at 500 cps and was designed to have a high diffusivity. The resulting plot of SPL versus frequency is shown in Fig. 15-44.

This is compared with Fig. 15-45 which gives a plot taken in the same room under similar conditions using a "good" quality 15 inch electromagnetic cone "woofer" combined with a horn "tweeter" in an 8 cubic foot infinite baffle enclosure.

As a matter of interest, several plots were taken for different locations of the ESLU. It was

241

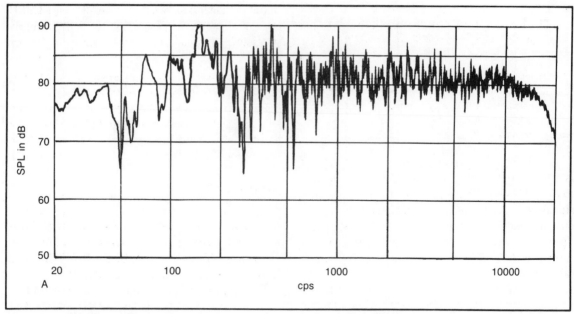

Fig. 15-44. Response of experimental ESLU in a small room, on axis 6 feet from ESLU.

discovered that the high frequency response would remain essentially constant, but the low frequency response was definitely influenced by the loudspeaker location. An ESLU mounted in a flat baffle of limited size has a $\cos^2\theta$ directivity pattern at low frequencies. The best location for a speaker of this type would be a position where both sound pressure lobes could be utilized with a minimum

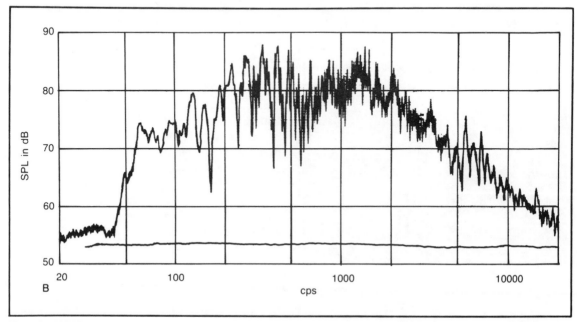

Fig. 15-45. Response of "good" quality electromagnetic woofer-tweeter combination in the room used for Fig. 15-44.

of cancellation from wall reflections.

The location fulfilling this requirement is the center of the room. Observations proved this to be true. The "best" location was not critical, however, as long as the speaker was not placed to near a wall or corner, an interesting contrast to the recommended location for a standard speaker.

CONCLUSION

A loudspeaker is not a musical instrument; it is a sound reproducer. It must, therefore, be able to translate electrical signals accurately into audio signals without imposing any extraneous tone color on the reproduced sound. Needless to say, this "perfect" transducer does not exist at present, but it is nevertheless the constant goal for experimental development.

The wide-range electrostatic speaker, while not a "perfect" transducer, does have many desirable features. The experimental loudspeaker described in this article has shown that the wide-range ESLU is not a practical possibility as was formerly predicted. There are, of course, many other factors which must still be investigated before the best design for a wide-range electrostatic loudspeaker is achieved. The present prototype is a long way from the living room, but it does give definite indication that the electrostatic loudspeaker can serve as a wide-range sound source for quality sound-reproducing system.

ACKNOWLEDGMENT

The work reported in this paper was done in the Research Laboratory of Electronics at Massachusetts Institute of Technology as an S. M. Thesis. It was supported in part by the Office of Naval Research under contract Nonr-1841(42).

The author wishes to express his gratitude to Professor Kenneth N. Stevens for his interest and encouragement in this project.

---

(1) Published by permission of the Audio Engineering Society and Mr. Charles I. Malme.

Appendix

SPEAKER MATERIAL LIST

The following is a list of materials that will be needed in order to build two 2-foot-by-4-foot electrostatic speakers.

Item No.	Qty.	Units	Description and source
1.	1	piece	15 feet of 1-×-12-inch pine board. (Local building supply stores)
2.	1		4-×-8-foot sheet of 1/8 inch ABS plastic. (Cadillac Plastics. Most large cities.)
3.	2	pints	Conductive Paint Part No. W0731. Wescorp. Corp. 144 S. Whisman Ave. Mountain View CA 94041.
4.	8	cans	Red "X" Corona Dope. This is made by General Cement and is available at most electronic supply houses.
5.	175	pieces	10/32 "T" nuts. Hardware Stores.
6.	4		10/32 × 2 1/2 inch screws. Hardware Stores.
7.	175		10/32 × 2 inch wood screws. Hardware Stores.
8.	16		6/32 × 3/4 inch screws. Hardware Stores.
9.	16		6/32 nuts for above screws.
10.	16		Washers. Plain and lock for 6/32 screws. Hardware Stores.
11.	20	ft	Mylar (1/2 mil.) Type A. (PLastic Supply Houses)
12.	68	ft	Foam Strips (1/2 × 1/2 inch open cell)
13.	1	roll	Masking Tape. 1/4, 1/2 and 2 inch size. The 1/4 inch masking tape may have to be ordered from a local tape supplier.
14.	24	pieces	Ratchett Fasteners. Part No. 47535 TRW 31 Ames St. Cambridge Mass. 02142.

ELECTRONIC PARTS FOR SPEAKER

The following is a list of materials that will be needed in order to build two 2-foot-by-4-foot electrostatic speakers.

Item No.	Qty.	Units	Description and source	Item No.	Qty.	Units	Description and source
1.	2	pieces	High Voltage Transformer. Stancor part number P 8179. Electronic Supply Stores.	4.	4	pieces	Diodes (High Voltage) Model VG10 Varo Semiconductor 1000 N. Shiloh P.O. Box 676 Garland Texas, 75040
2.	2	pieces	Step-up transformers. 40 :1 Stancor part number A3801. Electronic Supply Stores. 75 :1 (Mid-range or tweeters) Tranex Transformer Co. 2350 Executive Circle Colorado Springs, CO 80906 150 :1 (full-range) Tranex Transformer Co.	5.	1	piece	Resistor 20 megohms 2 Watts. Local Electronic Suppliers
				6.			Resistors (Used for equalization) Local Electronic Suppliers
				7.			High Voltage Wire Belden Manufacturing Local Electronic Suppliers
3.	4	pieces	Capacitors (High Voltage) Centralab DD60, Code 202 2000 pF @ 6 kilovolts. Electronic Supply Stores				

TOOL LIST

The following is a list of tools that you should have in order to build two 2-foot-by-4-foot electrostatic speakers.

Item No.	Description
1.	Table or radial arm saw.
2.	Mitre gauge hold down clamps.
3.	Dado blades for saw.
4.	Drill Press
5.	Assorted drill bits.
6.	#10 wood bit with pilot drill.
7.	1/4 inch wood boring bit (Also use a brad point bit in its place.)
8.	3/4 inch wood boring bit.
9.	Corner or mitre vise clamps.
10.	Fish Scale (0 to 10 lbs)
11.	Small Chain 9 feet.
12.	Small cloth roller. (3 or 4 inch size.)
13.	Hard wooden roller. (Used for wall paper seams.)
14.	"C" clamps 3 or 4 inch size. (4 required).
15.	1/4 inch dowel points. (4 required.)
16.	Bar Clamps 15 inch. (2 required.)

MATERIALS FOR STRETCHING FRAME

The following is a list of materials that are required for building the stretching frame described in Chapter 9 and shown graphically in Fig. 9-1.

Item No.	Description	Item No.	Description
1.	Speaker Plate.	14.	42 × 48 × 3/4 inch plywood.
2.	Mylar Diaphragm. (36 × 36 inches)	15.	1/4 inch guide rods (Hardware stores, as required).
3.	Tension Scale. (Hardware or fishing supply stores).	16.	2 × 27 × 1 inch wood strip.
4.	2 × 42 × 1 inch wood strip.	17.	Tension Scale.
5.	Base.	18.	2 × 27 × 1 inch wood strip.
6.	Flat washer. (1/4 inch, 12 pieces)	19.	2 × 42 × 1 inch wood strip.
7.	1/4 inch nuts. (12 pieces)	20.	Tension Scale.
8.	2 × 27 × 1 inch wood strip.	21.	2 × 27 × 1 inch wood strip.
9.	2 × 42 × 1 inch wood strip.	22.	2 × 42 × 1 inch wood strip.
10.	Speaker Locating Guide.	23.	1 1/2 inch 10/32 flat head machine screws.
11.	Hook for Tension Scale. (Hardware Store)	24.	2 × 27 × 1 inch wood strip.
12.	2 × 42 × 1 inch wood strip.	25.	2 × 42 × 1 inch wood strip.
13.	1/4 inch threaded rod (Hardware stores, as required).		

Index